Steaming through
BRITAIN

A HISTORY OF THE NATION'S RAILWAYS

Steaming through
BRITAIN
CHRIS ELLIS & GREG MORSE

GOLDEN
ARROW

CONWAY

A Conway Book

Text copyright © Navigator Guides Ltd
First published in Great Britain in 2010 by Conway, an imprint of
Anova Books Company Ltd
10 Southcombe Street
London W14 0RA

To receive regular email updates on forthcoming Conway titles, email
conway@anovabooks.com with 'Conway Update' in the subject field.

British Library Cataloguing in Publication Data
A record of this title is available on request from the British Library

ISBN 9781844861217

Distributed in US and Canada by:
Sterling Publishing Co., Inc
387 Park Avenue South
New York, NY 10016–8810

This book is produced under licence for NMSI Trading Limited. Royalties from the
sale of this product help fund the National Railway Museum's exhibitions and
programmes. The National Railway Museum Collection ® is a registered Trade
Mark No. 2309517

The National Railway Museum, York is the largest railway museum in the world.
Its permanent displays and collections illustrate over 300 years of British railway
history, from the industrial revolution to the present day. The NRM archive also
includes a fabulous collection of railway advertising posters charting the history of
rail. Visit www.nrm.org.uk to find out more.

The content of this book is the result of the authors' own research and reflects their
individual opinions. Both author and publisher would welcome the contributions of
readers with further information relating to the subject and they can be contacted
accordingly at the address given above.

Conceived, produced and designed by Navigator Guides www.navigatorguides.com
Printed and bound by 1010 Print International Ltd, China

Contents

Acknowledgements

Chris Ellis

I would take this opportunity to thank Tom Vine and his colleagues at the Science and Society Picture Library for choosing many of the fine illustrations from their archive for inclusion in this book. A further fine collection of photographs came from the picture library of the publishers of this book, Anova Books, with the help of John Lee, Matthew Jones. To Rupert Wheeler at Navigator Guides for the picture research and for bringing the book together. I would also like to thank Greg Morse for his contribution to chapters 6–10.

A select bibliography of books consulted (and very relevant to the subject of this book) is given on page 189 and these have been invaluable for checking dates and facts, and due acknowledgement is made to the authors of these books.

Greg Morse

I would like to thank Roger Badger, Alan Jones, Gary Mewis, and Gerald Riley for their assistance and advice on Chapters 6–10, David Brown for kick-starting my writing career and my late father Pete Morse for the life-long love of all things rail.

Picture Credits

Introduction

Contrary to general public perception, railway history did not start with George Stephenson and his Rocket locomotive in the early 19th century, nor the Stockton and Darlington Railway slightly earlier. It is true that Stephenson and the railways and locomotives he engineered had an important part in the history of railways and, indeed, were part of an important jump forward in development, but there is very much more to the story than that.

This book covers the history of the railway in Great Britain rather more comprehensively by going right back to the earliest days of movement on the rails, which happens to be in medieval times, and very probably much earlier that that, when miners, quarrymen, and others handling bulky loads found that by putting their wagons on the grooved trackways or wooden plank tracks, they could haul heavy loads more easily and more quickly than on rough roads. For several centuries after these early developments, traction was by man power or horse power, and by the late 18th century, with the Industrial Revolution well in progress, there was a surprisingly large network of horse-operated tram roads and tram ways, mostly serving mines and iron foundries, which were spreading across the expanding coal-field areas of Great Britain. By the early 19th century there were more developed railways, still horse drawn, such as the Surrey Iron Railway.

It took about a century of development before steam engines were compact enough and efficient enough to be used to drive wheeled vehicles, and in the early years of the 19th century steam carriages were built to run on roads, and the first steam locomotives appeared. By the 1820s steam railways became a practical reality and it was then that George Stephenson took a decisive part, overshadowing others that came before him and even some worthy contemporaries. Railways brought commercial, travel and work opportunities to the masses, and also led to urban expansion and an even greater spread of industry.

The whole sequence of development of all this achievement to the last years of British Rail is documented in this book. Fortunately for today's generation there remains a considerable wealth of relics of our railway heritage right back to the early days of 200 or more years ago, which collectively gives a vivid idea of the way Britain's railways have developed over this period. Official funding, both local and national, has also given us some fine museums principally the vast National Railway Museum (see page 176) at York, and several smaller museums, of which the one at Swindon is a good example.

If this book awakens your interest – which I hope it will – find your nearest preserved railway or rail and museum and make a visit soon.

Chris Ellis, 2010

chapter 1

The origin of movement by rail can be traced back to ancient times, with evidence of grooved trackways in Italy and Greece to facilitate the hauling of loaded wagons. Planked trackways were built in Europe during the Neolithic and Bronze age, over which sledges could be dragged without getting bogged down. Awareness of the added ease of movement made by trackways was soon exploited in Medieval times, mainly in mine and quarry workings and here can be established the first serious use of rails to facilitate wagon working, albeit by hand and later horse power. By the 18th century iron wheels were replacing wood on wagons and eventually iron rails started to replace wooden rails and flangeways. And the Industrial Revolution of the 18th century led to a big increase in tramroads, with wagons hauled by horses, serving mines and foundries.

Movement by rail

PREVIOUS PAGES
The Iron Bridge
at Coalbrookdale,
completed in 1779, was
the first in the world to
use cast iron structurally.
It was commissioned
because ferry traffic
on the River Severn
had become busy and
expensive. It was 40ft tall
and the span of its single
arch was 100ft 6in.

Ancient times

While movement by rail and using mechanical means of traction – steam, diesel or electricity – is thought of as a development of the Industrial Revolution in the 18th and early 19th centuries, the truth is that the idea of using some sort of track to make handling of the heavy loads easier can be traced back to ancient times. The traction then was by manpower, in essence pushing a laden wagon or trolley along a prepared trackway, enabling a man to push a very much greater weight, due to reduced friction on the trackway, than he could when pushing a similarly sized cart over rough ground.

The earliest discovered trackways did not involve actual rails, but were parallel grooves cut into stone-paved roadways, and traces of these were long ago found by archaeologists in Greece and Italy, dating from the time of the Ancient Greeks and Romans. This technique was clearly used elsewhere in later times before being superseded by better ideas, but at least one example of a grooved trackway, dating from as recently as the 1820s is preserved in an old quarry on Dartmoor.

Grooved trackways quite obviously involved a lot of intricate preparation work and were only really suited to short runs, such as those found in mines or quarries. Longer grooved trackways were found on important roads, however, and also on some mountain roads in difficult areas, seemingly to aid traction where the going was more hazardous. An interesting connection with modern railways is that most grooved trackways were roughly 4ft 6in to 4ft 9in apart (close to standard rail 'gauge' of 4ft 8½in matching the setting of Roman and Greek cart wheels.

An even more primitive early type of railway, dating back to the Neolithic and Bronze Ages, was to be found in Britain and Northern Europe whereby rough plank trackways were laid, mainly over soft or marshy ground, held together with wooden beams along the outside edges to form a basic path for hauling sledges without them becoming bogged down.

Plankways

Mines and quarries in Greek or Roman times were only developed on a small scale. It was in Medieval times that the development of trackways took a big step forward, and this came about due to the vast flowering of trade, enterprise and early industry across the centre of Europe, mainly in the states that today comprise Belgium, parts of France, Germany, Austria, Hungary and the Czech Republic. While mining for such minerals as silver, iron, lead, copper and other metals was taking place all through the Dark Ages, this was still on a small scale. By the early Middle Ages, however, mining and quarrying was being done much more intensively in what was, in effect, an early form of industrial revolution. From the end of the 12th century onwards, the value of coal as a fuel was discovered and by the 16th century it was also being mined in

A—RECTANGULAR IRON BANDS ON TRUCK.   B—ITS IRON STRAPS.   C—IRON AXLE.
D—WOODEN ROLLERS.   E—SMALL IRON KEYS.   F—LARGE BLUNT IRON PIN.
G—SAME TRUCK UPSIDE DOWN.

LEFT Plate taken from *De Re Metallica* (*On the Nature of Metals*, 1556) by Georgius Agricola (1494–1555). This was posthumously published in 1556, and detailed equipment, machinery and transportation methods used to extract and process ore.

increasing quantities in areas where coal fields were located such as Northern France and Northern England.

The early mines of ancient times were mostly just simple pits, but by the Middle Ages miners in the Germanic states had developed much more sophisticated techniques using shafts and horizontal galleries, and even making provision for keeping flooding at bay by using bucket hoists and, later, pumps. By the late 16th century these mining techniques had spread all over Europe, including Britain. Trading in valuable metals, and in iron and coal made the mining industry, for the most part, a key activity in the economy of the 16th and 17th centuries. In 1525 the Holy Roman Empire was said to employ over 100,000 men in mining and associated metal manufacturing.

It was this much increased mining activity (and more intensive quarry working too) that led to the next stage in the development of railways. In the shallow underground galleries of the mines, ore and diggings were put on wooden trays, sledges or wicker baskets and were either dragged or pulled along the floor, or carried by the miners. To reduce mud from poor drainage the gallery floors were planked over. This greatly improved the task of gathering the diggings, for wheeled barrows – usually four-wheeled – could now be pushed with considerably more ease along the planked floors. From here it was not long before the idea came of laying wooden rails along the planked floors along which the four-wheel barrows could be much more easily pushed. This greatly increased productivity because getting the ore or coal from the mine face along the gallery to the shaft where it could be hoisted to the surface was now a quicker and easier task. At the shaft the contents of the barrow could be tipped into a large bucket or box and hoisted to the surface.

With the efficiency offered by the use of wooden rails, the barrow could be made bigger and more robust, resembling a sturdy box on four wheels. In the German-speaking countries where these ideas originated, this bigger cart was most often called a 'Hund', though in English it was usually called a 'wagon'. Because every mine made

De Metallorum tranfmutatione. Cap. XXV.

ABOVE Hand-coloured woodcut from the *Origin of Thing*s section of the *Margarita Philosophica* (*The Philosophical Pearl*), by Gregor Reisch (*c* 1467–1525).

its own wagons, the size and style varied considerably, but the largest was, typically, about 4ft long, 2½ft wide, and up to 2½ft high, though many were rather smaller than this. A typical capacity was 4 cubic ft. Most wagons needed only one miner to push them, but where loads were heavy, as with iron ore, two men might be needed, one pushing and one pulling. The Hunds (or wagons) were generally strengthened with iron bands or corner plates, and usually had simple pulling handles on each end, and very often iron rings to allow ropes to be attached. A thick beam under the body was used to strengthen the construction and also to carry two wrought-iron axles on which wooden wheels were attached and held in place by pins so that damaged wheels could easily be replaced. Iron tyres were usually fitted on the wheel rims, though by the 18th century cast-iron wheels were used instead of wood. There was considerable variation in appearance and style of the wagons (or Hunds) depending on the region or maker. Some had very small wheels on short axles under the body and were hardly visible. Most had wider axles with the wheels conventionally positioned outside the body width, while some had a larger pair of wheels at the back and a slightly tilted body, seemingly to aid tipping when the wagon was emptied.

The actual wooden railway for these Hunds did not match today's style of rail tracks. The early mine railway actually comprised of two side planks, wider than the Hund, laid side by side with a gap between them. On the bottom of the Hund was a wrought-iron pin, called a Spurnagel (track pin) by the German users. This was about 2in long and 1in in diameter, projecting downwards. It fitted in the gap between the two planks that acted as the railway and so stayed on the centre of the planking as it was pushed along. It worked rather like the guide pin under an electric model racing car of the Scalextric type to keep the model on the track. The Spurnagel worked well enough in simple straight galleries, but as mines became bigger and more complex, some of the galleries curved and when the Hund went round a sharp curve the pin could chip away the adjacent wooden planking. By the late 18th century one way tried to overcome this was a small wheel, rather like a castor wheel, replacing the Spurnagel, which followed round the curve of the groove, hopefully doing less damage to the wooden planks. Another idea was to pivot one of the axles, and an improved variation on this was to put the Spurnagel on the end of an iron bar attached to the pivoted axle, projecting forward from the front end. The guide pin encountered the bend ahead of the wagon and turned the pivoted axle accordingly – an early forerunner of the moving bogie in common use today. This type of guide bar and pivoted axle on mine wagons was another late 18th century development, which was in quite common use in mines well into the 19th century.

Needless to say, the running of these wagons on the plank railways caused rapid wear even though hard wood was used. To get more use the worn planks were turned over and used until the other side was worn, then they had to be replaced. A later technique to protect the grooves at the bends from being damaged by the guide pin was to line the inside of the groove with thick iron plate.

Where their use was appropriate, the same sort of Hund (or wagon) was used with the same plank type of railway at the surface of the mine, for example to carry

Will. Boilby, Delineavit, a Newcastle. 1773.

Prevost Sculp.

the ore brought up by bucket to a nearby smelter (if there was one) or to a canal bank for loading into barges. Often the terrain was unsuitable for this and conventional horse-and-cart carriage was used. Also recorded, in some cases, were ropeways where several wagons were linked together and hauled by rope and capstan up an incline to, for example, a nearby smelter.

Flangeway developments

While the plank-type tracks with the guide pin running in the centre groove, were widely used, particularly in mine workings, there was a parallel development from at least the early 16th century, which came much closer, to the idea of using some sort of flangeway to keep the wagons on the trackway. A good number of surviving prints and engravings from about 1515–20 onwards show mining wagons running not on wide planks with a central guide pin, but on narrow plankways with upright strips affixed vertically either on the outer or inner edges giving an L-shape in cross-section, or with an upright strip on both edges giving a U-shape in cross-section.

One of the most famous surviving mine illustrations of the 16th century, portraying the heberthal mine at Ste-Marie-au-Mines in Alsace, from Sebastian Munster's book *Cosmographic Universals* of 1550 not only shows aspects of mining at the period, but clearly portrays a wagon being pushed along a wooden flangeway of U-shape (see page 14). According to Munster the wheels on the wagons in this mine were of iron.

It seems that there was a fair amount of variation in the way flangeway tracks were built, but many surviving prints show the L-shape flangeway with the vertical segment on the outer edge of the plankway. It is also well recorded that some of the plankway systems that used the Spurnagel (track pin) on plain wide planks were converted to flangeways by adding an outer vertical edging and dispensing with the pin. There were

ABOVE Coal wagon, Newcastle, Tyne and Wear, 1773. The wagon is going down a gradient controlled by the driver using his brake on the rear wheels. The horse follows behind, but is used to haul the wagon on the flat or up gradients.

also a few examples on record of double-track flangeways in the early 19th century so that wagons could be moved more efficiently in both directions in galleries and other mine workings. In a lead mine in Bleiberg the track gauge was recorded as about 2ft 6in.

One of the advantages of flangeway track was that the wagons stayed more firmly on the tracks than was possible with the wagons that ran on the unflanged plankways with only a pin to keep them on course. Each of these wagons needed a worker to guide it, stop it, and ensure it stayed on course. With a flangeway it became possible to link several wagons together with chains or ropes. In the early mines themselves it was usual to have a worker guiding each wagon but, on the surface, ropeways became even more practical with the possibility, where suitable, of hauling wagons by rope along tracks or inclines to smelters, canal jetties, or other nearby facilities.

Though not directly connected with railway development, another use of flangeways was in conjunction with canal barges and small boats. Canals often changed levels or small boats needed to be moved from one river to a nearby canal. This led to the early use of inclines where flanged tracks carried wheeled trolleys. The barge or boat was floated over the trolley in shallow water and hauled by winch or capstan up the incline to the higher water level.

ABOVE Mine and hard mining truck (left) running on U-shape wooden wagonway Ste-Marie-aux-Mines, Alsace, in 1550, from *Cosmographia Universalis* by Sebastian Munster. Note also, at the mining face (right), miners and shaft with bucket hoist (centre).

The final development of flangeway track came from Great Britain where John Carr, who had studied the logistics of coal mining in Sheffield collieries, suggested some further improvements. At that time many English mines were using a wicker basket, called a cart, to hold the coal, and this was placed on a low wagon running on L-shaped plankways (and in earlier days on sledges). Carr suggested that the collieries should change over to the larger wooden four-wheel wagons similar to those used elsewhere, notably in mainland Europe. The significant change, instituted at the same time was to replace the wooden flangeway track with iron flangeway track. This iron rail was fabricated in 6ft lengths and nailed to wooden cross-pieces – sleepers – to hold them in place. The first iron rails were installed in a colliery at Sheffield in 1787, and the idea soon spread to other British collieries in the following years. It was also quickly adopted in European mines. Carr's track system was 2ft gauge. There were several big advantages. The track was much more durable and tough, not requiring so much repair and frequent replacement as was the case with wooden flangeway. Also, friction was much reduced, and up to ten wagons could be chained together to make a train that could be pulled by a horse. The system worked as well underground as on the surface. A side effect was that it also reduced manpower. The old wooden plankways needed a man (or two men) to handle each wagon. With the new iron rails fewer men were needed to handle the wagons.

The coming of wagonways

An interesting technique developed in the late 16th century and early 17th century in some mines in Hungary, was a four-wheel wagon that ran on plain wood-beam rails, and was kept on the rails by four horizontal tree-running wheels attached to the underside of the body, so positioned that they revolved against the inner face of the deep beam rails and so held the wagon on the track. This was considered efficient by many at the time, and by the 18th century this type of wagon and track system, with the horizontal wheels known as guide wheels, was also in use in some mines in Sweden and Germany. There is no record of this idea being used in Britain however.

But the big idea that really revolutionised rail traction, and rendered all previous systems obsolete was mainly developed in Britain, and this was the flanged wheel, now universal on all railway systems. While British coal mines had used similar wagons to the various European designs, or cruder carriers like sledges or wicker baskets, these were almost always used underground in the galleries of the primitive early mines. In 1604, however, in Nottingham a surface wagonway was built at Wollaton to carry coal two miles from the pithead of one of the largest mines in England to a collecting point where dealers purchased it and took it away by horse and cart. Prior to that the carts had to come to the pithead and the road traffic around the mine at a time when demand for coal was rising was getting out of hand. The wagonway was the answer. While there may have been earlier attempts to build wagonways in Britain before 1604, the Wollaton line is certainly the earliest to be fully authenticated and recorded. And it appears that wooden wheels with flanges were used from the start, though it was some years later before this was put on record, and the rails were also of wood, with horses pulling the wagons. The wagonway idea quickly caught on and spread rapidly across England. An energetic mine manager, Huntingdon Beaumont, was the man behind this wagonway idea and he also used it to carry coals from another mine nearby, then went on to build three more wagonways in Northumberland in between 1605–08. These carried coal from the mines to staithes on the River Blyth for shipping away in barges. Through the 17th century wagonways carrying coal from mines, mostly to staithes in rivers or harbours, or to collecting points for transport by road were built in considerable numbers, most notably in the north east in the River Tyne and Wear area, in the Wyre Forest, Staffordshire, and near the River Severn in Shropshire, around Broseley and Willey.

Through the late 17th century and the 18th century the network of wagonways

BELOW View of Newcastle upon Tyne in 1783. In the foreground is the Parkmore Wagonway.

grew considerably, especially in the Tyneside and Shropshire areas, and also around Leeds and the Scottish Lowlands. As the coal trade became ever bigger, further boosted as the canal network grew in the late 18th century, so the wagonways became bigger and the equipment more technically advanced. In the Tyne area wagons were made much larger, with brakes, and assuming the outward sloping sides of a type called a chaldron. As even more pits were sunk the wagonway network increased and the engineering got more sophisticated. Wheels and rails were still almost always of wood at this time, but the track was more robust, usually of oak, pinned to sturdy sleepers about 2–3ft apart, and ballasted with stones, sand or gravel, or a combination of these. Proper level trackbeds were built and a pathway for workers was allowed for each side of the track. Full width of a single track trackbed was 14ft and 22ft for double track. Many wagonways were single track, but for the bigger collieries double track was preferred, allowing loaded wagons to use one track out to the riverside staithes, with empty wagons being hauled back along the other track. Sidings were also introduced in the 18th century to allow wagons to be stored, or to allow damaged ones to be taken out of service, or even to side-line a set of wagons to let another pass.

Track gauge had not been standardised at this time and could vary between 4ft and 6ft. Check rails on curves were also introduced in the 18th century to prevent the flanged wheels 'climbing' up off the rail as the wagon went round the bend.

The increasingly ambitious wagonways often needed to be taken over streams or rivers, so wooden bridges had to be built, and at the canal or riverside it was often necessary to build staithes out over the water so that coal could be tipped or shovelled straight into the barges. A notable feat of engineering was the 105ft long Causey Arch at Tanfield, built in 1725 to carry the Tanfield wagonway over the Causey burn (see page 17), but there were a number of other impressive bridges built in the wagonway era.

Though it did not affect the technical development of wagonways, a persistent problem for operators and mine owners was the matter of wayleaves – the fees charged by owners of the land over which the wagonways were built. There was much altercation and legal activity throughout the 17th–19th centuries over wayleave charges, sometimes involving Parliament to sort out disputes and settle fair fees. This led from the 1720s onwards to the formation of a number of associations of operators to negotiate fees, charges, and co-operative action. It was a complex subject mentioned here only for completeness.

Iron Roads and tram roads

While the first flanged wheels were made of wooden, it was not until the 18th century that cast-iron flanged wheels started to be introduced. Prior to that, however, some

ABOVE Staithe at Wallsend in the early 1800s. Wagons ran out along the staging and their weight caused the chute to drop, for the coal to fall into barges or boat holds below. A counter weight was used to haul the wagons back up again.

wooden wheels were given wrought-iron tyres on the tread to improve their running and reduce the extensive wear that wooden wheels suffered from.

A major wagonway system was built, starting in 1750, in Coalbrookdale to serve the major iron works and foundries established by Abraham Darby. Within a few years this had developed into quite a complex network, with large wagons used to carry coal, limestone and pigiron. It was here that the first cast-iron plate rails were made and laid by Richard Reynolds in a local furnace in 1767, and by the 1780s over 30 miles (48km) of wagonways at Coalbrookdale were running on iron rails.

Some wagonways had used cast-iron plating on their wooden rails to extend their life and improve running, but it was the building of the canals in the later part of the 18th century that boosted the number of wagonways being built, for rail connections were made to virtually all of them. This boosted the need for rails, and a combination of higher prices for wood and the expansion of iron foundries led to the making of more iron rail in quantity and its adoption by most of the new wagonways especially in South Wales and Shropshire. The first iron rails produced were, in fact, L-shape plate rail for flangeless wheels, a throwback to the old wooden plateway idea, and a good number of industrial lines used it well into the 19th century. The major supplier was Benjamin Outram, who from 1795, made it in his Butterly Ironworks. It was said that the word 'Tram' came from a corruption of Outram's name, and lines laid with iron-plate rail were often called 'Tramroads' or 'Tramways' rather than wagonways. Plate rail could easily crack or get blocked with debris, and many roads, particularly in the North of England, preferred to use flanged wheels on edge rail which was much stronger and was supported clear of ground level on sleepers. In about 1775, too, flanged wheels made in Britain began to be exported to mainland Europe where they were also used with edge rail. A variation on the single flange on the inner

ABOVE Causey Arch is the oldest surviving single arch railway bridge in the world. It was constructed to carry the Tanfield Railway across the gorge of Causey Burn.

Movement by rail   17

Wagonways

Increased demand for coal, even as early as the Elizabethan age, for use in the domestic fires of the better off and for such early manufacturing purposes as brick firing and glass making, gave a big impetus to the coal mining industry, with new mines being opened up, and exisiting ones dug down to the deeper seams. Getting the coal from the ine to the customer was a major problem. The Tyne area mines thrived because they had close access to the Tyne and Tynemouth, where even in the 16th and 17th centuries ships could carry the coal to London and the southern parts of the England. Pack horses carrying very limited loads, or horse carts struggling along rough country lanes, were a slow and unprofitable way of carrying the coal to the ships, and it was this that gave the major impetus for the building of wagonways where horses could haul the coal in larger wagons to the loading areas at the ports or river quays much more easily. Though the Tyne area led the way there similar developments in other parts of the country, such as the Nottingham and Coalbrookdale areas.

A major obstruction to early expansion that dogged development of wagon-ways and continued even with the pioneer railways of the 19th century was the need for what were called 'wayleaves'. A few coal-mine owners also owned adjacent land, in some cases allowing development of wagonways with no obstructions all the way to the railhead at river, port, or later (in the 18th and early 19th centuries) the canal basin. But in many more cases the wagonways had to be built over private land, involving permission to be sought and granted for the route and rentals or fees be paid. While some landowners were co-operative and reasonable a good number objected and negotiations were protracted and expensive in terms of legal fees. Some landowners tried to charge hefty rents, or were so obstructive that court cases ensued. So although the development

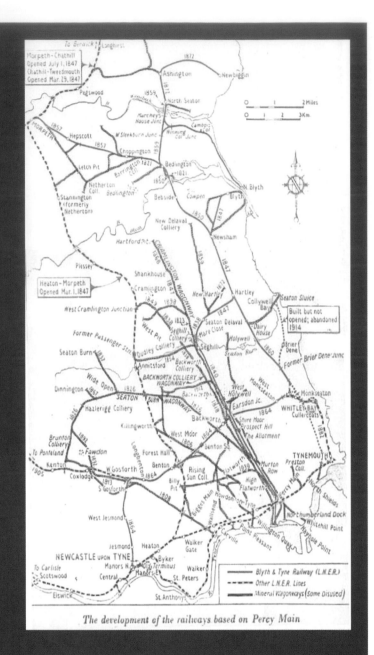

The development of the railways based on Percy Main

ABOVE A map showing wagonways in Northumberland.

of the first wagonways was impressive and eventually led to the development of today's railways, there was much more going on out of sight of the layman, than the building and operating of the system might imply.

face of the wheel was a flange on both faces, and this was used on a few quarry and mining lines, though not on any major lines. The edge rail proved so superior to plate rail that it had become the rail of choice by the time steam traction became a practical alternative to the horse in the 1820s. The first edge rail was produced in cast iron by another ironmaster, William Jessop, for a line connection with Leicester Navigation canal in 1793. An improved version was introduced in 1797 and came into use on one of the Tyneside railways. Because of the shape, with a bulbous underside, this was known as 'fish belly' rail. Because of its cost, edge rail was adopted quite slowly in the early years of the 19th century, and at least one line with the old wooden rails was still operating in 1840. By 1820 wrought iron, which was much stronger, had replaced cast iron. A major advantage of iron rails instead of wood, was that horses could pull a much heavier load on iron rails than on wood, and the maintenance and replacement of the track was much less with iron rather than wooden rails.

ABOVE Early plateway on the Ticknall Tramway, 1799.

Until the early years of the 19th century the motive power for all types of surface rail operation was the horse (or sometimes the mule) – except for ropeway operation – but the whole course of development was about to change radically with the coming of steam traction. By about this time the terms 'railway', 'railroad', or 'iron road' were already coming into use for lines with the superior edge rail.

Horse power

However, it is worth remembering that the horse as motive power on railways and tramways gave valuable service until well into the 20th century. By a strange reversal of duties, however, after steam traction became established, the horse was mostly used to haul passengers. In the days before steam traction, all the wagonways and tramroads were used solely to serve industry and horses hauled the freight loads, while passengers went by road in stage coaches or stage wagons.

With the coming of steam, on the Stockton and Darlington Railway for example, the steam operations were mainly concerned with the movement of freight, and it was only in response to public demand to ride on the line that led to the building of the first passenger coach named 'Experiment' which, however, was only run once each day in each direction, from October 1825. Meanwhile, other operators were allowed to use the line, and the horse-drawn 'Union', essentially a stage coach with flanged wheels and strengthened chassis, gave a half-hourly service on part of the route. Other railways, too, were dependent on horses for passenger, as well as freight haulage, in the early years of steam, particularly overseas, several of the early American railways on the eastern seaboard used horses, as did some early French railways, largely as a stop-gap until sufficient steam locomotives were available.

Aside from this, horses remained as the main form of haulage on surviving industrial tramroads for many years, and below ground in coalmines, horse haulage survived in some cases into the second half of the 20th century.

By the late 1820s as cities and towns expanded, and business grew, the need for efficient city transport started to become apparent. As early as 1829 a tramroad two miles long was laid down along Commercial Road in London, not for public transport but for horse carts hauling goods and building materials. In 1832 a public horse-drawn carriage tramroad was built in New York, though it was the 1850s before this idea was more widely taken up. Paris had one of the first lines in Europe. A line from Bayswater to the City of London was proposed (but not built) in 1858, a line in Liverpool for passenger carriage was built in 1859 and the same operator built a line in North London in 1860–61. In 1861 momentum was given to 'street railways' – as they were first called – by an American engineer, George Train, who built a line in Birkenhead, and three lines in London, which all opened in 1861. They lasted less than a year, however, as the rail rose above street level and impeded the movement of other horse-drawn vehicles. By about 1870, however, better planned and approved lines – by now generally called 'tramways', all horse-drawn, began to proliferate in London and many other towns and cities to provide municipal transport on a big scale. By 1876, steam-tram engines were slowly introduced, followed by other traction systems such as cable and electricity from the 1880s onward, but horse-drawn trams were still to be found on some routes and in some areas until well into the 20th century – 1912 in the case of London.

Surprisingly one horse tramway in the British Isles remained in service until 1957. This was the famous Fintona Tramway in Northern Ireland. The ¾ mile branch was built in conventional style in 1883 to link Fintona with Fintona Junction signal box. Another late-surviving horse-drawn operation was on the Port Carlisle branch of the North British Railway which was not replaced by steam traction until April 1914. In Douglas, on the Isle of Man, there are still horse-drawn trams operating today.

One aspect of horse-drawn traction that always attracted attention was the method of operation when gradients were involved. Many of the old wagonways and tramroads serving mines and industries were steeply graded in part. Grades of 1:40, 1:30, or even 1:20 were sometimes seen. Horses were used to haul wagons up these steep grades, but to bring the wagons down grade, the horse was not needed as gravity could be used. Very often the horses were tethered behind and had to follow, but this could be dangerous and a quite common alternative was to use a special cart that could be attached behind the wagon (or wagons) and for the horse to be tethered in the cart – usually called a dandy cart – and the train operator to use the brake to control the speed of descent.

Over the period covered by the 17th-19th centuries mining and related industries expanded greatly, gaining huge momentum with the Industrial Revolution, canal building, and the larger scale of manufacturing. This era saw the expansion of waggonways and tramroads serving all this commercial activity. Wooden railways were replaced by iron railways from the late 18th century, but for all this time until steam traction became practical in the early 19th century, it was the horse that provided the traction.

OPPOSITE The Fintona Tramway in Northern Ireland was the last horse-drawn tram in Ireland. It was used until 1957.

chapter 2

The 18th century saw the gradual development of practical working steam engines, albeit of primitive low pressure type. Newcomen's design of 1709 was the first really successful one, though it was not very efficient. James Watt was the key engine designer from the later part of the 18th century who greatly increased the quality and efficiency of the steam engine. All these designs were intended to operate pumps for the fast developing mining industry, and all were of the low pressure type. It was not until the last few years of the 18th century that other applications for the steam engine were considered and it took until the first two decades of the 19th century before high pressure steam was utilised and was used to drive and develop locomotives, thanks to the enterprise of such pioneers as Richard Trevithick, William Blenkinsopp, William Hedley and George Stephenson.

The coming of steam

PREVIOUS PAGES
Costumed men and
women of the London
and North Eastern
Railway company ride
in freight wagons hauled
by the early locomotive
'Puffing Billy' during
centenary celebrations
commemorating the 1825
opening of the Stockton and
Darlington Railway.

RIGHT Engraving taken
from *Experimenta Nova*
(1672) by the German
scientist Otto von
Guericke, showing
his experiment with
an evacuated sphere
being carried out at
Madgeburg, Germany. In
this demonstration sixteen
horses could not pull
apart the two halves of
an evacuated sphere,
which became known as
Magdeburg hemispheres.

The use of steam to generate power long preceded its application to railways. Indeed, steam power had been going through over one hundred years of development and application before the first steam railway locomotive was built.

Early experimenters in the 17th century realised the power of atmospheric pressure and reasoned that if pressure could move a piston inside a cylinder, then the movement of the piston could be linked to the moving of a weight. For the atmospheric pressure to move the piston down, there needed to be a vacuum in the cylinder below the piston. The first man to demonstrate this was a German inventor, Otto von Guericke in 1650. He used a hand pump to extract the air below the cylinder. Pressure from the air above it then forced the cylinder down, and a rope attached to the cylinder through pulleys could then lift a weight.

Several experimenters in France, Holland and England followed up this work. In England Robert Boyle (1627–1691) and Robert Hooke (1635–1703) made a similar device, essentially an air pump, based on Otto von Guericke's (1602–86) idea. A noted Dutch physicist, Christiaan Huygens (1629-1695), built a version of Guericke's machine, too, using gunpowder to blow out the air below the piston through leather 'valves'. While the demonstration was successful, the need for successive explosions for continuous operation made the idea far from practical.

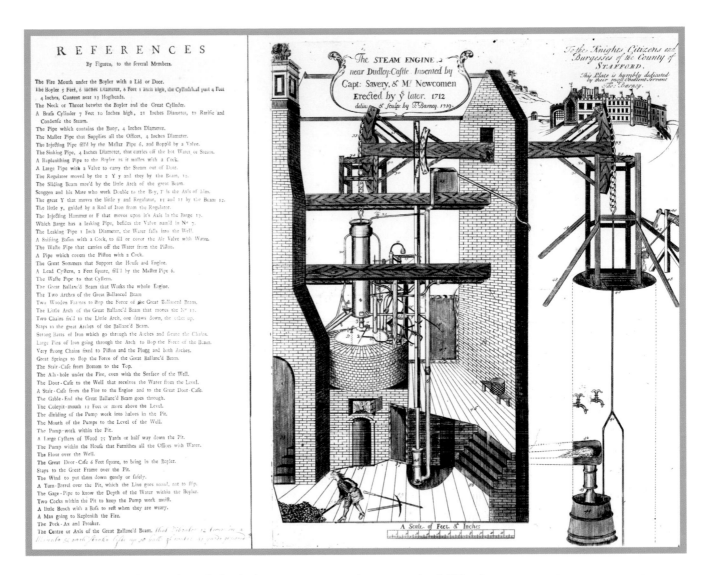

A major step forward, and the link to steam operation, came in 1690 when a French inventor, Denis Papin (1647–1712), who was a follower and former helper of Huygens, came up with the idea of using steam under pressure to create the vacuum. He made a model to prove that if steam was injected into the piston below the cylinder it then condensed and this created the necessary vacuum for the piston to move down the cylinder. If the steam was continuously injected the cylinder would continue moving up and down with each 'puff' of steam into the cylinder. An immediate suggestion by Papin was that this movement could be used to drive a pump, using steam power rather than men pumping by hand. An obvious use for this was in mining where flooding was a frequent problem.

Practical development

Demonstrating this idea with a model was one thing, but building it as a practical full-size machine was more challenging because metal-working techniques were still very primitive at this time, with iron forging and brass forming being done in the most basic way, and pipes able to stand high pressure being non-existent.

Cornish tin mining had become an important industry by the late 17th century and mines were becoming even deeper, and with it the problem of flooding. Better pumps were needed to combat this, and a Devonian, Thomas Newcomen (1663–1729), who was aware of Denis Papin's demonstration model using condensed steam, started work

ABOVE Newcomen's Steam Engine at Dudley Castle, 1719. Newcomen (1663–1729) invented the first practical steam engine. The first well-authenticated Newcomen engine, erected near Dudley in Worcestershire in 1712, was a mature and practical machine.

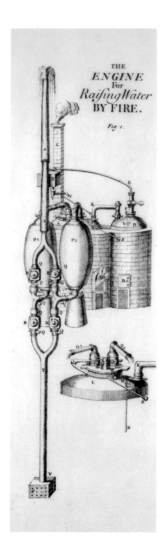

to try and build a full-size pumping engine. Meanwhile another West Countryman, Captain Thomas Savery (1650–1715), also set out to make a working steam pump and completed and patented his first, in 1698. This caused Newcomen to cease his work and join up with Savery. However Savery's design was something of a dead end in technical terms. His pump did not use a piston moving in a cylinder but instead depended on the vacuum effect created in a vertical cylinder when condensed steam was replaced by air. The vacuum sucked water upwards and a non-return valve stopped it falling back. The whole thing was inefficient, as large amounts of coal were needed to raise sufficient steam in the boiler, and the greatest height to which a load could be raised by this method was 80ft, and only in very slow time. This limited its use immediately for most mines by then were much deeper than 80ft.

These limitations encouraged Thomas Newcomen to resume his design work. By 1709 he had successfully built his first pump engine, based closely on Papin's original ideas. But Newcomen overcame the problem of transferring the movement of the piston in the cylinder to working a pump. He used a pivoted wood beam attached at one end to the piston end by a swivel join, with the other end attached to the pump arm.

Steam was forced into the cylinder pushing the piston up. It was then cut off and the steam was condensed by a water jet and the resulting vacuum caused the piston to drop. A valve allowed the exhausted steam to escape, and the sequence started again, giving the familiar continuous 'up and down' sequence still seen in steam-engine cylinders today.

The Newcomen steam engine, usually called an atmospheric engine at the time, proved to be a big commercial success. The first engine was operating at Dudley Castle coal mine in Staffordshire by 1712. As it turned out, coal mines became the main customers for the new steam engines, mainly because they needed a lot of coal – even though they were more efficient than Avery's original engine – and coal mines, of course, had a plentiful supply. Tin mines in Cornwall would have had to ship it in and that would have been an expensive business, added to by the tax on sea-coal at the time. With efficient pumps available to clear water, coal mines would be made deeper and bigger, and a tall engine house came to be a feature of the biggest 18th-century coal mines.

The earliest Newcomen steam engines were difficult to build, due to the problem of constructing the boilers and components, mainly hand-made from cooper for the boiler and brass for the fittings and cylinder. However, by the 1720s the Coalbrookdale blast furnaces were installed and in production, allowing cast-iron components to be produced. From about 1723 onwards, Newcomen's engines could be built using cast-iron for the cylinder and other parts, making production quicker and cheaper. Also engines could be made in different sizes to suit the task. One huge one of 1760 in a Newcastle coal mine could pump water in stages from over 500ft down and had a cylinder of over 70in in diameter. By contract small engines might be used to pump water supplies from streams to nearby farms or estates.

Several important improvements were made as the 18th century progressed. An engineer named John Smeaton (1724–1792) introduced a wheel with a moving chain as an alternative to the wooden beam, and designed a more efficient firebox fitted into the boiler. Originally the two valves on the cylinder injecting the steam and exhausting the condensed steam were operated manually but it was discovered that metal rods on the beam above the engine and attached to the valves could work these automatically as the beam moved up and down. The first thought of using a steam engine for any task other than pumping came in 1737 when an engineer put forward the idea that it might be possible to drive a boat by steam.

Improving the Engine

Two key figures who played a major part in steam engine development in the late 18th century were James Watt (1763–1819) and Matthew Boulton (1728–1809). Watt trained as an instrument maker, working at Glasgow University, and in 1763–65 as a young man he became involved in restoring an early model of a Newcomen atmospheric steam engine. He realised how inefficient it was in the waste of steam and the amount of coal needed to fire it. The cylinder was heated up with the steam injection, then cooled down when water was used to cause the condensation, then heated again for the next stroke and so on. Watt realised that a separate condenser was the answer allowing the cylinder to be lagged to retain the heat and also to be made more efficient by giving it a closed top. Less coal was now needed to supply the heat.

Watt made a model to demonstrate his improvements but no orders were forthcoming. A Scottish iron-master gave Watt backing in 1767, no doubt hoping for business from orders. This kept Watt going until 1769 when he patented the design. Following this, Watt built a full-size prototype of his improved engine and achieved a 50 per cent saving in coal compared with Newcomen's original design. The iron-master subsequently went bankrupt, and this brought James Watt into contact with one of the customers, an engineer named Matthew Boulton who ran a business in Soho, Birmingham. Boulton could see the potential of Watt's improved engine design, offered Watt a partnership in the business, and had Watt's first engine brought to the

BELOW James Watt's ten-horse-power patent rotative steam engine, as constructed by Messrs. Boulton and Watt, Soho, from 1787 to 1800. The term 'horse power' was first used by James Watt.

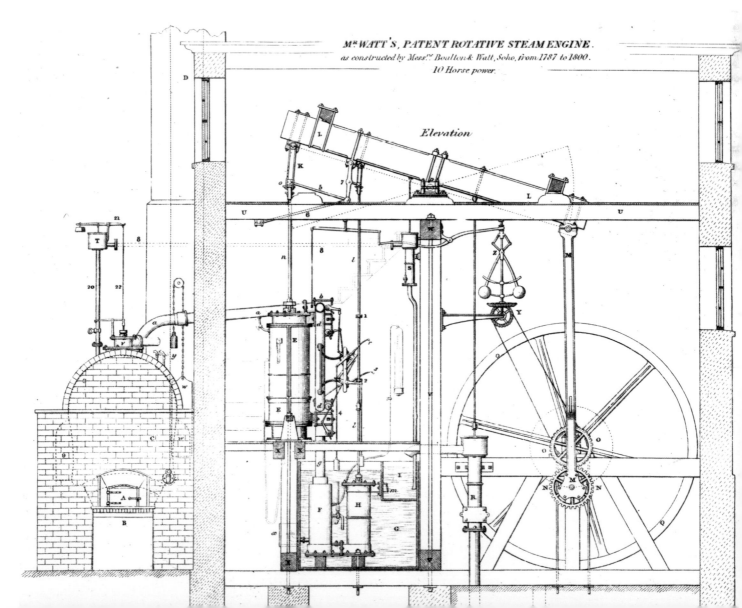

Mr WATT'S, PATENT ROTATIVE STEAM ENGINE.
as constructed by Messrs. Boulton & Watt, Soho, from 1787 to 1800.
10 Horse power.

Elevation

Soho works. Using more accurately bored cylinders made by a Midlands foundry, the engine was made even more efficient and from 1775 orders flowed in.

Many of the new engines went to coal mines, but they also went to Cornish tin mines for the much reduced amount of coal needed to power the Watt engine made them more economical when coal had to be brought in. In fact Watt and Boulton charged a royalty to users calculated from the money saved. Use of the engines for functions other than pumping also began to spread. For example, the first of Watt's engines built in Soho was used to re-circulate – by pumping – the water used to work the waterwheel at Boulton's Soho factory. Another was used to work bellows at the iron foundry of one of Boulton's customers.

In the meantime Watt developed further refinements to make the engine more efficient; in particular he improved the operation and timing of the valve gear and introduced the idea of condensing steam each side of the piston to give it better momentum. These changes, patented in 1782, made the engine more powerful and in this form it was known as a reciprocating double-action engine.

Wider applications

Another key innovation by James Watt was the use of a beam driven by the piston that transmitted movement by a crankshaft to a large diameter flywheel. He called this the 'sun and planet' method of transmission. The ultimate development was the addition of a 'governor' using balls on a spindle to regulate the admission of steam and vary the speed as required, while ensuring the speed stayed constant. The 'sun and planet' transmission opened the way for the application of steam engines to tasks other than pumping water. They were quickly adapted in coal and tin mines as winding engines, and could be used to power machinery of all kinds in mills and factories. They could also be used to operate ropeways and inclines at mines where horses or manpower had previously been used, and were used also on some of the inclined planes that carried barges to higher canal levels. By 1800 many hundreds of steam engines, mostly from Watt and Boulton, were in use at a time when the Industrial Revolution was reaching its peak.

High-pressure steam

Watt, himself, never ventured into high-pressure steam. The atmospheric engine, as its name implied, had a steam pressure of about 15lbs per square inch, virtually the same as steam from a kettle of boiling water. In the early days few realised the potential of the power of steam at higher pressures. Though James Watt knew of the idea late in his career, he never thought it necessary for his type of engine. It was left to others to develop this aspect of steam power. James Watt retired in 1800 (he died in 1819, and Boulton died in 1809), effectively ending his era of enterprise.

The same year, 1800, was something of a milestone in the development of steam. A key figure here was Richard Trevithick (1771–1833) of Redruth, Cornwall. He was an engineer in a Cornish tin mine. Watt and Boulton had protected their steam engine designs with strictly enforced patents, and Trevithick started looking at the idea of a high-pressure steam engine in the late 1790s to overcome the patent restrictions. He was aware, too, that an American engineer was thinking along the same lines.

Trevithick's first engine had a vertical cylinder with piston and a horizontal cylindrical high-pressure boiler. The piston turned a large flywheel that rotated a

ABOVE Model of sun and planet gearing, made by James Watt, demonstrating the action designed to produce a rotative motion.

wheel with a chain drive. This was used as a winding engine at the Cook's Kitchen mine in Cornwall. A safety valve was incorporated in the top of the boiler, activated if the steam pressure inside got too high.

The success of this mine engine led Trevithick to the idea of making a steam powered carriage in 1801. In fact Trevithick was not the first to have this idea, for in 1784 William Murdock (1754–1839), an engineer employed by Boulton and Watt, had built a model of such a vehicle, which had a vertical cylinder operating a beam that connected to a drive on the main axle. This was never built full-size, but Murdock was based as a mine engineer in Cornwall at the time and it is possible that this gave Trevithick his idea for a road vehicle. Even so, Murdock's design was not the first for, in 1769–70, a French engineer, Nicolas Cugnot (1725-1804), had built a three-wheel steam carriage intended to haul artillery pieces for the French army. This had limitations, including being hard to steer and needing frequent halts to refuel and replenish with water, so it was never a practical design, though a second vehicle was also built.

An advantage of a high-pressure steam engine was that it could be made smaller and still deliver as much power as a large atmospheric. This was the key to Trevithick's steam road carriage.

On road and water

The road carriage, built in 1801–3, made quite an impact, not least because it could run at the then high speed of 12mph. It had a horizontal cylinder inside a cylindrical boiler. Two huge 10ft diameter wheels were driven by gear wheels actuated by a flywheel linkage to the piston. The boiler was fired from the rear, and the boiler flue was also at the rear. The vehicle was steered by a single front wheel and a saloon body could seat eight passengers. Though demonstrated several times, including in London, Trevithick could not find a backer to enable him to build more, and after it crashed and caught fire the project was discontinued, although the compact engine design was patented for use in other applications.

However, Trevithick's efforts spurred others on to propose, or actually build, steam

RIGHT The common
road passenger locomotive,
London, 1803 from the *Life
of Richard Trevithick*.

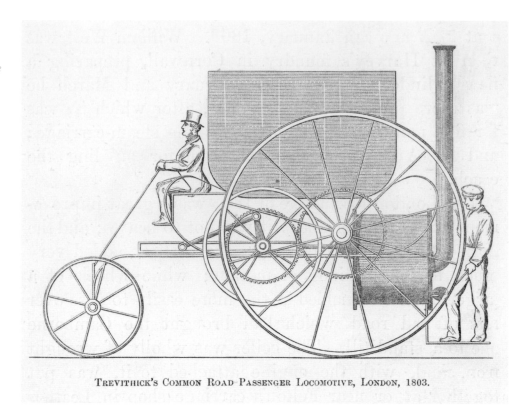

TREVITHICK'S COMMON ROAD PASSENGER LOCOMOTIVE, LONDON, 1803.

road vehicles in the early 19th century. Several were wildly impractical, including a steam stage coach that looked like a stagecoach with steam engine and drive at the back. A successful design by Sir Goldsworthy Gurney (1793–1875) was essentially a steam tractor that could haul an attached coach, substituting for a horse team. The Gurney steam carriage, called a 'Drag', was so safe and successful that several were made and ran passenger services in the Cheltenham and London areas in the 1820s. Walter Hancock (1792–1852) was a contemporary of Gurney who built a self-contained steam road carriage where the steam engine was fitted at the back with passengers in the front. A stoker and engineer tended the high-pressure steam engine in the back and a driver steered from the front. Hancock was based in Stratford, East London, and operated what were essentially the forerunners of bus services, with eleven vehicles in the London area, including routes such as Paddington to Moorgate.

From these early years onwards, steam road transport took its own path and departs some way from these early links with the railway pioneers. It is also worth mentioning that Watt had suggested the application of steam to both road and rail vehicles in the 1780s but had never pursued these ideas.

The other key element of transport, Water, was also beginning to harness steam in the early years of the 19th century. Most of the pioneering work here was by French engineers, though a British visionary called Jonathan Halls had made a primitive steam-paddle steamer, using a Newcomen atmospheric engine in 1737, but it had limited success or use. A Scotsman, Patrick Miller (1730–1815), built a very small steam boat in 1785, but subsequent designs were limited by a lack of suitable engines due to the patent limitations of Watt and Boulton. When the patent expired in 1800, William Symington (1764-1831), an associate of Patrick Miller, built the first really successful steam boat in Britain, the 56ft long 'Charlotte Dundas' of 1802, a paddle-driven vessel intended as a tug for barges on the Forth-Clyde Canal. From then on marine steam propulsion developed in its own way, quite distinct from steam for rail traction, but it is worth noting that railway pioneer Richard Trevithick also adapted

A Sketch of

MR GURNEY'S NEW STEAM CARRIAGE.

As it appeared at Hounslow on the 12th of August, with a Barouche attached, containing the Duke of Wellington and other Persons of Distinction. 1827

his high-pressure steam engine to power a dredger built for work in the London docks in 1806 and this engine influenced the work of some other marine engineers with new design features such as a water feed pump in place of a condenser.

On the rails

But Trevithick's lasting fame came with his move into locomotive design. He used a similar layout to the steam road carriage on his locomotives, essentially a high-pressure horizontal cylinder enclosed by the high-pressure boiler. The piston was connected to a large flywheel that, in the case of his first locomotive drove a toothed gear that, in turn, drove toothed wheels on the inner faces of the two left-hand wheels. This had been designed and built in 1802 at Coalbrookdale but appears never to have been operated. However, a second similar locomotive was built the following year.

This came about because Trevithick was engaged to install the high-pressure mine engines of his design at Penydarren Ironworks, Merthyr Tydfil). The owner asked Trevithick if it was possible to build a steam locomotive that could be used instead of horses on the ironworks tramway. The locomotive he built was tested at the ironworks on 13 February 1804, and ran at 5mph hauling loaded waggons weighing 20 tons in all. The locomotive weighed 5 tons and the cylinder was 8¼in in diameter with a stroke of 4½ft. A key feature of the design was to direct the exhaust steam into the tall upright chimney and this also acted to draw up the fire, which has been done on virtually all steam locomotives since then.

The Penydarren track led from the ironworks to the Glamorgan Canal at

ABOVE Gurney's steam carriage as it appeared in Hounslow on the 12th of August, with a Barouche attached, containing the Duke of Wellington and other Persons of Distinction.

ABOVE Steam engine
designed by the Cornish
engineer Richard Trevithick
and built in 1803. It was
the first steam engine to
operate on rails, running
at Coalbrookdale, near
Telford.

OPPOSITE In 1808
Richard Trevithick
established a 'steam
circus' in Euston Square in
London, charging members
of the public one shilling
for the opportunity to ride
in a carriage pulled by his
locomotive, the 'Catch Me
Who Can'.

Abercynon, 9¾ miles. From late February 1804 the locomotive was in general, but showed an early limitation in that the track broke several times under the weight of the locomotive, and much undergrowth and tree cutting alongside the track was needed to give clearance for the locomotive which, of course, stood much higher and wider than the horses. The locomotive had flangeless wheels to run on L-shaped plate rail, 4ft 2in gauge.

In 1805 a third 'Locomotive Engine' of the same type as the second was built in Newcastle for use on the Wylam tramroad. This differed from the Penydarren locomotive by having its cylinder at the opposite end with the gearing and drive re-arranged accordingly. It also had flanged wheels to run on edge rail. However, it was never put into service to haul wagons and was used solely as a stationary steam engine.

Trevithick's final locomotive made the biggest impact. This was a smaller machine with a vertical cylinder and horizontal boiler very similar to the original Trevithick mine winding engines, and it was described at the time as a 'portable steam engine'. A rod from the piston head was attached to the rear wheels to provide the drive. Prints show a platform at the rear for an engineer and stoker. By comparison drawings of the earlier Trevithick locomotives show no provision for a crew. This suggests that a small platform *may* have been provided at the opposite end to the piston for a crew but was omitted from the drawings, *or* no provision was made for a riding crew and the engineer and stoker walked along and tended the locomotive from the trackside.

The new 'portable steam engine' was called 'Catch Me Who Can' and the publicity slogan said 'Mechanical Power Subduing Animal Speed'. It was brought to London in July 1808 and set up on a fenced-off circle of track on a site at the top of Gower Street in what is now Euston Square. The locomotive towed a barouche round the track and public could ride behind the engine at speeds of up to 12mph for a one-shilling fare, or could watch the proceedings inside the high fence for 5d. The event certainly publicised the idea of railways and gave many the first ever glimpse of a train. However, the proceedings did not pay and after a few weeks of operating

Richard Trevithick's Railroad Euston Square 1809

Canals

The relevance of canals to the development of railways should always be remembered. Canal construction preceded railways, canals being mainly built in the 18th century, and in the early years of the 19th century. At the time the canal movement started, they were seen as the way to speed up communcations and transport to meet the needs of the Industrial Revolution, which was the same reason put forward later for the construction of railways. There were over 100 canals totalling over 2,500 miles of length when the canal system was at its zenith in 1875. Many canals only served local areas, but a few 'trunk' routes were formed, some of them like the Grand Union connnecting London with the Midlands and the North. There was also the Trans-Pennine Bridgewater Canal and also canals west and southwest of London. In the 18th century canal boats carried large numbers of passengers, with subsequent opposition from turnpike operators who feared the loss of business – just as they later opposed railways. The problem with canals was the slow transit time, making canal boats unsuitable for perishable or urgent cargoes. They were suited to coal, sand and similar loads. As with the railways, canals needed a Parliamentary Act to be built and were always hedged about with legal requirements concerning fees and carriage.

When the first tramroads and waggonways were built, however, many of them served nearby canals, interchanging loads with canal boats, typically coal or other minerals, and in this respect they gave canal use a boost. Later still, warehouses were built at canal basins for the handling of more general cargoes, and in the 1840s, a number of canal companies were bought up by railway companies giving an early form of 'integrated transport' and leading incidentally to rail company canal boats in railway company livery and lettering.

a rail broke, the locomotive was derailed and damaged, and the enterprise was abandoned. At this point Trevithick withdrew from any further railway activity and moved into marine engineering, later working as an engineer in South America.

After Trevithick

The Trevithick era was something of a false dawn for steam railways. The main drawback was that his locomotives were too heavy for the rails that had been laid for horse-drawn waggons, and all his efforts were thwarted sooner or later by broken rails. So for a short time there was no further progress.

However, prices of horse fodder were rising due to the Napoleonic Wars, and in 1811 this caused John Blenkinsop (1783–1831), manager of the Middleton Colliery to introduce steam haulage. He designed a track system intended to prevent the problem of rail breakage. This used toothed rack rail laid outside the running rails with cog wheels arranged to run along the rack rails while the unflanged main wheels ran along the plateway. A 3½ mile line range from the colliery to carry coal to Leeds and this was relaid with the rack rail. Matthew Murray (1765–1826) of an engineering works in Leeds designed a locomotive to suit this system. It used Trevithick's high-pressure boiler design, but with two vertical cylinders inside, operating vertical cranks that drove the centrally placed cog wheels on each side by means of gear wheels on the axle. The locomotive wheels were not driven but ran on the plateway, simply carrying the weight of the locomotive which was 5 tons. Water and coal were carried in an attached tender. On test in June 1812 the locomotive pulled 27 loaded coal cauldrons with a weight of about 100 tons. It was a successful design and four locomotives were built, remaining in service until 1835. Further locomotives of this type were built in 1813 for the collieries at Kenton and

Coxlodge on the Tyne. Two further locomotives were built in Berlin in 1816 and 1818, the first steam locomotives in Germany, but these were unsuccessful. Two of the Blenkinsop engines were said to do the work of 14 horses.

Though rack railways were built in later years, and are still to be found today, the Blenkinsop locomotives and rack system was a dead end at the time and was not more widely taken up. The next stage of development was pursued by William Hedley (1779–1843) of Wylam Colliery who, in 1813, had designed and built a locomotive named 'Puffing Billy', assisted by Timothy Hackworth (1786–1850), which is preserved today in the Science Museum, London. This locomotive also used two cylinders working vertical cranks on beams, but this time the cylinders were outside the boiler. This was actually a second attempt, for the first locomotive built had only one cylinder driving wheels on one side only, which proved inadequate.

'Puffing Billy' was so successful that a second locomotive was built, 'Wylam Dilly', also preserved, this time in the Royal Museum of Scotland. In preparation for the locomotives the 5ft gauge wood tracks at Wylam had been relaid with iron-plate rail, but even so track breakages still occurred. To avoid this, in 1815 four more wheels were added to an extended frame, these being geared to the two main driving

ABOVE 'Puffing Billy' and its sister locomotive 'Wylam Dilly' are the earliest surviving locomotives in the world. Both were built by William Hedley.

OPPOSITE Hand-coloured aquatint by Robert Havell of the earliest known representation of Blenkinsop's 'Salamanca' on the Leeds and Middleton Railway.

axles, and intended to spread the weight. Later still, in 1830, edged rail replaced the plate rails and locomotives reverted to four wheels, this time flanged. A short tender to carry water was also attached. The draughting arrangement using exhaust steam directed up the chimney, as devised by Trevithick, was used, a feature omitted from the Blenkinsop rack locomotives, which were less efficient as a result. The Hedley locomotives, too, had the firebox set into the boiler with its hatch next to the chimney and the smoke flue which ran to the back of the boiler, doubled back to give a maximum heating surface for the water in the boiler.

Enter George Stephenson

While all this was going on George Stephenson (1781–1848), was working as an engine-wright maintaining the stationary engines at Killingworth on the Tyne. His father had worked on the stationary engines at Wylam. Stephenson was interested in Hedley's locomotive work at the nearby Wylam Railway, and the Blenkinsop engines used on the adjacent Kenton and Oxlodge Railway. So he was keen to make a start when the owner of the Killingworth collieries asked him to build a steam locomotive to run on the Killingworth Railway. In 1814 he built his first locomotive, 'Blücher', at Killingworth. This copied many of the features of the Blenkinsop locomotives with which he was familiar, but the cog wheels and rack feature were abandoned and flanged, driven wheels were fitted instead to run on edged rail. There were two in-line cylinders of 9in diameter and 24in stroke fitted into the boiler with the connecting rods from the top of the pistons driving the wheels direct on the wheel crank-pins. Toothed wheels on the axles were connected by a chain so that the cranks were synchronised. The firebox was the opposite end to the chimney and a small attached tender carried coal, the water supply, and also the crew. The drive arrangement was noisy, so a second engine in 1815 had connecting rods driving the wheels and the axles had sprockets and were coupled together by a chain. On this engine the cylinders were moved from being embedded in the boiler to a position above the wheels so that they could drive the connecting rods direct.

Stephenson built another locomotive in 1816 that had six wheels instead of four and had a new feature in which the axle bearings could move freely up and down guides and were attached to pistons that ran in small cylinders fitted vertically below the boiler. Filled with steam, these cylinders gave a good degree of springing which equalised wheels over roughly laid track, ensuring a much smoother ride, especially at low speed with a laden coal train. Several more were built, some being sold to other collieries, and by 1823 Stephenson set up his own locomotive works in Newcastle, in time for the next period of railway development.

chapter 3

The period from about 1820–30 was the key decade that finally established steam railways as a practical and more efficient alternative to horse-drawn transport and the slow transit of the canals that preceded them. Two railway undertakings in particular, Stockton and Darlington (S.D.&R) and Liverpool and Manchester, pioneered the way ahead, and in the same decade locomotive design moved on rapidly from the underpowered early efforts like 'Puffing Billy' and 'Locomotion' to the 'Rocket' which first established principles used in most steam locomotives. The most famous and prominent designer and builder of locomotives in this period was George Stephenson who, with his son Robert, also established the first properly organised locomotive building company. George Stephenson's early experience was with colliery railways, another important feature of the period.

The first railways

PREVIOUS PAGES Detail
of the rods and wheels
of George Stephenson's
'Rocket', winner of the
Rainhill Trials in 1829.
This famous locomotive
subsequently ran on the
Liverpool and Manchester
Railway from 1829–1836
and the Midgeholme
Colliery Railway in County
Durham between 1836 and
1840.

BELOW A view of the
railway that connected
Hetton Colliery with
its depot on the banks
of the River Wear, near
Sunderland in Durham.

The key developments in steam locomotive design that George Stephenson initiated during his time at Killingworth were drive by connecting rods from the pistons in place of the complicated gearing and chains used on earlier engines, and springing by means of his 'steam-springs', which gave a much superior ride. As it happened 'steam-springs' had a limited life as an idea, but the principle of sprung axles for locomotives was established and was followed later by the use of laminated metal springs. At Killingworth, Stephenson and his assistants built at least 12 locomotives, and possibly 16, both for use on the Killingworth Railway and for other colliery lines. One of them, in 1816, was for the Kilmarnock and Troon Railway, serving a colliery owned by the Duke of Portland, and this was the first steam locomotive to run in Scotland. Aside from locomotives, Stephenson was also busy building steam-worked stationary and winding engines, and also developed a miner's safety lamp, though this was soon eclipsed by the almost contemporary Davey safety lamp.

In 1819 George Stephenson was asked to build a new railway at Hetton Colliery, County Durham. This he engineered from the start as a steam railway with edge rail. It was about eight miles long, but because of the terrain only 3½ miles was level enough for locomotive haulage, and the inclined lengths were worked by hauling the chaldrons by winding engines or letting them descend by gravity. Two locomotives of the Killingworth type were used at first though the other improved designs were ordered later. The building work for the Hetton Colliery Railway took until 1822.

Public railways

Up until this time most tramroads and steam railways were built to serve collieries or mines concentrating on the haulage of coal or minerals only. But some non-colliery railways, albeit horse-drawn, had existed since 1803 and about 19 had been authorised and built by 1820. The first of these to make an impact was the Surrey Iron Railway, which was authorised in 1801 and opened in July 1803, running six miles from Wandsworth in South London to Croydon and Carshalton. It largely followed the course of the River Wandle and to some extent was built as an alternative to a canal for which the Wandle was unsuitable.

The Surrey Iron Railway was a plateway serving industrial customers only and was interesting in that it was an early forerunner of an 'open access' line that became the custom in the late 20th and early 21st century in Britain and parts of mainland Europe whereby the track was owned by an infrastructure company and operators paid fees to use it. The Surrey Iron Railway was open to individual firms who were charged tolls (or fees) to use, such as 3d per mile per chaldron of coal and 2d per mile for other loads such as bricks, clay or stone. A similar type of operation was built in 1820, the Stratford and Morton Railway, which also charged users. A wagon and stretch of rail from this is preserved at Stratford-upon-Avon. The line was, however, a much truncated version of an original grand ambition to build the line through to Cheltenham and then on to London. The builder of this railway, William James, also suggested a horse-drawn railway from Liverpool to Manchester as early as 1803, possibly influenced by the Surrey Iron Railway.

In fact, the Surrey Iron Rail seems to have fired the imagination of a number of thinkers. A test on this line showed that a horse could haul as many as 12 chaldrons loaded with stones to bring each one to three tons. These could be pulled at 6mph, and on test further chaldrons were added until the load had grown from 36 tons to 55 tons at the end of the journey. This was compared with typical load of 15cwt

SURREY Iron Railway.

The COMMITTEE of the SURREY IRON RAILWAY COMPANY,

HEREBY, GIVE NOTICE,- That the BASON at *Wandsworth*, and the Railway therefrom up to *Croydon* and *Carfhalton*, is now open for the Ufe of the Public, on Payment of the following Tolls, *viz.*

For all Coals entering into or going out of their Bason at Wandsworth,	*per Chaldron,*	3d.
For all other Goods entering into or going out of their Bason at Wandsworth	*per Ton,*	3d.

For all GOODS carried on the said RAILWAY, as follows, viz.

For Dung, - -	*per Ton, per Mile,*	1d.
For Lime, and all Manures, (except Dung,) Lime-ftone, Chalk, Clay, Breeze, Afhes, Sand, Bricks, Stone, Flints, and Fuller's Earth,	*per Ton, per Mile,*	2d.
For Coals, - -	*per Chald. per Mile,*	3d.
And, For all other Goods, -	*per Ton, per Mile,*	3d.

By ORDER of the COMMITTEE,
W. B. LUTTLY,
Clerk of the Company.

Wandsworth, June 1, 1804.

BROOKE, PRINTER, No. 35, PATERNOSTER-ROW, LONDON.

ABOVE Announcement of the opening of the Surrey Iron Railway, together with toll charges for carrying goods. The goods were transported between Wandsworth, Croydon and Carshalton, villages at the time but all now part of Greater London.

that a horse could pull on a road at that time, though it must be said that the test described was much heavier than typical loads on the line that were more often one to five chaldrons.

One witness of the test was Sir Richard Phillips (1767-1840) who said that the money then being spent by the government fortifying Malta could have been better spent building 'double lines of iron railway from London to Edinburgh, Glasgow, Holyhead, Milford, Falmouth, Yarmouth, Dover and Portsmouth.' While this happened eventually it was many years later in the steam age, though a horse-drawn railway from London to Portsmouth had been suggested in 1799, but by 1803 this scheme had been abandoned due to its high estimated cost of nearly £½ million.

A visionary who was ahead of his time was Dr James Anderson (1738–1808) who in 1800 published a treatise suggesting that horse-drawn railways should be built alongside existing turnpike roads, for heavy loads at one rate and faster journeys at a higher rate. He proposed a trial installation from London to the Isle of Dogs where, at the time, it was planned to build new docks for London. The other trial installation, he suggested should be west from London to Hounslow. If these were successful, he said, the route to Hounslow could be extended along the turnpike to Bath. He was clearly also in favour for 'open access' for he said the lines should be 'kept open and patent to all alike who shall choose to employ them as the king's highway as it shall be found necessary.' A key advantage he saw for the railway was that heavily loaded waggons could be hauled at an estimated one-tenth of the force and cost of hauling them on the road. Anderson also suggested some engineering features for these roadside railways, covering height, width, gradients, bridges and tunnels, all some years ahead of his time.

Another thinker in the early 1800s, Thomas Gray (1788–1848) of Nottingham, visited one of the colliery lines in the north where the tramway hauled coal from the mine to a wharf for shipping out. He watched all the movement of wagons and horses with fascination then asked the engineer of the line 'Why are not these tramroads laid down all over England, so as to supersede our common roads, and steam-engines employed to convey goods and passengers along them so as to supersede horse-power?' The engineer looked sceptical and replied, 'Just propose you that to the nation, Sir, and see what you will get by it! Why, Sir, you will get worried to death for your pains.' Gray became obsessed with the idea and wrote and talked about it extensively, but was mostly dismissed as a bore and eccentric. Later, in 1820 he put his thoughts into a book *Observations on a General Iron Railway*, suggesting the Blenkinsop type of rack locomotive for haulage (see page 34). One key route, he thought, would be Liverpool to Manchester.

However, in March 1807 there was a significant step in the right direction when the Oystermouth Railway or Tramroad Company (as it was first called), running from Swansea west to the Mumbles, started operating. It had been authorised by Act of Parliament in 1804 and built in 1805–6 by Benjamin French. It ran alongside the turnpike to which an operating fee was paid. It was, of course, horse-drawn and was the first to carry both freight and passengers. An early passenger described a coach mainly built of iron with four wheels, an 'easy and light vehicle' pulled by a single horse. Ironically the line ceased to carry passengers in 1826 when a horse bus company started running along the turnpike and attracted custom. It is worth noting that the Oystermouth Railway started business over a year before Trevithick first demonstrated his steam locomotive 'Catch Me Who Can' in London in July 1808. The Oystermouth railway eventually closed in 1960.

The Stockton and Darlington

The Stockton and Darlington Railway is generally considered to be the undertaking

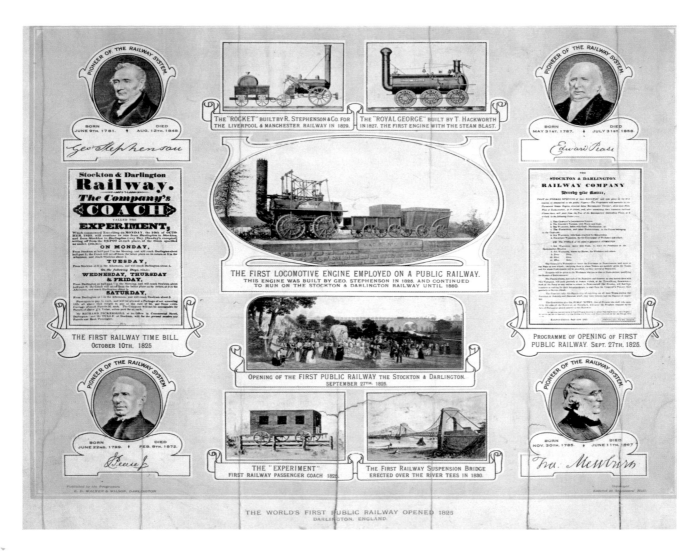

that advanced the development of railways by a quantum leap, starting the concept of route building and operating that has been followed to the present day. The line actually had a long period of gestation. And the commercial reasons for its importance were related directly to furthering business in one of the largest coalfields. This was at Bishops Auckland. Mining the coal here was fairly easy, but transporting it was not so straightforward. It was close to the River Wear, which would have made a water route for carrying the coal, but was not suitable for barge navigation south of Durham. And even if it had been, the River Wear ran far north to the sea at Sunderland. The alternative was to carry the coal south to ship it out on the River Tees which reached the sea at Middlesborough. Carting the coal south east to the River Tees was a long and difficult business over variable ground, some of it hilly, with the coal carried by pack horse, and priced higher accordingly than coal from better placed collieries. At various times in the late 18th century, a canal was mooted but nothing was done until 1810 when a group of traders and businessmen convened a meeting in Darlington to promote the idea of a canal or railway to run west from Stockton via Darlington, and in 1812 they appointed an engineer, John Rennie, to survey the route and report on the relative merits and costs of the two alternatives. He recommended a canal as the best option, but the Darlington businessmen hesitated, jibbed at the cost and came to no decision.

In 1816 at the instigation of Edward Pease, a Darlington businessman, some initial proposals were drawn up for a wooden tramway over which chaldrons could be hauled by horses, or on ropes by stationery steam engines as appropriate to the

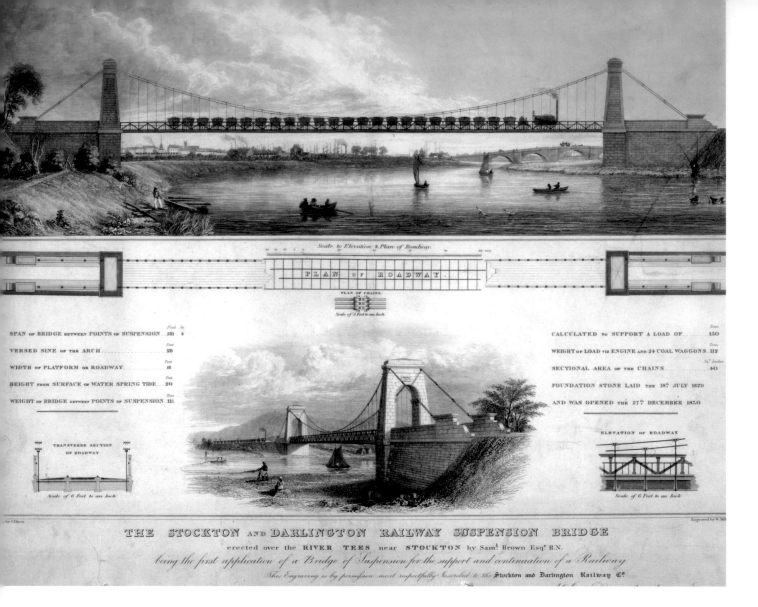

SPAN of BRIDGE between POINTS of SUSPENSION 281 4

VERSED SINE of the ARCH 28

WIDTH of PLATFORM or ROADWAY 16

HEIGHT from SURFACE of WATER SPRING TIDE....20

WEIGHT of BRIDGE between POINTS of SUSPENSION .111

CALCULATED to SUPPORT A LOAD OF 150

WEIGHT of LOAD viz ENGINE and 24 COAL WAGGONS .112

SECTIONAL AREA of the CHAINS 40

FOUNDATION STONE LAID the 18th JULY 1829

AND WAS OPENED the 27th DECEMBER 1830

THE STOCKTON AND DARLINGTON RAILWAY SUSPENSION BRIDGE

erected over the RIVER TEES near STOCKTON by Saml Brown Esqr R.N.

being the first application of a Bridge of Suspension for the support and continuation of a Railway

This Engraving is by permission most respectfully Inscribed to the Stockton and Darlington Railway Co

ABOVE The Stockton bridge on the Stockton to Darlington, which was opened on 27th December 1830, was the first suspension bridge to be built for the purpose of supporting a railway line. The Stockton to Darlington Railway, built by George Stephenson, was the world's first public steam railway line when it opened in 1825.

route. The report said '... one horse of moderate power could easily draw downwards on the railway, between Darlington and Stockton, about ten tons, and upwards about four tons of loading exclusive of empty wagons.' It was estimated that the export trade for coal '... might be taken, perhaps at 10,000 tons a year', which represented probably about one cargo a week. No mention of passenger carriage was made, and this early scheme clearly envisaged a horse tramroad similar to others that had gone before it. By the end of 1816 a company was formed, and a start was made at raising capital. However, the idea was largely ridiculed by other businessmen and only 20 shares were sold originally in Stockton. The project was kept going by support from two leading Quaker families, the Backhouses and the Richardsons, who admired the efforts of Edward Pease, a fellow Quaker. Other Quakers added their support so that the company could to fully established. This led to the nickname 'The Quaker Line' for the Stockton and Darlington Railway, in its early years.

There were still some advocates of the canal scheme, and in 1818 the company asked George Overton (1775–1827) to survey a possible route for both options and report as soon as possible. This he did on 20th September 1818, and on 13th November the company decided on the railway option, and applied for an Act of Parliament to give assent 'to make a tramway on the plan and estimates given by Mr Overton'. George Overton was the engineer who had supervised the Pen-y-darren Tramway back in 1804 on which Trevithick's first locomotive ran.

Locomotion

'Locomotion' was the first locomotive on the first steam operated railway, the Stockton and Darlington, and was built by Robert Stephenson and Co and delivered in September 1825. The price was £600 and was one of the two 'Locomotive Engines' ordered by the Stockton and Darlington Railway. The engine was ready on 13th September 1825 and was delivered by horse-drawn wagon from Stephenson's Newcastle works, to the most northerly part of the S and D, a considerable road journay, with the locomotive weighing 6¼ tons empty as built.

When first in service the locomotive did not carry its famous name, nor was it known by that name for some time afterwards. The name 'Locomotion' was not applied until 1833. The second engine of the same type was delivered in November 1825 and eventually called 'Hope'. Two more, 'Black Diamond' and 'Dilgence', were delivered in April and May 1826. The workmanship was rough, partly because it was relatively new technology and partly due to a casual and haphazard management style at Robert Stephenson and Co. This led to complaints and requests for assurances that the workmanship would be improved.

Despite this, 'Locomotion' remained in active use until 1846, and then was used as a stationary pumping engine until 1857. Fortunately its historic significance was recognised by the North Eastern Railway, who by then had absorbed the Stockton and Darlington Railway, and the withdrawn locomotive, its tender and a contemporary old coal wagon, were placed on a stone plinth at Darlington North Road station, so saving it for posterity.

Opposition to the Stockton and Darlington proposal was vociferous. A leading opponent, Lord Eldon, said 'I am sorry to find the intelligent people of the north country gone mad on the subject of railways'. Another said 'It is folly: you will not get your waggons to travel on the railroad'. To this the company replied, 'On our two parallel bars our horse shall carry eight tons at twice the speed your horse can carry one.' One pessimist said, 'It is all very well to spend money; it will do some good, but it will eat all the coals that your railroad will carry.'

In Parliament itself there was much opposition to the Act, notably from those whose landed interests would potentially be affected by the line. These included the Lord Chancellor, Lord Eldon, whose estate was nearby and the Earl of Darlington and Duke of Newcastle because the line crossed their fox-hunting country. Owners and trustees of turnpikes in the area also opposed the Act on the grounds that they would get a reduction in toll income, which would affect their mortgage payments. Edward Pease solved this problem by a public notice that the company's solicitors would purchase these securities at their original price.

The preface to the Act said that the line would 'be of great public utility, by facilitating the conveyance of coal, iron, lime, corn and other commodities'. Edward Pease was still thinking in terms of horses of the main mode of haulage at this time and the wording asked for the power to provide 'for the making and maintaining of the tramroads, and for the passage upon them of wagons and other carriages with men, horses, or otherwise'. This last word probably meant steam winding engines, but was vague enough for almost any interpretation. The word 'loco-motive' did appear elsewhere but was deleted from the Bill because the clerk concerned did not know its meaning. At any event the Bill was defeated in Parliament in 1819 and the company had to try again.

The second application for a Bill was very diplomatically worded, emphasising the lower cost of coal and the reduction of congestion by horses and carts on the roads when all the coal went by rail. However, the use of locomotives was included as a requirement. The Bill went forward in 1820 but was delayed by the death of the king, George III, and Royal Assent was finally given by his son, the new king, George

IV, in April 1821. Included in the wording of the Act was the historic statement '... it shall and may be lawful to and for the said Company ... to make and erect such and so many loco-motives or moveable Engines as the said Company ... shall from Time to Time think proper and expedient, and to use and employ the same in and upon the said Railways or Tramroads ...'.

On the day that Royal Assent was given there was another important event. George Stephenson visited Edward Pease, the driving force behind the Stockton and Darlington Railway project, and the two men met for the first time. Until that time Pease was still thinking in terms of horse power for the line, but Stephenson persuaded him that steam locomotives were a much better option. He invited Pease to Killingworth to see for himself how a steam road could perform. At the time Stephenson was also supervising construction of the Hetton Colliery Railway (see pages 40–41), which was due to open at the end of 1821. He suggested that a similar mode of working that he had devised for Hetton could be used on the Stockton and Darlington Railway. This was locomotive haulage on flat sections or easy gradients below 1:300. For steeper gradients steam winding engines would be used to haul loaded wagons up, and gravity could be used for letting wagons down.

Edward Pease was sufficiently impressed by Stephenson's ideas, and after his visit to Killingworth he asked Stephenson to re-survey the route originally suggested by Overton. This he started in July 1821 and completed in January 1822. Stephenson's route was much more direct that Overton's and came further south into Darlington. The more circuitous route suggested by Overton was probably chosen because he only envisaged horse haulage. Following the survey, George Stephenson was immediately

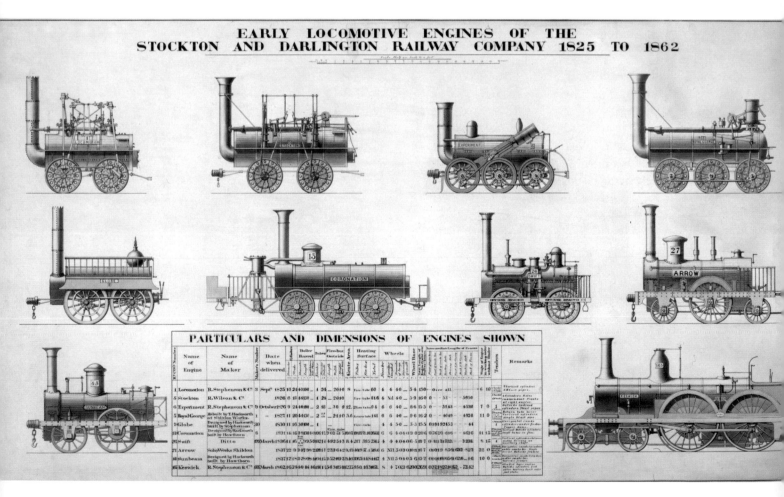

asked to engineer the line. In April 1822 work started on preparing the route and the first rails were laid down in Stockton. But as Stephenson had altered the route a further Bill was presented to Parliament in 1823 to cover Stephenson's new route and other changes, and to confirm the use of steam locomotives. This Act was passed in May 1823 and cleared the way for completion of the line.

The engineering work required on the route of the Stockton and Darlington Railway was of considerable magnitude. It included long high embankments from Dinsdale to Eggescliffe, some up to 48ft high, a high stone bridge over the River Skerne, and a marshy area, Myers Flat, which needed a huge amount of filling to give a stable track bed. Stephenson chose long straight sections and gentle curves for most of the route. However, two collieries served at the west end of the line, Brusselton and Etherley, could only be reached by steep gradients worked by steam winding engines. The route between these two inclines, which crossed the River Saunless by another bridge, was worked by horses.

Yet another historic development was linked to all these endeavours. In 1823 the company headed by George Stephenson was set up in Newcastle to build locomotives and named Robert Stephenson and Son, with George's 20-year old son Robert as manager (he had just left university), and George Stephenson, Edward Pease and Michael Longridge (a local iron-master) as directors. The new company, of course, was able to build the locomotives needed for the new railway. In theory a conflict of interests could be said to exist, but as George Stephenson was the foremost locomotive builder of the time he was also best placed to supply the companies he worked for.

Robert Stephenson had a disagreement with his father after a short time and left the company within a year. Timothy Hackworth, who Stephenson knew from his work with Hedley, replaced Robert for a time while the new locomotives were built, and later became the chief steam engineer for the Stockton and Darlington Railway.

The first locomotive built for the Stockton and Darlington Railway in 1824 was the famous 'Locomotion' which is still preserved. It cost £500 and weighed 6½ tons. It also had connecting rods on the wheels worked from vertical cranks from the cylinders set within the boiler. There were no brakes and stopping was achieved by putting the locomotive into reverse. Three more of the type were built for the S. & D. R. ('Hope', 'Black Diamond' and 'Diligence') and two similar engines were supplied to the Hetton Colliery Railway.

The official opening of the Stockton and Darlington Railway took place on 27th September 1825 and was a big and memorable event. Huge crowds turned out along the route to watch. A witness later said 'The scene on the morning of that day sets description at defiance. Many who were to take part in the event did not the night before sleep a wink, and soon after midnight were astir. The universal cheers, the happy faces of many, the vacant stare of astonishment of others, and the alarm on the countenances of some, gave variety to the picture.'

The opening run started at the west end of the line from the foot of the Brusselton incline, after a demonstration first of the incline's winding engine. The train moved off heading east for Stockton, with Locomotive No 1 'Locomotion' driven by George

Stephenson himself, and Timothy Hackworth as train guard. Behind the engine were six wagons loaded with coal or flour, next a covered coach carrying the directors and guests, then 21 wagons fitted with seats for passengers, and finally six wagons loaded with coal which were to be detached at Darlington. The witness said, 'Off started the procession with a horseman carrying a flag at its head. A great concourse of people stood along the line. Many of them tried to accompany it by running and some gentlemen on horseback galloped across the fields to keep up with the engine. The railway was descending with a gentle incline towards Darlington, the rate of speed was consequently variable. At a favourable part of the road, Stephenson determined to try the speed of the engine and he called upon the horseman with the flag to get out of the way, and Stephenson put on the speed to 12 miles, then 15 miles per hour and the runners on foot, the gentlemen on horseback, and the horseman with the flag were soon left far behind. When the train reached Darlington it was found that 450 passengers occupied the wagons and that the load of men, coals and merchandise amounted to about 90 tons.' A sad aspect of this celebration was that Edward Pease, whose efforts had brought the line to fruition, missed it all, for his 22-year-old son Isaac suddenly died that morning.

It took 65 minutes to reach Darlington in actual running time at an average speed of 8mph for the 8¾ miles. The journey actually took longer for there were stops to repair a wagon and clear a feedwater pump on the engine. When the coal wagons were removed at Darlington, a wagon carrying a band was added at the end of the train for the journey on to Stockton. At Stockton a 21-gun salute was fired on the new wharf by the River Tees, where the journey ended. On the approach to Stockton the railway ran alongside the road and for a time a stagecoach ran alongside the train with the passengers in both cheering and waving to each other. At Stockton celebrations and dinners for all involved, workers, directors and guests, took up the rest of the day. It is interesting to note that though 450 passengers, and possibly more, were counted on the train, only 300 tickets had been sold based on the number of seats fitted in the wagons!

Despite the initial optimism, there were numerous problems both with equipment and operations in the early years of the Stockton and Darlington. The locomotives caused problems with breakages (including wheels) and some were found to be deficient on delivery. The long route mileage led to a frequent loss of steam pressure. To combat this drivers started to lash down the safety-valve lever, a dangerous practice, but in turn this caused the chief steam engineer, Timothy Hackworth, to develop the sprung safety-valve, which henceforth, became a standard design feature. With only a limited number of locomotives, horses still had to be used for many of the coal trains, typically with one horse pulling four wagons. This caused problems down the steeper grades, leading to the use of dandycarts for the horses to ride in down grade, as also used on some other horse-operated lines (see page 20). Traffic was sometimes chaotic since some individual operators could use their own horses and wagons on the line. Congestion led to some trains being held in sidings, and complaints were made about the time some wagons were delayed in transit from the collieries to Stockton, occasionally four days or more. Some delays were due to inadequate facilities at Stockton wharf, making ship loading protracted, but these were overcome early in 1826 when the wharf was fully finished and fitted.

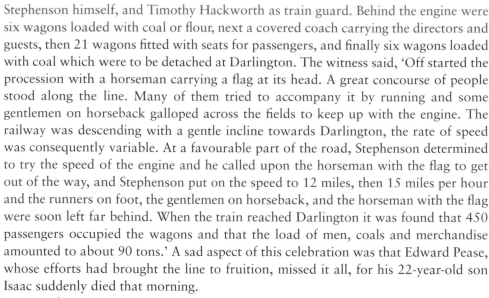

BELOW A steam locomotive is shown hauling a train through the Olive Mount cutting, on the Liverpool and Manchester Railway (L.M.R). The cutting, was one of the first extensive cuttings on any railway, and is still considered one of the most formidable. It is approximately two miles long, and in some parts nearly 80ft deep.

LIVERPOOL STATION

MOORISH ARCH

THE TUNNEL

SANKEY VIADUCT

ENTRANCE INTO MANCHESTER

ENTRANCE OF THE TUNNELS

CHAT MOSS

NEWTON VIADUCT

RAINHILL SKEW BRIDGE

PANORAMA OF THE LIVERPOOL AND MANCHESTER RAILWAY.

Liverpool and Manchester railway

While the Stockton and Darlington Railway put the potential of trains carrying goods and passengers firmly in the mind of the public, it was essentially built solely for industrial purposes. The idea of a railway to further wider applications came from two Manchester businessmen, Henry Booth and Charles Lawrence. On 29th October 1824, they issued a prospectus that said ' ... railways hold out to the public not only a cheaper but far more expeditious mode of conveyance than any yet established ... in the present state of trade and commercial enterprise is no less essential than economy. Merchandise is frequently brought across the Atlantic from New York to Liverpool in 21 days; while owing to various causes of delay, goods have in some instances been longer (than that) on their passage from Liverpool to Manchester. The advancement in mechanical sciences renders it unnecessary; the good sense of the community makes it impossible. Let it not be imagined that were England to be tardy, other countries would pause in the march of improvement.' They went on to point out that a railway would speed up despatch and transit of merchandise in the Manchester area with a saving to traders, that coal would be better available at lower prices, and farm produce could be sold over a wider area, and more markets could be found for minerals and agricultural produce. They ended by saying, '... as a cheap and expeditious means of conveyance for travellers, the railway holds out the fair prospect of a public accommodation, the magnitude and importance of which cannot be immediately ascertained.' This was a shrewd prophecy.

A Bill was put to Parliament for an Act to build the Liverpool and Manchester Railway (L.M.R.) in March 1825, while work was in full swing building the Stockton

ABOVE A print showing nine views of the Liverpool and Manchester Railway, including some of its major engineering feats.

and Darlington Railway. Predictably enough there was massive opposition from landowners, canal owners, turnpike owners and many others who considered their property or interests threatened by the railway. George Stephenson was called as a witness for the Bill and testified to the safety and potential of steam locomotives and operation. He had been engaged at that time as engineer for the proposed line, despite his other work at the same time. The Parliamentary Committee sat for 38 days, but they were not convinced that steam locomotives were safe, and a major stumbling block was taking the line across the marshy Chat Moss, which they also thought unsafe. The survey was also found to be grossly inaccurate in places. So the Bill was rejected.

Undaunted, the promoters engaged John (1761–1821) and George Rennie (1791–1866), who had a good reputation as engineers, to re-survey the route. The original construction cost of the line was estimated at £400,000. But the Rennie proposals and a new survey by Charles Vignoles (1793–1895) led to the route being changed slightly, requiring a tunnel and a rock cutting at Olive Mount, bringing the cost up to £510,000. Under these modified proposals, which also avoided some of the property of land and canal owners, progress was made. A very influential figure in this was William Huskisson, MP for Liverpool and President of the Board of Trade (1770–1830), who took an enthusiastic interest in the project. He knew the Marquis of Stafford, owner of the Bridgwater Canal and a major opponent of the railway scheme. Huskisson enlisted his co-operation – and indeed some investment – in the railway plan in return for useful concessions. When the Bill was re-submitted to Parliament with all these changes, it was passed in July 1826.

Now came the problem of locomotive procurement. Joseph Rastrick (1780–1856), heading the committee deciding on the means of haulage in the spring of 1829, announced a competition for 'locomotive engine' designs to be used on the new railway with a 'premium' of £500 to the winner. The trials were to be held at Rainhill on a 1½ mile length of run, with 200 yards added at each end for stopping and starting. Each locomotive was to run ten double trips. After more coal and water was loaded, it was to do another ten trips, equivalent to the distance of the line from Liverpool to Manchester. The locomotives had to be on site by 1st October 1829 and the trials were scheduled for 8–14 October. The now famous Rainhill Trials captured the imagination of the press and public and thousands attended to watch.

An interesting selection of prototype machines were entered. 'The Novelty', built by John Ericson (1803–1889) and John Braithwaite (1797–1870), was little more than a simple vertical boiler road carriage with flanged wheels. It failed early on after only two runs of the course when the boiler joints gave way. Timothy Hackworth (1786–1850) entered the 'Sans Pareil' which was disqualified as being too heavy, at 4.77 tons, for a four-wheel engine under the rules that had been promulgated. It was a very efficient locomotive, however, achieving 14mph on the trials and hauling 14 tons. Despite not being eligible and bursting its water pump on test, it was purchased by the company after the trials and used for some time before being sold in 1832 to the Bolton and Leigh Railway. 'The Perseverance' by Timothy Burstall also failed. It was another design with a simple vertical boiler. It could only achieve a top speed of 6mph while the competition terms demanded 10mph. Another failure was the 'Cycloped', an ingenious vehicle that was powered by a horse walking on moving tread, thus turning the wheels. It was also too slow, and did not meet the requirement of being steam powered.

The outright winner, however, was the now famous 'Rocket' built by George Stephenson with much input and assistance by Henry Booth, secretary of the L.M.R. and George's son, Robert. The 'Rocket' was a leap forward in locomotive design. Booth suggested the use of copper fire tubes in the boiler to carry the heat of the firebox through the water. 'Rocket' had 25 of these – earlier locomotives had no more than two. The other new idea was a separate firebox behind the boiler rather than fitted into it, and angled pistons driving the front wheels directly rather than transmitting movement vertically by means of levers. Steel springs were also used, first tried by Stephenson on an earlier engine, 'Lancashire Witch'. The design principles first applied to the 'Rocket' were used in almost all later steam locomotives on a much larger scale. One further development was a smokebox at the front of the boiler to more efficiently evacuate the fumes from the firebox. This was a later addition to 'Rocket' which also had its pistons set at a much lower angle later on.

Opening of the line

With construction of the line virtually complete – it had meanwhile been extended further towards Manchester by a bridge over the River Irwell – the opening was fixed for 15th September 1830 when the Duke of Wellington, the Prime Minister, and William Huskisson were among many politicians and distinguished guests assembled to travel on the first train, which consisted of 33 coaches, starting from the Liverpool station. Bands, bunting and many spectators were there celebrating the occasion. The occasion was marred by the death of William Huskisson, probably the first casualty on a public passenger carrying railway. While the train was stopped at Parkside station to take on water many passengers took to the track to view the proceedings, Huskisson among them. Another train came up and as Huskisson tried to get clear of it he stumbled, was run down, and died later in the vicar of Eccles' house.

Despite this tragedy, everyone who experienced the day recognised that a new age of engineering achievement had arrived, not only in the trains themselves but in the impressive design and building of the infrastructure. On the following day, 16th September, the Liverpool and Manchester Railway opened for business, with the first train carrying 130 passengers from Liverpool to Manchester in an hour and fifty minutes. Six trains ran daily, replacing 30 daily horse-drawn stage coaches over the same distance, and carrying 1,600 passengers on average instead of the 500 who could cram into the stage coaches. The day of the steam railway had now arrived.

ABOVE Page 16 of the notebook belonging to John Urpeth Rastrick which was used to record details of the Rainhill locomotive trials in 1829. This page concerns Timothy Hackworth's engine 'Sans Pareil'.

chapter 4

Railways in Britain continued to develop at a great pace in the period from about 1835 to 1845. The earlier lines were promoted by those with a genuine interest in the districts or areas they served, and can be said to have contributed greatly to the social and economic fabric of Great Britain. However, their success and stability as long term investments brought the investors good returns on their shares, usually between 10 and 15 per cent. By 1844–45, when Britain was experiencing an economic boom and the Bank Rate was only 2½ per cent, financiers realised that railways could be a profitable investment. Huge numbers of new railways were promoted, many of them bogus or impractical, and millions of pounds worth were sold to speculators. Many business men made huge fortunes from all this. The most famous man involved in this 'railway mania' bubble was George Hudson who had a short but spectacular reign as the 'Railway King'.

Railway mania

PREVIOUS PAGES
Coloured lithograph by
John Cooke Bourne (1814–
1896) after his original
drawing, showing an
engine house near Camden
Town on the London and
Birmingham Railway
(L.B.R.), the first railway
into London.

RIGHT The 'Planet'
locomotive was designed by
Robert Stephenson and
Co for the Liverpool and
Manchester Railway and
was first used in December
1830, four months after the
line's opening.

Though the 'Rocket' was a major step forward in efficient locomotive design, George Stephenson's company advanced the design even further in the batch of new locomotives built for the opening of the Liverpool and Manchester Railway. First of these was the 'Northumbrian', effectively an enlarged version of the 'Rocket'. It had cylinders of 11in diameter and 16in stroke compared with 8in by 17in on the 'Rocket'. It weighed more than twice as much as the 'Rocket' and it had the firebox and a smokebox built into the same shell as the boiler, establishing the style used on most later locomotives. The boiler had more tubes also. The two driving wheels were larger at 5ft diameter and the cylinders were set at a lower angle above the trailing wheels – the 'Rocket' was later altered to give a similar position for the cylinders. It was 'Northumbrian' that hauled the first long train at the opening of the Liverpool and Manchester Railway (L.M.R) carrying the Duke of Wellington and distinguished guests. The 'Rocket' followed behind with a second train and it was the 'Rocket' which injured Huskisson. The power of the 'Rocket' was still impressive and its hauling power up grades showed that the winding engines could be dispensed with.

More important, however, than 'Northumbrian' was the 'Planet', another big jump in locomotive design. On these new locomotives Robert Stephenson was carrying out the refinements. The 'Planet' was the first locomotive with a heavy wood frame (or chassis) to carry the suspension, axle boxes and wheels, and also the mount for the boiler and firebox. This locomotive had cylinders the same size as 'Northumbrian', set under the smokebox at the front of the engine, working direct on to a double-cranked driving axle. The two driving wheels were, therefore, at the rear, with two small leading wheels, giving the locomotive a 2–2–0 (**For a complete explanation of wheel notation please see page 104**). There were 80 boiler tubes and the boiler was lagged with wood stripes. There was a door on the front of the smokebox, too, making it easier to clean out the boiler tubes, another feature that became usual on most subsequent locomotives. Cylinders inside the frames to

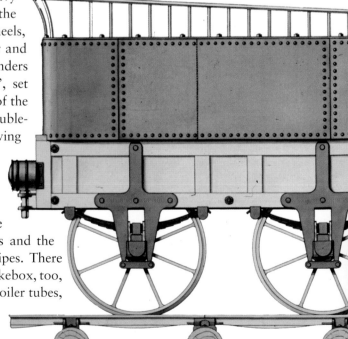

drive the axles became a popular alternative to outside cylinders, particularly in Britain. Many locomotives of the 'Planet' type were built, besides the initial batch for the Liverpool and Manchester Railway, and later ones intended specifically for freight haulage were built to 0–4–0 configuration with the wheels coupled together. The 'Planet' weighed 8 tons. Though a key stage in the development of steam locomotives, no 'Planet' engine was ever preserved so they can only be seen in contemporary illustrations. As it happened the 'Planet' type did not quite pioneer the idea of inside cylinders, as Gurney's steam road carriage was the first with this arrangement.

Economic effects

Eight more engines of the 'Rocket' type but with minor changes were also built for the Liverpool and Manchester Railway. One was called 'Phoenix' and the last 'Majestic'. Initially the line carried only passengers and parcels in trains of coaches, but in November 1830 the company started carrying mail as well by contract with the Post Office who switched over from stage coaches on the Liverpool–Manchester run. This was when the term 'guard' came into use, copied from the stage coach guard, as this official was responsible for the security of the mail while on railway transit. While the company planned to carry freight, such as coal, cotton, and general goods, this was not possible initially due to a shortage of locomotives. With the delivery of 'Planet' in December 1830 some freight trains started to run, but it took a year or two before it became more intensive.

Meanwhile passenger traffic had been a much greater success, spurred on by the immense publicity given to the opening of the line. Trains of first-class and second-class coaches ran separately, not mixed as became common later. All the passengers who previously travelled by stage coach switched over to the trains, and many people who had never travelled before took advantage of the trains to now do so. So many passengers were carried that fares were reduced and this increased custom even further, with around 460,000 passengers in the first year. Stage waggons, carrying

goods by road, went out of business as well as the stage coaches; turnpike takings fell dramatically and it became difficult to attract turnpike operators. When freight haulage commenced, business on the Bridgewater Canal slumped by about 30 per cent, though the economic effect of this was not so great because canal freight rates still gave a profit.

More railways and locomotives

Though the Liverpool and Manchester Railway got huge publicity, and was a successful undertaking commensurate with its cost and the quality of its engineering, there were several other railways being either promoted or, indeed, built in exactly the same 1828–30 period. In fact more than 20 were authorised though not all were built. They were the forerunners of a flood of railway development across Britain, which was to follow in the next decade, and carried on with great intensity through the 1840s. Ten more railways were authorised by Parliament by 1832.

The Bolton and Leigh Railway actually pre-dated the Liverpool and Manchester, opening for business in August 1828, though it was a much smaller operation. George Stephenson was involved with this undertaking, supplying their first locomotive 'Lancashire Witch', a predecessor of 'Rocket' and the first he built with metal springs, and driven by inclined cylinders like the 'Rocket'. It weighed 7 tons and reached 8mph with a 50 ton load. It was fired with coke with bellows for draughting, and it had a firebox at each end of the boiler. Several more locomotives of this design were built.

Another designer who made his mark around the 1830 period was Edward Bury (1794–1858) whose 0–4–0 locomotive Liverpool also had inside cylinders placed under the smokebox and a tall domed firebox, actually D-shaped in cross-section. It also had strong cast iron wheel hubs and the cylinders were 12in diameter with 18in strokes. The performance was good, with a speed of 25mph recorded, while hauling a 125 ton train. The Liverpool was purchased by 1831 and used for a time by the Liverpool and Manchester Railway. Bury went on to design and built many more locomotives and tall domed firebox became something of a feature of his engines.

Up until this time almost all locomotives had only four wheels – Hackworth's four-wheel 'Sans Pareil', later sold to the Bolton and Leigh Railway, is such an example. The four-wheel locomotives, all of very short wheelbase, suffered from much pitching and general rough riding at anything but the slowest speeds. Four wheels also limited the tractive effort as trains became longer and heavier. Even the 'Planet' locomotives were inadequate in this respect. It was to overcome these limitations that Stephenson designed and built in 1833 a new longer six-wheel locomotive, the 'Patentee'. This was another major step forward in locomotive development which set the standard for designs into the 1840s and the basic concept was copied by many other makers who got round Stephenson's patent by omitting some of the features in his patent such as steam brakes and flangeless main driving wheels. The first engine built was purchased by the Liverpool and Manchester Railway who actually called it 'Patentee', the name that became generic for the type. Stephenson had not given it a name.

In essence the 'Patentee' was a longer version of the Planet, built as a 2–2–2 with the cylinders driving the centre large pair of flangeless main wheels. Wheels on the outer axles had flanges and were simply small carrying wheels. While the 'Planet' had a heavy wood frame carrying iron plates for the axle-boxes and with iron strapping on the corners, the Patentee had a 'sandwich' frame of wood with ¼ inch thick iron

ABOVE The 'Sans Pareil', designed by Timothy Hackworth (1786-1850), competed in the Rainhill Trials of 1829. and though unsuccesful there, it was later sold to the Bolton and Leigh Railway.

plating along each side, and later locomotives that copied this design had thicker and heavier frames as locomotive size increased. The firebox, a much longer boiler, and the smokebox were carried between the frames with support brackets attaching them to the frame. The cylinders were carried below the smokebox with the pistons driving the centre pair of wheels.

Patentee weighed 11½ tons with an axle-loading of 4.3 tons on the main driving wheels and slightly more on the loading wheels which made it slightly nose-heavy, but not sufficiently so to cause trouble. The driving wheels were 5ft 6in in diameter and the overall wheelbase was 10ft, almost double that of the 'Planet'. Cylinders were 11in diameter with 18in stroke. In the following years, by both Stephenson and other makers, the wheel arrangement was sometimes altered to 0–4–2, or 0–6–0 by the necessary changes of coupling wheels and altering wheel diameters. A few Planets were altered with longer frames and extra axle to follow the 'Patentee' style, and one of these, 'Hercules', converted to 0–4–2, went to another of the new railways, Leicester and Swanington. This company also ordered a 0–6–0 'Patentee' from Stephenson in 1834, named 'Atlas'.

By the later 1830s several engineering firms were in business as locomotive builders, among them Sharp, Hawthorn, Rothwell, and Haigh Foundry, and as the

ABOVE The 'North Star' 2–2–2 was designed by Robert Stephenson and Co for the Great Western Railway in 1837, a later variation the 'Patentee' type.

OVERLEAF The Canterbury and Whitstable railway showing the 'Invicta', which was built by Robert Stephenson and Company.

railway network expanded the larger companies also founded their own workshops to build locomotives. The dominant type of those years, in some cases into the 1860s, was the basic 'Patentee' design, mostly in 2–2–2 form, though the fittings and style improved. They all copied the Stephenson concept, though all used flanged driving wheels and the Stephenson firm changed over to this in 1842. The original idea of having flangeless driving wheels was to eliminate thrust on the wheels as the locomotive went round sharp curves. This could fracture crank axles, which, in the early days, were often poorly cast.

Edward Bury (1794-1858) was one of the few locomotive builders to ignore the 'Patentee' concept and continue with his own original ideas. All his locomotives, like 'Liverpool', continued to be built as 0–4–0s or 2–2–0s, with inside cylinders, inside bar frames, and the dome topped fireboxes. Bury's company, Edward Bury and Co, enjoyed a good reputation for the quality of its locomotives, which most considered better made than Stephenson's. However, by the time Bury came around to building 0–6–0 engines in the late 1840s he had been long overtaken by rival builders already offering the larger engines. His most famous engine, still preserved, is 'Old Coppernob' (from the polished domed firebox), built for the Furness Railway in 1846.

Building the network

By the time the Liverpool and Manchester Railway was in full operation, other railway

lines were either operating, too, or were being built and were close to completion. Some of the new railways used horses, at least in their opening years, and several also had cable-operated steep sections. Among numerous new railways that opened were Canterbury and Whitstable (1830), Edinburgh and Dalkeith (1831), Warring and Newton (1831), Garnkirk and Glasgow (1831), St Helens and Runcorn (1832), Wigan Branch Railway (1832), and Leicester and Swannington (1832), while several more were authorised by Parliament in 1833–34.

The Canterbury and Whitstable Railway was notable in being the first railway built in the south of England after the considerable activity in the north. However, the Canterbury and Whitstable Railway, linking the cathedral city to the then busy port of Whitstable on the north Kent coast, was only 6 miles long. Engineered by George Stephenson it was mainly cable-hauled over steep grades, but the 1¼ miles nearest the coast was flat, and Stephenson built a 0–4–0 locomotive for this section. Called 'Invicta', it had inclined cylinders high on the front. From the start it hauled passengers, beating the Liverpool and Manchester in this respect by a few months. The 'Invicta' turned out to be a much less successful locomotive than the 'Rocket' with a poor performance. Modifying the boiler made it even worse, and the line reverted to horses, though the 'Invicta' is still preserved.

While there was a primitive railway in the London area from 1803, the Surrey Iron Railway, running from Wandsworth to Croydon, this was only a horse tramroad

ABOVE The 'Adler' (Eagle) locomotive, driven by English driver William Wilson, pulls a train past large crowds of spectators during the opening of Germany's first railway between Nuremburg and Fürth. The 'Adler' is a good example of the original 'Patentee' design.

with plate rails serving industries along the route. The first steam railway was the London and Greenwich, which received Parliamentary assent in 1833 and was built in the 1834–1836 period. It was an ambitious engineering feat, being built on a long brick viaduct carrying it high above the low lying land of south-east London. This viaduct was 3¾ miles long with 878 brick arches mostly 18ft wide and 22ft high. The line started at Tooley Street station – which was later greatly expanded to become London Bridge Station – and ran to Greenwich. Some of today's commuter trains take the same route into London Bridge. Opening date was 8th February 1836. Locomotives of the 2–2–2 'Patentee' type were mostly used. In the early days there were no Sunday trains because of a shortage of locomotives, but for a small fee passengers were allowed to walk along the line.

A junction was built at Corbett's Lane, Southwark in 1839, when the London to Croydon Railway opened, branching off the London and Greenwich Railway. The two companies were amalgamated and a signal box was built to control trains at the junction, possibly the first ever purpose-built signal box. In 1845 the line became part of the expanding South Eastern Railway.

Foreign connections

The influence of British engineers on the introduction of railways in several other countries in the mid-19th century was quite considerable.

Horse-drawn industrial railways, mostly serving mines had been built in France just as in Britain, but in 1830–32 a fully engineered main line was built to link

Lyons and St-Etienne. Its chief engineer, Marc Seguin (1786–1875), had visited Britain, met Stephenson, and ordered two locomotives from him. But from here on Seguin used his own ideas, mainly based on fans driven by the locomotive axles to achieve the draughting. He did, however, use wheels, cylinders and other fittings based on Stephenson's designs.

Germany came to railways later, mainly due to the enthusiasm of King Ludwig of Bavaria. A couple of Blenkinsop cog locomotives had been imported by German mines in 1816 but were not much used. Stephenson was called in by King Ludwig to oversee an 8-mile line from Nuremburg to the adjacent town of Fürth, which was Germany's first railway. A 'Patentee' type 2–2–2 locomotive 'Adler' (Eagle) was supplied from Stephenson's works, along with an English driver, William Wilson, and the railway was opened in 1835. After that German firms moved quickly into the railway business and a second line, from Dresden to Leipzig, was built in 1837–39. In 1935, to celebrate the centenary of German railways, a replica of 'Adler' was built to the original Stephenson plans, and it and its train is kept at the DB Museum in Nuremburg, and still runs on special occasions.

Four locomotives were imported into the USA from Britain in 1828–29 by the company that operated the Delaware and Hudson Canal. One was a Stephenson engine, 'John Bull' and the others were built by Foster and Rastrick of which 'Stourbridge Lion' was the first. This engine was the first practical locomotive to run in America, in August 1829, but it was too heavy for the lightweight rail, and when the track broke the British locomotives were set aside and American companies built lighter ones.

Jumping ahead slightly, the first really successful American locomotive builder was William Norris of Philadelphia (1802–67) who made some unsuccessful locomotives in the early 1830s, but by 1834–35 had developed a 4–2–0 design with domed firebox, which was very efficient and had good hauling power. They sold well to American companies and good export orders were received, with locomotives being sold to five countries, including Germany, Austria and England. The Birmingham and Gloucester Railway bought four and they were used mostly on the steep Lickey Incline. Engineering companies in Europe copied the Norris design, rather as other British companies copied Stephenson's design.

In the 1830s George and Robert Stephenson also advised on the building of a quite extensive railway in Belgium, and in 1846 Robert Stephenson advised on the building of railways in Norway and Sweden. And for the rest of the steam era, British locomotive builders enjoyed big export business all over the world, ranging from South America to China and Japan.

Locomotive Design

It is interesting to note the differing time lags in the way cross-border influences in locomotive design were taken up. Rigid frame locomotives designed by Stephenson, the 'Planet' (2–2–0) and 'Patentee' (2–2–2) types, were popular on mainland Europe and a number were exported, or copied in various ways by European builders. They suited the European way of building stable and well levelled track beds, and 'Patentee' derived designs were built and used for many years will into the 1870s.

Early American lines were much more lightly laid, and altogether rougher, often with sharper curves. Hence the relative failure of the British locomotives exported to America in 1829, where they were too heavy and rigid for the track. Lighter four wheel locomotives built in America such as 'De Witt Clinton' and 'Tom Thumb' proved more successful in those early days. Bigger more powerful locomotives were needed, however, and the first engineer to tackle this was Henry Campbell (1810–70) of the new Philadelphia and Georgetown Railroad, who designed in 1836 a longer locomotive, essentially a 0–4–0 with an extended wood frame supporting a smaller wood fram holding four smaller carrying wheels within it ahead of the four coupled driving wheels. It was in effect, the first 4–4–0 though the leading wheels were flexible to aid running round curves rather than being in a swivelling bogie (or truck in American terms). The actual locomotive was built by Brecks of Philadelphia in 1837 and it was probably the biggest locomotive in the world at that time with the then very high boiler presssure of 90lbs. Other American makers quickly took up this 4–4–0 idea and immediately improved it, most notably by putting the leading four wheels into a proper swivelling bogie, with sprung suspension to create the true 4–4–0 format which remained the most popular well into the 20th century.

ABOVE Lithograph by John Cooke Bourne, of the construction of the London and Birmingham Railway (L.B.R.) showing the tremendous scale of the works necessary to link Camden Town, (originally intended to be the site of the railway's London terminus), to Euston station. Beginning at Curzon Street station, Birmingham, and finishing at Euston station, London, the 112 mile long line took 20,000 men nearly five years to build. All the earth was shifted by labourers using picks, shovels and wheelbarrows. Horses helped to pull the men and barrows up the sides of the embankment.

Spreading the network

Despite several visionaries suggesting that railways should be built linking all the major cities in Great Britain, most of these early proposals were made before steam traction had been developed well enough to be fully practical. While new local lines were being built and opened in the mid-1830s, among them the Newcastle and Carlisle, Warrington and Newton, Durham and Sunderland, Stanhope and Tyne, and several more – the real prize was the building of major rail routes linking Manchester to Birmingham and Birmingham to London, and from London to the south, southwest, and west.

First attempts to get Parliamentary assent for lines from Manchester to Birmingham (in 1824) and Birmingham to London (in 1830) were rejected due to huge opposition from canal and turnpike operators. There were 27,000 miles of turnpike by then, and a big network of stage coaches and coaching inns along the turnpike routes. Land owners and farmers along the routes were alarmed and warned of people losing their jobs or harm to animals. Doctors warned of the dangers to health of travelling by rail. A politician said that a railway was 'the most injurious that can be conceived to the public good.' Another said 'I hate these infernal railways as I hate the devil.' A leading engineer was sceptical and deprecated '... the ridiculous expectation ... that we shall see engines travelling at a rate of 12, 16, 18 or 20mph. Nothing could do more harm ... than the promulgation of such nonsense.' The overall hostility to the trunk routes was on a much vaster scale than that experienced by the promoters of the earlier local lines. For example, the promoters of the London and Birmingham Railway were forced to change their planning to avoid Northampton on the grounds that smoke from the locomotives would ruin the wool on sheep in adjacent fields. To

overcome this objection the route had to be altered, necessitating the boring of the Kilsby Tunnel, adding £300,000 to construction costs. Eventually, after very lengthy arguments and amendments, the Parliamentary Acts assenting to the building of the first trunk routes, the London and Birmingham Railway and the Grand Junction Railway, were passed together in May 1833, and work could begin.

The through route from London to Liverpool would be achieved in three sections, London to Birmingham, then Birmingham to Warrington, linking up to the Warrington and Newton Railway, and from there connecting on to the Liverpool and Manchester Railway. George Stephenson was appointed the chief engineer of the Grand Junction Railway and his son, Robert, was chief engineer of the London and Birmingham project. George Stephenson was engaged in many other projects at this time, such was his fame, and assistants were brought in to oversee most of the work. On the Grand Junction this was Joseph Locke (1805–60), a young and competent engineer, who upstaged Stephenson and took over from him completely in 1834. Building kept to both schedule and budget and the Grand Junction Railway was completed and opened in July 1837. The terminus in Birmingham was at Curzon Street, and the route was 78 miles in length.

The London and Birmingham route, which was 112 miles long, ran from Euston in London to Curzon Street to link with the Grand Junction. Because there was a steep 1:70 grade for one mile from Euston to Camden Bank, Robert Stephenson installed a cable-hauled section there, with locomotives taking over at Camden. On the rest of the route grades were gentle, none exceeding 1:330. Joseph Locke acted as assistant engineer on the northern half of the route and John Rastrick (1780–1856), covered the southern half. Total cost of the project was £5½ million, about twice the

cost of the short and simpler Grand Junction Railway. An elegant station at Euston was built, and, at a cost of £35,000, a grand classical arch that became an icon of the railway age until it was demolished by 'modernist' politicians in 1962 against much opposition.

The London and Birmingham Railway was opened in June 1838, and one reason for its high cost was the amount of engineering in the way of embankments, cuttings, and viaducts in order to keep to the gentle gradients that had been specified. At the time it was the greatest and most expensive engineering project the world had ever known. It also brought home to the public the complexity and enormity of building railways, for the grand scale of the project made it hard to miss. In those days before mechanical diggers or excavators, all the digging was done by hand labour with thousands of workers using picks, shovels and wheelbarrows, and with horses and carts (sometimes on rails) to carry away the diggings. This was the time when the word 'navvy' became well-known, short for navigator, which was the term used for the labourers who built the canals. Some of the first men to work on railway building had, indeed, previously worked on canals, and the name stuck. Many navvies were rough, hard-working, and hard-drinking men. They lived in huts or camps near the railway workings, often with their families in the same primitive dwellings. The navvies got a reputation for coarse behaviour and drunkenness in towns and villages along the route of the railway, and added to public opposition to railway projects. Some order was achieved with the rise of the railway contractor who took over management of stretches of line under construction on behalf of the company. The most famous and successful of these contractors was Thomas Brassey (1805–70), but there were several other major personalities in the same business.

More trunk routes

Close upon assent to the London and Birmingham Railway were other key routes. First of these was the London and Southampton Railway, for which assent was given by Parliament in 1834. The first engineer appointed for this project proved ineffective, and the efficient Joseph Locke (1805–60) took over. The first section of the line, Nine Elms (the London terminus) to Woking was opened on 1st May 1838. The line was not extended to its more famous London terminus at Waterloo until 1848. Once again there was fierce opposition by rival interests and land owners along the route. A famous example was at the key market town of Kingston-upon-Thames in Surrey. The railway's planned route was to be taken in a curve through low-lying land by the Thames with a station at Kingston. At the time Kingston was a major staging post for coaching routes south and southwest with 26 stage coaches a day changing horses at the big coaching inns in the market place. This brought in a lot of business, and the town corporation opposed the railway because it would ruin the coaching trade. So the route was replanned to bypass Kingston with a major cutting built through Surbiton Hill instead. A station at Surbiton – then a tiny village – led to it becoming a major town attracting prosperous merchants with business in London. Kingston did not get a rail connection and station until the 1860s, and then only as part of a local line serving the area. The full rail route to Southampton opened in 1840, leading to the expansion of that destination to a major seaport. Further extension from this route led to lines to Portsmouth and Fareham in 1848, Weymouth in 1857 and Exeter in 1860.

Also south from London, the London and Croydon Railway, previously noted as a link to the London and Greenwich Railway (see page 60), became the starting point for an extension to Brighton on the south coast by an Act of 1837, and from Brighton branches were built to Lewes, Newhaven (a port for cross-channel shipping) and

OPPOSITE ABOVE
Navvies at work building the Scarborough and Whitby Railway, with horse-drawn wagons to carry away the spoil.

OPPOSITE BELOW
Navvies at work on the Great Central Railways goods yard at Rugby.

ABOVE Isambard
Kingdom Brunel's goods
station yard in Bristol.

Shoreham. This latter branch was quickly extended to Worthing, then all along the coast to Portsmouth to serve the great naval port. Lines southeast from London took a little longer to plan and build, but the key South Eastern Railway, engineered by Sir William Cubitt, was opened from London Bridge to Tonbridge in May 1842.

But the most spectacular of the new trunk routes was the Great Western Railway (G.W.R.), which was first proposed to Parliament in 1832 but rejected in 1834 after much opposition all along the route from all the usual rival interests and land owners. Famously the head of Eton school objected to a station at Slough because it might bring from London '... the most abandoned of its inhabitants to come down by the railway and pollute the minds of the scholars ...'. He also thought the railway would lead to boys playing truant, with trips to London. Oxford University would not allow the Act to be passed without insertion of clauses to prohibit the building of any railway branch to Oxford. An amended Act was passed in August 1835, forbidding a station at Slough and requiring a high fence for 4 miles each side of the line at that point to keep the Eton boys from contact with the railway. When the line was built and the company stopped the train briefly on the track to pick up and set down passengers for Slough (despite the absence of a station) they were sued by Eton for infringing the Act.

The engineer supervising the building of the G.W.R. was Isambard Kingdom Brunel (1806–59), the most famous name after Stephenson as a railway builder. Much of his elegant civil engineering – bridges and tunnels, etc. – remain in use today on the old Great Western route to Bristol. The first part of the line, from London to Taplow was completed in 1838 and Bristol was reached by 1841. By 1844 extensions by associated companies took the routes to Exeter and Bridgwater, with a branch to Oxford from Didcot and to Cirencester from Swindon. The latter became a key centre for the G.W.R. for it was here that the company workshops were set up to build locomotives and stock. The chief locomotive engineer was the energetic and innovative Daniel Gooch (1816–1889) who set high standards for the company's locomotive designs.

The most unique feature of the G.W.R., however, was the use of what was called 'broad gauge', of 7ft ¼in instead of 4ft 8½in. Brunel considered, rightly, that the wider gauge gave a smoother and safer ride and allowed faster speeds. While this proved to be the case when put to the test, it made the G.W.R. out of step with all other lines. Where the G.W.R. interchanged with standard gauge lines through running was not possible and passengers, and freight, all had to be moved from one train to the other. George Stephenson had early on commended that all new railways being built should be to 4ft 8½in gauge, because he foresaw the day (which by 1840 was fast approaching) when Britain would be covered by a network of railways.

The broad gauge became such a problem that in 1846 Parliament passed an

BELOW The 'Battle of the Gauges', where passengers had to change between the two systems between Birmingham and Bristol: a comic version of the chaos that ensued is depicted here. Passengers and luggage are being transferred from broad-gauge to narrow-gauge carriages at Gloucester station, on their way to Birmingham.

act making 4ft 8½in the standard gauge and anything wider illegal, except for lines already built. The G.W.R. did not finally give up broad gauge until 1892, converting remaining lines to standard gauge in a swift operation, though all lines they built after 1846 were to standard gauge. A few other railways were built to odd gauges, notably the Eastern Counties at 5ft, but they quickly converted to standard gauge in the early years of operation.

Perversely, Irish railways were treated differently. The first three railways built in Ireland were all to different gauges – 4ft 8½in, 6ft 2in, and 5ft 3in. To sort this out a Royal Commission was set up and fixed Irish standard gauge at 5ft 3in, with 3ft allowed for secondary lines, and from 1846 all new Irish lines followed these rules.

In addition to those railways that might be considered the most important in Britain, either in terms of development or con-ception, by 1840 there was a vast amount of further activity with 76 railway companies established and nearly 2,500 miles of route authorised, of which about 1,300 miles were still being built and the rest either open or nearly ready to open. An incidental development at this time was the telegraph system, which the G.W.R. was first to install along its route in 1839, followed closely by all the other major routes.

De Seinkamer te Londen van binnen.

Gedeelte van den Spoorweg tusschen Londen en Portsmouth.

Among many other important companies of this period were the Taff Vale Railway (1840), the first railway in South Wales, Manchester and Leeds (1841), York and North Midland (1839), Glasgow, Paisley, Kilmarnock and Ayr Railway (1840), Edinburgh and Glasgow (1842), and Eastern Counties (1840-44) from London to Colchester, and later into East Anglia.

OPPOSITE The 'Acheron' 2–2–2 locomotive emerging from a tunnel near Bristol, 1846 on the G.W.R. which was built in 1835 to provide a route from Bristol to London, using broad-gauge track developed by Isambard Kingdom Brunel. The line opened fully in 1841.

LEFT Colour lithograph showing a group of men operating telegraph equipment in the signalling room in London, and a view of the railway and the electric telegraph between London and Portsmouth.

Regulation

With such a profusion of activity, the need for regulation soon became apparent. The first substantial Act for Regulating Railways was passed in 1840, which required all extensions or alterations and accidents to be reported to the Board of Trade. In 1842 the Board of Trade set up the Railway Inspectorate that not only checked and

OPPOSITE English cartographer, printer and publisher George Bradshaw (1801–1853) was the originator of the railway timetable. *Bradshaw's General Railway and Steam Navigation Guide for Great Britain and Ireland*, commonly known as 'Bradshaw's' was published between 1839 and 1961 and was the traveller's bible.

BELOW 'Can you tell me how to make £10,000 honestly in Railways?' One of the many cartoons published during the 'Railway Mania' period.

approved new railways and extensions before they were allowed to operate, but also investigated and reported on accidents.

Another key step forward, also in 1842, was the setting up of the Railway Clearing House (R.C.H.), which was to operate until the railways were nationalised in 1948. The R.C.H. had the task of logging all monies received and movements of stock across the network so that income could be allocated to the correct company when passengers, freight, or wagons, moved over the rails of more than one company in the course of a journey. In later years, too, the R.C.H. regulated designs for wagons used by private owners over the rail system to ensure common standards throughout the network.

In 1844 came the important Railways Act instigated by William Gladstone that regulated minimum standards for passengers, with the obligation to run trains for poorer 3rd class passengers a 1d per mile fares, and in properly enclosed coaches with seats and ventilation. These became known as 'Parliamentary Trains'. They were sometimes run attached to goods trains, and a certain number had to be run each day. The railway companies themselves were quick to regulate smoking and arrange 'smoking' and 'non-smoking' carriages, but even this requirement was later incorporated as a law.

The railway 'bubble'

A railway boom of a sort was already taking place in 1836–37, following the success of the early lines, notably the Liverpool and Manchester, which led to a swift presentation of bills for Parliamentary assent for the new companies and trunk routes already discussed. The idea of rail travel was rapidly being taken for granted by the public and in 1843 the Board of Trade was able to report that 24 million journeys were being made by rail passengers for an average length of 15 miles. The Post Office, too, was using rail for carrying the mails whenever the route was practical, so communication in general was being rapidly speeded up by the early 1840s. An early report by the then new *Railway Magazine* in 1838 told how a Manchester cotton merchant shipped 300 tons of cotton by rail from Liverpool in two consignments, for sale in Manchester on the day it was landed in the port.

Investors in the new railway companies up to about 1843–44 were generally local businessmen or institutions who could see the advantages to trade or well-being that the new lines could bring to their areas. Also the economic circumstances of the nation were not good in the late 1830s, and most investments were made with caution. It is fair to say, therefore, that up to 1843 and the first half of 1844, the new railways were built in an honest attempt to serve the public good and be socially valuable to the areas they covered. They were also regarded by their promoters as long-term investments.

However, these conditions unintentionally led to what became known as 'railway mania'. The new railways, from the Liverpool and Manchester onwards, were in general so successful and profitable that they offered great financial security and returned very large dividends to shareholders, 10 per cent for the York and North Midland and Liverpool and Manchester, 11 per cent for the Grand Junction and an enormous 15 per cent for the Stockton and Darlington. This caught the attention of bankers and city financiers.

By 1844, Britain was enjoying an economic boom. Bank rate was 2½ per cent

and shares were giving good yields. Manufacturing in general was expanding at a great rate, and there was plenty of money about. The temptation of the high return on railway shares was hard to resist, and soon financiers, engineers, lawyers and speculators were talking up the big money to be made from railway shares. This rapidly led to a 'bubble', the greatest since the South Sea Bubble (and not unlike notorious 'bubbles' of more recent years), where exaggerated forecasts of the profit to be made from railway shares were widely promoted. This led to a frenzy of share buying and new company promotions, with activity and investments multiplying almost literally by the week towards the end of 1844.

The process for what next happened was facilitated by the Joint Stock Company regulations of the day, which were very loose (and coincidentally were being scrutinised with a view to reform by a parliamentary committee at the time). In 1844 it was possible to issue a company prospectus, without the names of directors being revealed when the company was advertised. Share applications could be made

RIGHT Watercolour by Sean Bolan depicts the broad gauge locomotive designed by Sir Daniel Gooch (1816–1889) in 1847. Gooch designed a total of 340 locomotives, including the 'Iron Duke' and the 'Great Western'.

and the money taken with a receipt. The company bankers accepted money from all comers, with few questions asked. Many shareholders then sold on their shares at a profit, and were not around in 6 or 12 months time when the company could be wound up and declare itself bankrupt with all monies eaten up in 'expenses'.

In such circumstances unwise speculators could (and did) lose a lot of money. But the financial regulations made it easy to operate and keep the mania going. In January 1845 16 new railway companies were registered and this number more than doubled in both February and March, with 52 new companies formed in April. This all kept the market bubbling away and, though some companies formed were genuine projects, a great deal were bogus companies intended to prey on gullible investors. The capital needed to form a company was small, and a company could be given a plausible railway name with the proposed route shown on a map. Some 'respectable' directors could also be listed, and dividends of at least 10 per cent were promised on shares sold at £2 or £2 10s. each. Once purchased by some investors the shares were talked up and sold at much higher prices. Yet the entire scheme could be intentionally bogus with the sole intention of making a fast profit from the investors. The mania continued, such that 89 new companies were registered in a single week, which would need a capital investment of £84 million if built. Later still, 357 new companies were registered in a single month, calling for a capital investment of £352 million.

People throughout society acquired shares, including vicars, servants, spinsters, MPs, QCs, clerks, milkmen and every other calling, and most ended up with nothing.

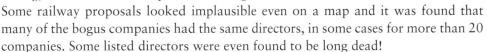

LEFT Engraving by James Andrews after his own painting. Railway chairman George Hudson who was known as the 'Railway King'.

Some railway proposals looked implausible even on a map and it was found that many of the bogus companies had the same directors, in some cases for more than 20 companies. Some listed directors were even found to be long dead!

Eventually, of course, it all ended in tears even when the bubble burst and the great mania crashed.

There were many crooked speculators in this great 'bubble', but the most significant of all was George Hudson (1800–71). He was a successful draper in York when he was left a good sum of money. After noting the success of the Liverpool and Manchester Railway he used his money to promote what became the York and North Midland Railway, which opened in May 1839. He then got involved in a network of schemes that gave him pecuniary advantage but were difficult for others to follow. He came up with plans for new railways as the railway bubble developed and encouraged some mergers, which extended what had started as the York and North Midland as a 600 mile route from Rugby to Newcastle, and was one of those who started the trend towards company amalgamation.

In this respect he aided the development of the British railway system. Hudson soon became a respected business man, then an MP and was even courted by royalty and the rich. But his downfall soon came. He was involved in the expanding Eastern Counties Railway and it was found that as financing became more difficult he was paying dividends out of capital and taking expenses too. Further investigation proved that this and other irregularities were also applicable to other companies controlled by Hudson. He had become known as the 'Railway King' but he was now charged with financial crimes, was imprisoned, and went abroad afterwards, fading from the railway scene even quicker than he joined it.

The mania was really brought to an end when Parliament ruled that any outstanding schemes for new railways had to be deposited at the Board of Trade by the night of Sunday, 30th November 1845. This led to frantic activity on the part of promoters and by this date 815 schemes had registered. But the way railways were set up and operated was changing and the railways of Britain moved into a new era.

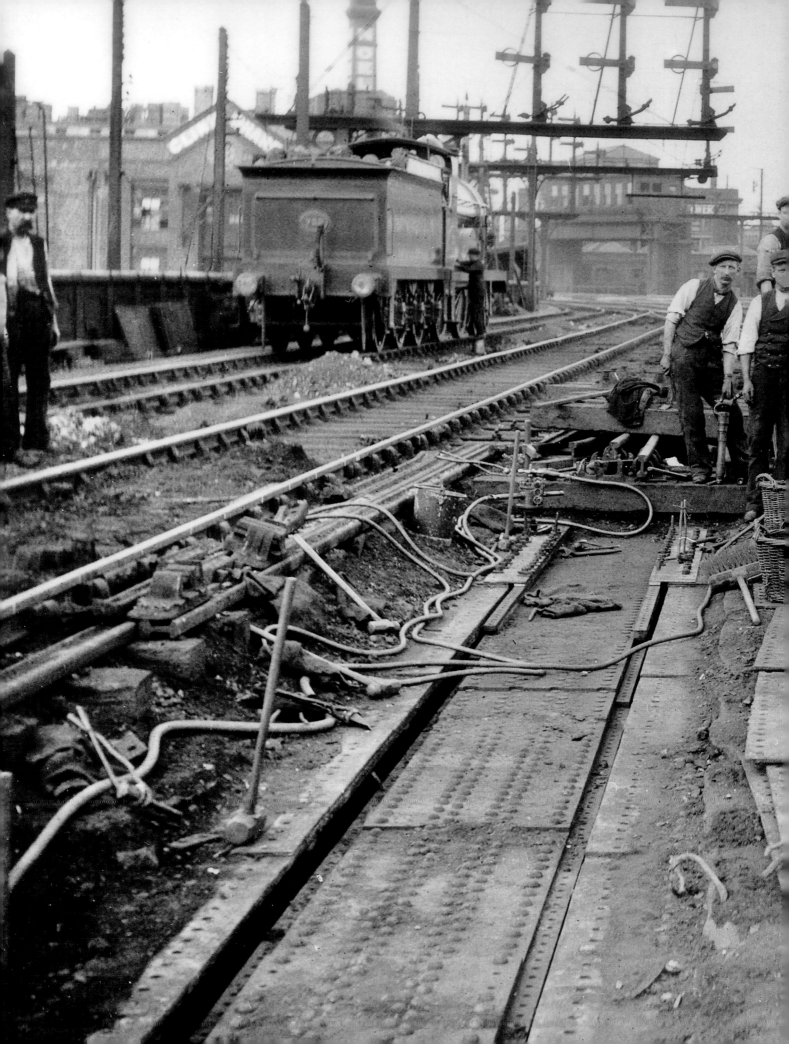

chapter 5

The last half of the 19th century and the first two decades of the 20th century saw the rail network in Britain expand to its greatest extent. Technical progress also took place at a steady rate, bringing comfort, safety and efficiency to the transport of passengers and goods throughout the land. It changed the face of the countryside, but it also brought prosperity, more employment and opportunities to travel that had never before been possible. Steam locomotive development had almost reached a peak by 1920, though there was a little more progress to come. Coaches, too, and rail travel, generally, had reached a height of perfection that has hardly been bettered since.

The first age of the train

While the latter part of 1845 was the peak of 'railway mania' in terms of the number of new lines projected, it was another four years before it could be said to have petered out, with sanity restored to ambition and progress. A total of 1,428 lines had been authorised, registered, or simply announced by 30th November 1845. Of these, around 450 had actually been authorised by that date, but only 47 had been built and opened by then, and 118 (totalling 3,543 miles) were under construction. Including all the many more new lines that had been announced, the total capital invested, or due to be invested, in railways in Britain was the then huge sum of well over £701 million. This was over ten times the amount being earned each year by the British export trade at that period.

Ironically, the Railway Act of 1844 that had been drawn up by W.E. Gladstone, then President of the Board of Trade, which even included provision for possible government control, had, as an unintended consequence, the effect of encouraging the 'railway mania' rather than bringing order and regulation to railway development. Long-term regulations for railway-company taxation, if profits were 10 per cent or more over a long period, suggested to investors that railways would be yielding good profits for years ahead. And the need for a deposit of 10 per cent of capital when a new company sought Parliamentary authorisation was reduced to only five per cent of capital after successful lobbying by the railway interests, prominently led by George Hudson. This made it easier to raise the money needed to register a company, adding to the flood of new companies being formed in 1845. In addition to this, over a hundred MPs were directors of railway companies (Hudson himself became MP for Sunderland in 1845), and Prime Minister Robert Peel favoured railway development and thought Gladstone's proposals too restrictive, so the Parliamentary attitude to 'railway mania' was somewhat benign.

In addition to all this, railway companies were not required to submit properly audited accounts to the Board of Trade until 1849, which made it easy for any published (or unpublished) accounts to be fraudulently adjusted or fictionalised. George Hudson did this in a big way and in the 1845–47 period his frenzy of activity as he tried to buy up rival companies, or float new ones to block rival projects (such as the projected Great Northern Railway from London to York), led to his financial transactions being carried on in cavalier fashion. Share prices were fiddled or hidden liabilities were discovered. Assiduous shareholders investigated and exposed him, and in 1847–48 his dubious activities were found to be so corrupt that he was forced out of his position by 1849. As it happened these events coincided with a new recession in Britain, partly caused by railway speculation, but also by adverse overseas trading conditions and increasing commodity prices. Several banks failed, interest rates rose greatly, and political events abroad, such as the overthrow of the French king in 1848, caused even more economic uncertainty. Share prices collapsed, and many of

the projected railway schemes collapsed with them. Parliamentary assent for new rail companies was greatly reduced to only 17 in 1849, which really marked the end of 'railway mania'.

Railway amalgamation

The one important legacy that survived from the days of George Hudson's railway management was the idea of amalgamating several small adjacent railways into one ownership to form a bigger company. His creation was the Midland Railway, formed in May 1844 by extending his York and North Midland Railway to take over the North Midland (which ran south to Derby), the Birmingham and Derby Railway, and eventually the Midland Counties Railway to reach Rugby. The Midland Counties Railway was built in 1839–40. Similarly Hudson extended the York and North Midland Railway further north by a branch to Bradford and leasing or taking over three small companies to reach Harrogate in 1848.

Amalgamation would probably have happened anyway, though Hudson showed the way. By 1845–56 there were a number of important amalgamations under way as companies realised the economies of scale, and as it became clear that through workings would be more profitable for both passenger and freight traffic, and more convenient for the customers, too. Sometimes amalgamations were protracted as rival companies argued over terms and sometimes sought alternative partners. Sometimes, too, larger companies extended their routes by leasing small companies which connected – or could be connected – to their routes.

A major amalgamation which took place over the 1845–46 period was the link up of the Liverpool and Manchester Railway with the Grand Junction, and these then joined with the London and Birmingham Railway to become the mighty London and North Western Railway (L.N.W.R.), a major trunk route, and by the late 19th century the L.N.W.R. was the largest joint-stock company in Britain.

ABOVE Construction on the approach to the London and North Western Railway's Liverpool Lime Street station. The image shows a locomotive hauling away the spoil.

In these early decades of railway history it is necessary to remember that new companies were receiving Parliamentary assent for building right up to the end of the 19th century, and in a few cases into the early years of the 20th century. A few examples from hundreds illustrate the time scale, such as the Findhorn Railway (1860), Esk Valley Railway (1867), Cowes and Newport Railway (the first on the Isle of Wight, 1862), Wallingford and Watlington Railway (1866), North Pembroke and Fishguard Railway (1895), and Elsenham and Thaxted Light Railway (1913). However, as the years went by the provenance of some of the new railways was not always so straightforward as the names might imply. Of the above, the Findhorn Railway was taken over in 1862 by its main line neighbour, the Inverness and Aberdeen Junction Railway, itself merged with the Inverness and Perth Junction Railway in 1865 to the form the Highland Railway which was another example of amalgamation.

Extending the routes

The diversity apparent in just these few random examples was typical of what was happening all over Britain as the railway network continued to expand at a steady pace. And all the while railways were amalgamating to form the trunk routes that

still exist today. Of all the original major companies, only the Great Western Railway (G.W.R.) kept its name intact through all the period of amalgamation right up to nationalisation in 1948. The original London terminus was a rather basic looking collection of tracks and huts centred around the Bishop's Bridge Road with the booking office and entrance under of the arches of the bridge itself. But by 1845 it had moved fully into Brunel's imposing new station, which still exists at Paddington, a little further east from Bishop's Bridge Road. The G.W.R. absorbed about 150 smaller companies in the West of England, Thames Valley area, West Midlands, Wales and Oxfordshire by 1923, and then absorbed even more at the time of the 'Big Four' grouping. This was amalgamation on a grand scale.

A pattern of extension was happening all over Britain. For example, the Midland Railway built south from Rugby to reach St Pancras, which opened in 1868 with a large freight station alongside it, now the site of the British Library. The Midland took over a number of adjoining smaller companies such as the Birmingham and Gloucester (in 1846) and the Birmingham and Derby Junction Railway (in 1844), and eventually had over 5,000 miles of trackage as a major company.

An important amalgamation in 1854 resulted in formation of the North Eastern Railway when the York and North Midland, Leeds Northern, and York, Newcastle and Berwick Railway joined together, and took in later one or two minor railways. The company had a junction with the Great Northern Railway (G.N.R.) via York, and this completed the East Coast route up to Berwick. The G.N.R. was a major route, 285 miles long from London King's Cross to York, while also diverting to serve Boston and Lincoln, and built in stages from 1848 to 1852, the year in which it reached

ABOVE Before the advent of motor traffic, the railways made extensive use of horses for collection and delivery to and from their stations. Sommerstown Milk & Fish Depot, alongside St Pancras Station is now the site of the British Library.

The first age of the train   79

King's Cross. Its building was opposed by George Hudson, and a deal was done by the G.N.R. to take over one of his companies to make the final link into York. The G.N.R. was engineered by William Cubitt (1785–1861), and the elegant King's Cross station was designed by Lewis Cubitt. On the west coast, the main route north from Manchester was the Lancaster and Preston Railway and the Lancaster and Carlisle, both engineered in succession from 1840–46 by Joseph Locke (1805–60), the latter being one of the longest single section projects, at 69 miles, then undertaken. These two companies merged, were then leased by the L.N.W.R. from 1859 who finally took them over in 1879.

The L.N.W.R. also took over the Chester and Holyhead Railway (engineered by Robert Stephenson) within a year of its opening in 1858, thus moving into North Wales. Several small railways built into Central Wales were also taken over by the L.N.W.R. in the 1868–73 period, eventually getting the company a good foothold in South Wales. The G.W.R. got into South Wales by ferry across the River Severn in 1863, with a company called the Bristol and South Wales Union Railway, fully absorbed into the G.W.R. in 1868. The ferry was finally replaced in 1886 by the Severn Tunnel, a massive engineering feat at the time. The famous Cambrian Railways running up the Welsh coast to Barmouth resulted from the merger in 1864 of several smaller undertakings and the Cambrian itself merged with the G.W.R. at the 'Grouping' in 1923.

The most important route from England to Scotland was the Caledonian Railway, built from Carlisle across Beattock to Glasgow, and via a junction at Carstairs to Edinburgh, which was all constructed in 1847–50 period. With its completion, passengers could, for the first time, take a train directly from London to Glasgow or Edinburgh in a fastest time of 12½ hours, with no need to change or break the journey. The Caledonian gradually absorbed a number of smaller railways and eventually reached Aberdeen on the North Sea coast, and then Ballachulish on the Atlantic Coast by taking over the Callander and Oban Railway in 1880. The Caledonian network was the largest in Scotland with nearly 3,000 miles of trackage at its final extent. The formation of the Highland Railway has already been mentioned, but the other important Scottish railway was the North British, the first section of which, 57 miles from Berwick to Edinburgh, opened in June 1846. The North British expanded mainly by absorbing the many small railways around Edinburgh, including the Edinburgh and Glasgow Railway in 1865, and totalling eventually about 50 other undertakings. The Tay (1878) and Forth (1890) bridges were built by the North British Railway and, prior to these, train ferries were used to cross both rivers. The Great North of Scotland Railway opened in 1854, and covered routes north of Aberdeen, Banffshire, and Deeside, absorbing several smaller railways as it expanded.

BELOW Glasgow–Carlisle train at Beattock summit in the early 1900s hauled by a Caledonian Railway McIntosh 4–4–0.

Railway buildings

Civil engineering work of all kinds was needed in constructing the railway network, ranging from great river bridges, to long viaducts, tunnels, small bridges, culverts, retaining walls, and the cuttings and embankments along the route.

To operate the railway, much more had to be built, taken for granted today, but

new to public perceptions when the railways were first built. Stations for picking up passengers came with the early railways. On the first railways, effort was made with the termini at each end of the line, and these were often quite substantial and included company offices, parcel offices and the like. Along the line in the early days stations could merely be stopping places with no shelter at all though this became less usual after a few years. Sometimes a passing station would be little more than a shanty offering basic shelter for waiting passengers. By the 1850s, however, most wayside stations were of higher quality and often in a company 'style' as architects were appointed to the work. An example is the series of neat Italianate style intermediate stations, and Brighton station itself, designed by David Mocatta. On the Great Western Railway, the line's engineer, Isambard Brunel, also designed the handsome stations, though in varying styles, often Gothic. Famous too, was the work of Philip Hardwick who designed the famous London Euston arch and the Curzon Street, Birmingham terminus of the London and Birmingham Railway, both in classical Greek style. And there were many other architects at work for all the major companies and much of their work still stands today, anything up to – and even beyond – 160 years on.

With the stations came ancillary buildings such as company houses adjacent to country stations for local railway and station staff, and also for the station master where accommodations was not provided on the upper floor of the station building itself. At termini and major junctions there was usually a railway hostel somewhere nearby where train crews from outside the area could sleep over before the next day's duty took them on elsewhere. And along the route shelters or cottages were built for crossing keepers, plus huts and tool stores for track workers.

At all major terminus stations and many junctions a large hotel was invariably built

ABOVE The public turn
out in large numbers for the
opening of Padstow station,
Cornwall on 27th March
1899.

to accommodate travellers of better means. Often this was built within the footprint of the station itself, such as the Grosvenor Hotel at Victoria station, London, or else immediately adjacent such as the Great Western Hotel at Paddington. These were all company-owned hotels. And at almost every station in the land a nearby inn or public house was built, frequently called 'The Railway Hotel', but privately owned, again mainly intended for travellers but also frequented by locals. Many of the hotels and railway inns still stand today, though no longer in company ownership in the case of hotels. A class of building near railway stations, almost completely forgotten and disappeared now, was the 'commercial hotel' – usually with that wording in its title – intended for commercial travellers (salesmen) and more basic in amenities, because in the days before cars, sales representatives travelled with their samples by train to call on customers in the towns in their areas over a period of days.

Freight operations also needed special buildings, most importantly what were often called goods (or freight) stations, or alternatively goods depots. In practice the latter term was most often applied to sheds and platforms for local goods transactions at small stations along the route, while major termini and junctions had much larger facilities that were sometimes even bigger than the nearby passenger stations, certainly in London and other big cities. They featured long, covered sheds, cranes and warehouses, including bonded warehouses for wine and spirits, and specialised warehouses in some places for such commodities as tea, sugar, cotton or wool. As rail operations increased in scale through the 19th century, trackage at freight stations could become very complex and crowded. Wagon turntables were used extensively to move wagons quickly into designated loading bays and horses made a comeback to hauling rail wagons, this time as inexpensive and always available shunting horses, complete with stables and facilities. An echo of the old stationary winding engine for wagons also returned in the form of capstans, also used for shunting wagons in freight stations. Horses, too, were of course used in their thousands by the railway companies to haul the carts that delivered or collected

The Monorail

The monorail idea (using only one rail) originated in France in the 1870s. Several diferent types were built, but the only one to be tried in the Great Britain was the Lartigue system, which was originally used in France and Algeria. It was used for an industrial line on the 9 mile long Listowel and Ballybunion Railway in Ireland and opened in 1887. The locomotives were 0–6–0 and like the coaches straddled a central rail and were all built as twin units to ensure balance. The locomotive, therefore, had two separate boilers and fireboxes, as is apparent in this view. They were also fitted with powered tenders for use when going up hills. Also shown is the complicated point system, involving a pivoted track section. One of the major problems with the design was that in populated areas it was not possible to install level crossings and a drawbridge had to be constructed.

In 1907 a British engineer, Louis

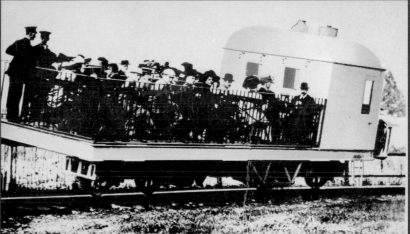

Brennan, designed a monorail locomotive that used an oil-fired (diesel) engine and ran on a single rail at ground level, with gyroscopes each side to balance the unit. Though tested it never progressed further for two reasons. Firstly the government could see no use for it in a war situation and secondly the rail companies of the day would not support it because it would mean their existing infrastructure would become obsolete.

ABOVE The Lartigue monorail on the Listowel and Ballybunion Railway in Ireland.

BELOW The Brennan Gyroscopic Mono-Rail car.

local goods despatches handled at the freight station. Some horses for both shunting and haulage were, in fact, still being used well into the 1960s.

A spectacular feature of some larger freight stations was the wagon lift, seen at a number of big city freight stations to enable multi-level operation. For example, the approach to the freight station might be at high level, and the wagon lift would be used to carry wagons down to tracks at ground level for unloading or loading for road deliveries. It could also be used where one company had a yard at high level adjacent to another rail company with a yard at low level. A wagon lift allowed interchange between them. There were even some examples of wagon lifts in large warehouses so that wagons could be hoisted to upper floors for loading or unloading.

In a number of locations old passenger stations that were superseded were turned into freight stations. Two notable examples were the original terminus of the London and South Western Railway at Nine Elms, which became a big freight station when Waterloo was built as the new passenger terminus and the Great Northern terminus at York which was similarly used when the imposing new York station was opened. Both these examples were still in use as freight stations into the early 1980s, but there were many more.

Aside from general goods, railways carried specialist loads, most notably cattle

(and some other livestock such as horses and sheep) and coal, both of which were big business. This involved the building of cattle docks for the transhipping of the cattle, not only at stations serving country market towns but also in city goods yards. Related to the extensive use of horses in 19th century towns and cities were regular manure trains from collecting points to certain yards, the consignments being taken to country destinations for use as fertilisers. But coal carriage was a major business of the railways, for in the 19th century and the first half of the 20th century it was the key fuel for domestic use in house heating, for town gas works, and later also for electricity-generating stations. The railway companies, too, were major users for steam locomotives, and also for heating their own numerous properties. Nearly every town in the land had a coal merchant and an office and storage pens built in the town goods yard. In every city there would be these coal merchant's premises in every goods yard of every rail company serving the city, and their proximity to each other, sometimes as little as two miles apart, reflected not only the huge numbers of houses, schools, shops and offices to be supplied, but also the working radius of the horses used to haul the coal-delivery carts.

Virtually every colliery in Britain had a railhead where the mined coal was sorted and loaded by tipplers into wagons – indeed coal-mining had been the industry to first

Barnstaple Town station showing Lynton and Barnstaple narrow-gauge train on left and standard gauge L.S.W.R. line on right in about 1908.

ABOVE A goods train at Oakengates station, Shropshire, 1911. The train is carrying mining equipment. The coming of the railways was of enormous help to the coal mines, as trains could bring heavy equipment to mines and carry coal away to its destination.

build the original plateways to carry coal to canals or harbour wharfs – but in the age of the railway, network coal could now be carried all over the country more quickly by rail. At least one colliery, Clay Cross, was built new specifically to ship coal by rail, the seam having been discovered while a cutting was being dug in Derbyshire, and the first coal by rail for London came via the Midland Railway to the St Pancras goods yard. Prior to that London's coal had come by canal or by coaster up the Thames from the northeast. There were many thousands of coal wagons owned by collieries, coal factors, and coal merchants, most painted prominently with the owner's name, and long trains of these wagons could be seen bringing coal from Welsh, Scottish and English coal fields towards the big cities, from where wagon loads for town coal merchants or other users would be dropped off by local mixed goods trains on their daily runs. The rail companies also had wagons for coal consignments, and also for carrying their own 'locomotive coal'.

Another significant user of rail was the agricultural business, where warehouses for farm produce, and 'provender stores' for animal feeds were built in most country goods yards. Produce for city markets was shipped out, and animal feed, seed and fertilisers were shipped in. Some towns and cities had railway sidings laid directly into market areas. Canal and rail interchange also became more common as the rail network grew, leading to the building of larger canal basins, sometimes roofed over, where railway wagons could run right alongside canal boats to tranship loads. Many of these basins had chutes where coal could be discharged from wagons directly into the boats, again reflecting early plateway practice but now on a bigger scale.

Beyond the need for structures and facilities for handling passengers and freight, the other big category of extensive building was to service the needs of the railway itself. From the earliest days, there were sheds for servicing, cleaning and repairing locomotives. As the railways grew so did the sheds which ranged in size from a

LEFT Milk churns and mail sacks on a platform at the Great Western Railway's Paddington Station, Christmas 1908.

The first age of the train   87

single-road structure housing one or two locomotives at a branch line terminus to huge depots stabling scores of locomotives at a big city terminus. Some locomotive depots were multi-track sheds of great width and length, within which there might be turntables for turning locomotives, or traversers – side moving sections of track – for moving locomotives to adjacent tracks, but a very popular and favoured structure was the 'roundhouse', a circular shed with a turntable in the centre serving numerous tracks that radiated from it so that the locomotives were housed like petals round a flower. Some of these survived until the end of steam traction or beyond and a preserved example (no longer used for rail services) is at Camden Town in London. The turntables in locomotive sheds were long enough, of course, to hold even the longest locomotives. In the early days they were turned manually, but later steam or electric power was used. Smaller wagon turntables were commonly used in goods yards and warehouses well into the 20th century, but in the early days of railways,

up to the 1860s-70s they were also used in passenger stations, and a larger radius version, sometimes called a 'turnplate' was used in some stations to move carriages across from one track to another.

In addition to the locomotive depots, every company built huge workshops where locomotives were built, rebuilt, or overhauled and repainted. These were lavishly fitted with forges, every kind of machinery for turning wheels and axles, overhead cranes, fabricating shops, paint shops, and much else. Many of these were legendary, well-known to all rail enthusiasts past and present, such as Swindon (G.W.R.), Eastleigh (L.S.W.R.), Crewe (L.N.W.R.), Derby (M.R.), Stratford (G.E.R.), Ashford (S.E.R.), Brighton (L.B.S.C.R.), and many others. Of these Ashford still exists to its full extent giving a good idea of how big railway workshops could be. Added to these there were other large workshops building, repairing and overhauling railway carriages and goods rolling stock of all kinds. Most of the larger companies had their own facilities of this type, plus further depots dealing with signal equipment, trackside maintenance, station equipment, advertising hoardings and all other requirements needed to run an efficient system.

Auxiliary equipment at locomotive sheds included coaling platforms, and later tall coaling towers, plus water cranes and water towers, the key elements of steam operation. All but the smallest station halts also had water cranes or water towers, and in later years water troughs, with associated pump houses, were a feature of most main lines so that express train locomotives could pick up water on the move, the key to enabling the later famous express trains line the 'Flying Scotsman' to run non-stop. And finally every locomotive depot and goods yard had offices built for managers and mess rooms for workers going on and off duty, or awaiting the call to duty.

Signals, signalling and safety

In the early days of railways signalling was almost non-existent as were ideas of safety. Apart from the accident to William Huskisson on the opening day of the Liverpool and Manchester Railway in 1830, there was another serious accident not long after which led to calls for stricter attention to safety.

On this occasion four passengers stood on an adjacent track watching the train they had just left, and amid the swirling steam and noise they were unaware of a fast approaching train that ran them all down, as the driver did not spot them until too late.

Accidents like this, and several others, caused the first safety and signalling measures, initially on the Liverpool and Manchester Railway with the employment of look-outs called 'railway policemen' on the station approaches and other places along the route. They used their arms to signal whether the line ahead was clear or occupied by hand signals, and later by flags in various colours. If passengers were waiting to be picked up at a station a red flag was hoisted in daylight or a swinging lantern at night. Also at night a train carried a red lantern on the end of the last coach or wagon when running. If the train stopped, the lantern was turned around to show a blue light to the rear, warning any following train to stop. Roads crossing the track were gated and guarded by gatekeepers to stop people wandering along the track. There was also a 20mph speed limit for trains.

In 1833 the company started using more flag poles for the coloured flags to be hoisted so that they were visible to locomotive drivers at a greater distance, and from 1834 coloured lights were hoisted at night. In 1837 signal boards that could be turned to either face the oncoming train or be set parallel to the track were introduced on posts. A facing board indicated 'stop' and a parallel board 'proceed'. In 1840 about 10 other new railway companies got together, with others following, and decided to use the same signals and operating methods used by the Liverpool and Manchester Railway, an early attempt at standardisation. The L.M.R. already ran passenger trains to a set timetable with goods trains run 'as required'. These took second place to passenger trains, and goods trains were sidelined into storage tracks if a passenger train was due. Shelters were provided for the 'railway policeman' who also operated points by hand along the route. On double track, separate signal posts were used on each track. On the Liverpool and

ABOVE Early semaphore signals and box for controlling a junction.

RIGHT Auxillary 'distant' signal.

OPPOSITE ABOVE A railway accident at Sevenoaks station in 1884. Accidents of this severity led to the regulations making continuous train braking mandatory.

Manchester Railway, whether on flags or boards, white was indicated as safe passage, green indicated 'caution', and red indicated 'danger – stop'. The main signal board was painted red one side and green the other, the appropriate side being turned towards the engine driver. A lamp showing the same lights was linked to the post and showed the same colours at night or in fog. When a train had passed through a station the red signal board was shown for three minutes, followed by the green board for five minutes to stop (or warn) any following train. On other lines the red and green boards were often shown for longer periods, typically five and 10 minutes respectively. Soon after this auxiliary, or 'distant' signals were installed placed some way ahead of the station (or 'home') signals, typically 200 yards. These also displayed the board and the lamp on a single post, and the board (and lights) displayed white ('safe to proceed') and green ('caution') colours. These signals could be worked by wires and a lever by the policeman at the station ('home') signal.

Despite these advances there was still wide variety in signalling systems and signal types across the country. The Great Western Railway, London and Birmingham Railway, and others, were still depending to a great extent on railway policemen with hand or flag signals in the mid-1840s, but on the other hand the G.W.R. had the useful idea of using small signals to indicate the direction in which points were set as early as 1839.

The next major stop was the development of the semaphore signal, originally a useful idea for controlling diverging lines at junctions. Here arms were pivoted in slots at the top of a mast, with one arm each side to control traffic in each direction. The arm facing the driver was painted red, and its reverse side white. With the arm kept

ABOVE After an accident a mobile crane has been put in place to lift the locomotive off the road below.

horizontal it indicated 'danger – stop', dropped to 45 degrees it indicated 'caution'. and dropped vertically into the slot into the mast it indicated 'proceed'. These signals were on a raised platform and were controlled by levers and wires, while linked wires and chains changed the points for the desired routes. A box was provided to shelter the signalman, and also the levers in many instances, so starting the idea of signal boxes. The idea of semaphore signals spread from 1841 onwards, with lamps attached to give night-time signals in red, white, and green, but again there was a deal of variation in the detail and such matters of height, etc.

The technical development that improved signalling and safety was the coming of the electric telegraph, surprisingly early in 1837 where it was first installed for trials on the G.W.R. between Paddington and Slough and on the London and Birmingham Railway between Euston and Camden to control the incline. It took a little while to work out the best way to use it, but by 1841 the inventors of the system had designed instruments to show if the line section was clear or occupied by a train. This was particularly useful in indicating whether long tunnels were clear or not. One of the inventors, William Cooke (1872–1939), went on to suggest how a route could be divided up along its length in sections from station to station with the telegraph signals being passed along the sections so that all the signalmen in their

BELOW Crewe North junction all electric signal boxin 1906 showing an extensive array of block instruments.

boxes knew exactly where the trains were, and could control the distances between them by means of the signals. This became known as the 'block system', a key advance in train safety that did much to reduce the accidents and collisions that were so frequent in the early days. The block system also made single line working (with trains running in both directions on the same track) a more practical and safe proposition, and this was backed up by a token system controlling the interlocking that ensured only one train could occupy a single-line track at one time. The telegraph system was later improved by adding bell codes. The G.W.R., S.E.R., and Eastern Counties were early users of the telegraph, but it spread all over these systems and many others through the 1840s and 1850s. The idea of interlocking came in the 1850s, too, came, a foremost developer of which was John Saxby (1821–1913) which ensured that signals could not be set until the route had been correctly set first. This also allowed larger signal boxes to be built that controlled long stretches of track, and signals and points some distance away. Prior to that a signalman had to control every location where signals and points were needed. In turn all these changes allowed more frequent train services, and more stations along the route, all adding to the fast-developing economic conditions of the 19th century. Other safety features, among many, included point locking, fully gated and attended level crossings and the fencing off of all tracks and railway yards to prevent public trespass and accidents. As a result of the universal use of the block system, semaphore signals were changed so that a horizontal arm (with red light visible at night) indicated 'danger – stop', and a 45 degree downward angle (with green light) indicated 'safe – proceed'. The one area of confusion thatremained was the system of bell codes and procedures in the block system that tended to differ from company to company. This was solved by the Regulation of Railways Act of 1889, which made the block system and interlocking mandatory over the whole British railway system, with standardised bell codes and procedures common to all companies.

Social and economic effects

A major change that affected the travelling public, and eventually the whole country, was the matter of time. Until the coming of the railways each town or area kept its own time based on its distance from the Greenwich meridian. This caused time differences across the land of up to 30 minutes at the extremities from east to west. When the first railways carrying passengers were built local time did not cause much of a problem, but as the network expanded and trains covered greater distances, time variations became a problem, not least when producing a timetable. The secretary of the Liverpool and Manchester Railway suggested to the government in 1845 that Greenwich time be adopted across the land. The Railway Clearing House backed this idea and most, but not all, companies took it up. To assist in keeping to the correct standard time, signals were sent out from Greenwich via the railway telegraph system. Gradually through the 1850s all companies fell into line, but it was not until 1880 that standard Greenwich time became established by law. In the meantime, it had become fairly standard practice to have clocks prominently displayed on stations, and for train guards to be issued with watches so that train punctuality could be observed.

As the rail system grew there were a lot of public benefits. The nation as a whole became more mobile and far less static. Travel by train brought the classes into much closer contact than they had ever known before, though some members of the upper classes were still travelling in their private coaches on carriage trucks well into the 1850s. By train, families could take holidays away from home and seaside resorts began to boom. Excursion trains became common, allowing day trips to the seaside, beauty spots, or sporting events at attractive low prices. A very early effort in this direction saw excursion trains from Nine Elms to Surbiton in 1838, within a week of the opening of the London and Southampton Railway, enabling over 5,000 people to watch the Derby – so long as they walked more than five miles across the fields from Surbiton to get to Epsom.

A good train service, too, allowed people to get work further away from home, and train routes to ferry ports, some of which were developed due to the railway, made travel abroad much easier for those who could afford it. Workmen's

BELOW Porters loading luggage into the baggage van of a London and North Western Railway train as the guard looks on, Euston Station, c 1907.

trains were being introduced by the 1880s with very low price tickets, examples being 2d for a 7–9 mile journey or a weekly return ticket of 1s. Railways, too, led to the development of suburbs around big cities, or completely new towns where country stations had been built and cheap fares encouraged workers to move out from city centres to the suburbs. In 1859 there were 58 million passenger journeys by rail with receipts of nearly £6 million. By 1880 journeys had reached 540 million with receipts of £20 million. Receipts dropped relative to the number of journeys largely because more people were travelling 3rd class (more than five times 1st and 2nd class journeys combined) and more were travelling on workmen's trains. In 1881, 623 million journeys were recorded of which 520.5 million were 3rd class. All this travel led to extensive publication of railway timetables, both by the companies themselves, and commercially, notably by Bradshaw.

The railways themselves generated an enormous number of new jobs of all types, from porters to engine drivers, cleaners, gangers, mechanics, carters, shunters, labourers, skilled engineers, clerks, officials, and much more. In the 1880s Crewe locomotive works alone employed 6,000 workers. Then there were companies with contracts with the railways, such as caterers and newsagents (of which W.H. Smith was the most famous), and cartage companies delivering parcels. Communications were speeded up with most mail going by train, plus the daily newspaper and milk trains running through the night. Even the stage and mail coach companies did not entirely lose out. Though displaced by the railways from their trunk routes there were still mail coaches being hauled on carriage trucks for onward journeys by road to places not yet served by rail, and enterprising stage coach companies set themselves up to meet the trains at key stations and carry passengers on to destinations also not served by rail. Some of these horse-drawn coaches were still running until the 1920s, notably in Scotland and the Lake District.

BELOW Locomotives in the erecting shop at Horwich works. This shop was where the locomotives were put together. It was equipped with 20 cranes, tools for repairs and drilling machines. Horwich works opened in 1886 as the locomotive works for the Lancashire and Yorkshire Railway.

One other aspect of railways that affected passengers was the ticketing. In the earliest days of rail travel companies issued paper tickets with hand written information, and the counterfoil was kept as a record for the company. This was time consuming, and in 1837 a railway booking clerk, Thomas Edmondson, devised a compact card ticket system with pre-printed journey details and cost marked on, and the date printed on at the time of issue. This speeded up the issuing process but it also made accounting easier. These card tickets, or half of one in the case of returns, were collected up by staff one stop short of the terminus, or at special 'ticket collecting platforms' in some cases (for example just short of Victoria station in London), or at the barrier of intermediate stations, and the collected tickets were sent to the Railway Clearing House where 2,000 clerks sorted them and allocated receipts to the railway companies concerned.

Locomotive development

Stephenson's Patentee design, with its well-balanced 2–2–2 wheel arrangement and sturdy frame first appeared in 1833 (for the Liverpool and Manchester Railway) and locomotives by Stephenson to this design were widely sold and even more widely copied by other locomotive builders. More developed locomotives to this basic design were built well into the 1850s, and in the case of the G.W.R., the 1870s. For the G.W.R. the first Patentee locomotive built in 1837, to broad gauge of course, was the famous North Star which performed well and on a test run from Paddington to Maidenhead in 1838 achieved 30mph with a 80 ton train. Pleased with this, Daniel Gooch the chief built over 60 more Patentee type 2–2–2s between 1840–42 for express passenger work. Gooch lengthened the valve on the cylinders on these engines to give a more expansive use of the steam and a freer exhaust, making the locomotive more economical of fuel and faster. In 1839 a locomotive builder, Isaac Dodds, developed a new way of securing a locomotive boiler without bolting it to the frames (which could stress both boiler and frames), by attaching the boiler only to the smokebox and with the firebox and allowed to slide on the frames. This became standard practice for the rest of the steam era.

The Stephenson company developed a 'long boiler' in 1841. This was used with a small firebox set behind the rear driving wheels, mostly on 0–6–0 type locomotives. This necessitated a short wheelbase, and gave good traction for the size of the locomotive plus ability to take sharp curves. The long boiler held a large volume of steam, useful for starting a heavy load, while the small firebox was economical on fuel which in the 1840s was coke rather than coal. This arrangement was ideal for locomotives which spent time between short moves, as when shunting freight yards or acting as station pilot engines. While both 2–2–2 and 0–6–0 goods engines were built with long boilers (the last 0–6–0s not scrapped until 1923), this type was not taken up by many British companies but was much used by locomotive builders in mainland Europe, notably in France and Germany.

For a long boiler passenger engine, Stephenson built in 1845 a locomotive with an extra pair of carrying wheels, making it a 2–2–2–0, the third pair of wheels being the large diameter drivers which were driven by outside cylinders set between the two leading axles. To achieve this layout the outside frame of the 'Patentee' design was replaced by inside plate frames, and this was a design advance which was taken up by other builders leading to a proliferation of types with a large pair of driving wheels with non-driven carrying wheels in front and behind, in 2–2–2 layout.

The Crewe type built from 1846 by the L.N.W.R. and developed by Joseph Locke with design and assembly work by W.B. Buddicom, Richard Trevithick and Alexander Allan, was the most successful and significant. Apart from the inside frames which bore the driving wheels and axleboxes, there was added a much lighter outside frame with the axleboxes for the leading and trailing wheels. The outside cylinders were sandwiched between the two frames. With later increases in size this became a standard type for the L.N.W.R. built by them until 1857, but locomotives of the same Crewe type were built by or for many other companies including the L.S.W.R., Caledonian Railway, Great Eastern and others up to 1883 when the last were built for the Manchester, Sheffield and Lincolnshire Railway. Over this long period the locomotives got longer and heavier and the driving wheel diameters increased from

6ft, 6ft 6in, and 7ft, up to 8ft 2in or even 8ft 6in on the L.N.W.R. engine Cornwall. Some were exported and there was a smaller 2–4–0 version and a 2–4–0T and 2–4–2T tank engines with a coal bunker and well tank replacing the coupled tender.

These large wheel engines were generically called 'single drivers' or 'single wheelers' and another significant design of this type was the 'Jenny Lind' 2–2–2, designed by John Gray with the first built in 1840. This had a higher pressure boiler than most other locomotives of the time, set high on full length outside frames and partial length inside frames, with cylinders set between them with is own patent valve system and 6ft diameter driving wheels. This was an efficient and widely used type, starting with locomotives built for the L.B.S.C.R. in 1847 (where Gray became chief engineer) and others were supplied to other leading companies such as the G.W.R., M.R., L.N.W.R., Great Northern, and Eastern Counties Railway, with bigger versions still being built in the late 1850s.

Between them the features of the Crewe and Jenny Lind designs, in particular the framing method of the latter, plus the use of bogies in the Norris style, showed the way forward in British locomotive design. Bigger and more powerful single wheelers for express work were built for all the major companies from 1860 on. onwards bigger and more powerful single wheelers for express work were built for all the major companies. Patrick Stirling's famous series of single wheelers for the Great Northern Railway started in 1870 with a 2–2–2 of elegant appearance using the Jenny Lind type of framing. But experience with these engines led Stirling and others to conclude that plain inside-framing was sufficient, and on the Stirling 4–2–2 locomotives of 1882 this was done. For a time both styles of construction were to be seen. For example, Great Eastern single wheelers built in 1879 followed the Stirling inside-frame style, while Midland and L.N.W.R. single wheelers followed the old Crewe style in enlarged form, and William Dean's Cobham class 2–2–2 of 1878 still followed the old Patentee style, albeit with modern boiler type and cab. The best G.W.R. single wheelers, however, also designed by William Dean were the Lord of the Isle class 4–2–2 of much more elegant appearance and power, built in 1894. The last single wheelers to be built were 4–2–2s designed by H.A. Ivatt, Stirling's successor, for the Great Northern Railway and delivered in 1900–1, but scrapped in 1918. The last single wheeler to run in Britain was Caledonian Railway No 123, built in 1886 as a one-off for an exhibition. It was not withdrawn until 1935, by then in L.M.S. service.

What made the single wheelers still viable as good fast haulers was the invention of the steam sanding apparatus in 1886 which blew sand under the driving wheels to greatly assist adhesion in wet weather or on gradients. Other developments included the vacuum brake (though a few companies preferred the American Westinghouse air brake), better wheels, I-section coupling rods, better packing for piston and valve rods, bigger and more protective cabs, a number of developments in more efficient valve gears, including the first use of the Walscheats valve gear in Britain in 1890, and improved blast pipe chimneys.

An interesting technical development was compounding a French idea of 1885 that used two inside high-pressure cylinders driving one axle and two outside low-pressure cylinders driving the other axle on a four-coupled locomotive. It worked well and a number of British compound engines were built, most notably a big class of 4–4–0s by the Midland Railway, but it was never used as extensively as it was in France. More important was superheating whereby steam passed through superheater tubes to reach a very high temperature before being supplied to the cylinders. The first ones were fitted in 1906–7 to the new powerful Star class 4–6–0s designed by G.J. Churchward for the G.W.R., also being fitted to later express locomotive types as they appeared. At about the same time Churchward started installing 'top feed' equipment on more and more locomotives, supplying feed-water to the steam space at the top of the boiler.

By this time locomotive design in Britain had reached a very high standard, only really improved on by the more powerful larger 4–6–2 locomotives introduced friom the 1920s onwards. By the time of 1923 'grouping' milestones in locomotive types and design included the 4–4–0, the 4–4–2 'Atlantic' (both first developed in USA), small but efficient 2–4–0s and 0–4–2s, 0–6–0s in great numbers, mainly for freight work, and 0–8–0s for heavy freight, and there were both tank and tender versions of these types. The first British 4–6–0 (for the Highland Railway) appeared in 1894, with more for the N.E.R. in 1899–1900, and the G.W.R. Stars in 1906. On the technical side the first four cylinder engines, the Belpaire firebox, double chimneys and water-tube firebox all appeared in 1897.

ABOVE A 'Pug' shunting 0–6–0 saddle tank loco of the Neilsland Colliery in about 1905, typical of hundreds of small industrial locomotives operating on light railways. Note the wood block 'dumb' buffers.

Standardisation

Aside from standard classes of locomotives, sometimes built in hundreds, and standard designs of coaches and wagons, built in hundreds or even thousands (in the latter case), the railway companies of the late 19th century and later, used standardised designs in a big way for almost every part of their activity. These included fences, lamp posts and lights of all types, station buildings and halt shelters, platform seats, uniforms, luggage trolleys, platelayers' hats, storage sheds and much else, even including advertisement hoardings. Many of these early standard designs remain to this day, added to by standard designs by the 'Big Four' companies from 1923, and B.R. from 1948.

Light railways, tramways, industrial railways and narrow gauge

While public attention and awareness was mostly fixed on the glamour and drama of the big railway routes and the companies who ran them, there was a truly massive development of minor railways on a scale unimaginable to the modern reader. Virtually every major seaport had its own private rail system, including Southampton, Hull, Manchester, Liverpool, and London, whose Port of London Authority had one of the biggest of all, with huge track mileage. Manufacturers had private rail systems, as did collieries, quarries, breweries (particularly at Burton-on-Trent and Dublin), power stations, waterworks and large gasworks. A notable example of the latter was at Beckton in East London. In the early 20th century the first 'business parks' were being built such as Trafford Park (Manchester) and Slough, and these, too, had rail systems serving the factories and warehouses on the estates that also connected them to the main line. Virtually all of these systems closed down at various times in the 20th century, though a few are preserved, or partly preserved, today.

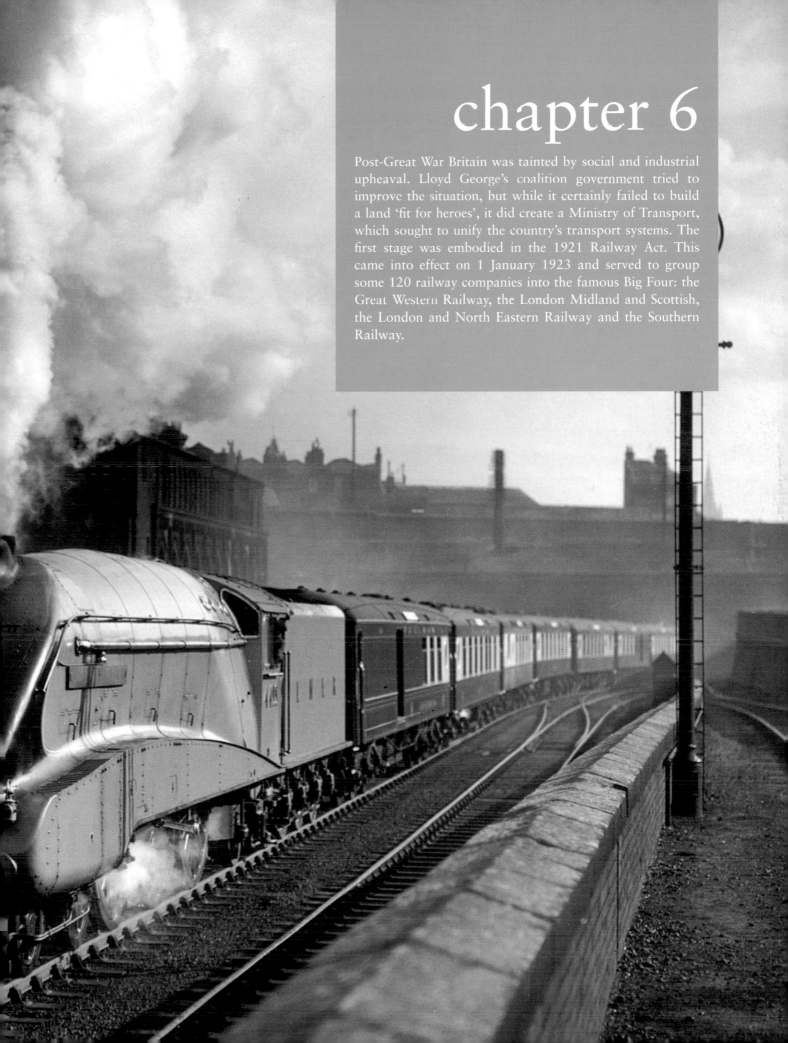

chapter 6

Post-Great War Britain was tainted by social and industrial upheaval. Lloyd George's coalition government tried to improve the situation, but while it certainly failed to build a land 'fit for heroes', it did create a Ministry of Transport, which sought to unify the country's transport systems. The first stage was embodied in the 1921 Railway Act. This came into effect on 1 January 1923 and served to group some 120 railway companies into the famous Big Four: the Great Western Railway, the London Midland and Scottish, the London and North Eastern Railway and the Southern Railway.

The grouping into the big four

PREVIOUS PAGES
Class A4 engine No. 4499 'Pochard' hauling the down Yorkshire Pullman, Kings Cross to Hull. The locomotive on the left is the first large boiler 4–4–2 of the G.N.R.

RIGHT Poster produced to promote deluxe daily pullman service between Victoria Station and Paris.

OPPOSITE ABOVE Great Western Railway poster showing a harbour scene in 1937.

OPPOSITE BELOW Poster produced for the London, Midland and Scottish Railway (L.M.S.) to promote the Euston to Holyhead Irish mail trains.

The Britain of the early 1920s was shrouded by the grey aftermath of the Great War. Many lives had been lost and many of the lives that continued would do so with indelible scars.

It was against this backdrop that the post-war coalition government tried to build the land 'fit for heroes' of which its leader, Liberal MP and former Chancellor David Lloyd George, had spoken in his 1918 election campaign. Sadly, the plan failed, and by 1921 the coalition was being wrenched apart by ideological differences. But before it bowed out in 1922 and Lloyd George gave way to the Tory Andrew Bonar Law, it created a Ministry of Transport, whose first minister was Eric Geddes.

Nationalisation was mooted at this stage. The railways had been sequestered into government service to ease the movement of troops and supplies during the war and had provided such sterling service that even Winston Churchill could see the advantage of running them 'at a loss to develop industries and agriculture'. Inflation caused the railway wage bill rise threefold between 1913 and 1920, while a coal strike in 1921 had lost so much trade that the system was thrown £60m into the red.

And yet there remained an acceptance that the benefits of unified operation should be retained. As Geddes put it, 'under a system of cooperation not only did one railway strive to divert traffic from another, but trams sought to wrest traffic from the railways, railways to wrest traffic from canals and so on'. 'In future,' he went on, 'our effort will be to encourage each agency of transport to undertake that part of the work which it, owing to its own special qualities, can most efficiently and economically perform.' It was a grand and admirable scheme of integration, whose first stage was embodied in the 1921 Railway Act, which came into effect on 1 January 1923.

Some companies – like the Midland and Great Northern Joint and the Somerset

 CORNWALL

"SPECIAL" IS PADDINGTON STATION, LONDON, W.2.   PRINTED IN GREAT BRITAIN BY JORDISON & CO LT. LONDON & MIDDLESBROUGH   JAMES MILNE, GENERAL MANAGER

THE IRISH MAILS
By Bryan de Grineau

LMS

8.30 a.m. EUSTON to HOLYHEAD	12.15 noon HOLYHEAD to EUSTON
8.45 p.m. EUSTON to HOLYHEAD	12.13 night HOLYHEAD to EUSTON

and Dorset Joint Railways – retained their own separate entities, but the Act served to amalgamate the rest – around 120 of them – into the famous Big Four: the Great Western Railway (G.W.R.), the London Midland and Scottish (L.M.S.), the London and North Eastern Railway (L.N.E.R.) and the Southern (S.R.) – each to be forever synonymous with their initials.

An uneasy marriage?

The Biggest of the Four was the L.M.S., a sprawling monolith which brought together old rivals in an uneasy, forced marriage. Its size was reflected in its operating area, which included London, the Midlands, the North West of England, Wales, Scotland, and a separate network in Northern Ireland (which it had inherited from the Midland Railway). Its principal routes were the West Coast Main Line from Euston to Glasgow, and the former Midland line from St Pancras to Leeds, Nottingham, Sheffield and Manchester.

The early years of the company were characterised by financial difficulty and infighting – generally between its two largest constituents: the London and North

Western and the Midland. The will of the latter generally prevailed, many Midland practices being adopted as policies by the L.M.S. Board. Sometimes this was beneficial, such as the decision to follow that company's centralised train control system; sometimes it was less so, as in the continuation of the M.R.'s small-engine policy. The man behind many of the locomotives which adhered to this edict was Henry Fowler, who took over from George Hughes as Chief Mechanical Engineer (CME) in 1925. Fowler had been a Midland man, and perpetuated many Midland designs, such as the 2P and 4P 4–4–0s, the 3F 0–6–0Ts and the 4F 0–6–0s – a type which went on to haul freight trains almost until the end of steam in the 1960s.

A problem with the small engine policy was that it forced the widespread, and uneconomical, use of double-heading, as single locomotives could not cope with heavy loads and steep inclines. This was particularly evident on the West Coast Main Line, where punctuality was becoming an issue, and on the Somerset and Dorset, where pairs of engines would struggle to haul long holiday specials up over the Mendip hills and down to Bournemouth during the summer months. Problems were also created when the company tried to standardise on certain components, as many locomotives were left with short travel valves and small axle boxes; inefficiency was endemic and hot axle boxes not uncommon.

In order to try to improve the situation, Fowler came up with a radical idea, proposing the construction of a compound 4–6–2 Pacific for express passenger work. Sadly, he was thwarted by the Superintendent of Motive Power, James Anderson,

OPPOSITE The Royal Scot, *c* 1935. The train is being hauled by a 'Princess Royal Class' 4–6–2 No 6211 'Queen Maud'. The spray seen beneath the train is caused by the water scoop apparatus picking up from the trough visible between the front wheels.

BELOW Driver with the Princess Royal class 4–6–2 locomotive number 6204 'Princess Louise', 1938. The driver is with a young boy holding a Hornby model locomotive of the same class, number 6201, 'Princess Elizabeth'.

Wheel notation

STEAM The notation for steam locomotive wheel arrangements used in this book was devised by F. M. Whyte of the New York Central Railway in 1900. It is a simple system, which counts the wheels on a locomotive from front to back, taking the leading wheels first, followed by the driving wheels and finally the trailing wheels, each group being separated by a dash. So, a Great Western King is a 4–6–0, as it has a non-powered 'bogie' of four wheels at the front, followed by six powered wheels, but no trailing wheels. A Princess Coronation is exactly the same, except that it has a single trailing axle (to help distribute the weight of the locomotive etc) at the rear. It is thus a 4–6–2 (which, in common with all other 4–6–2s, is termed a 'Pacific' class of engine). The humble 0–4–0 (no leading or trailing wheels, but four powered wheels) is likely to be a tank engine; as such, it would be noted as an 0–4–0T. There are variations on this theme, PT meaning 'pannier tank', WT meaning 'well tank' and so on. Some diesel shunters also feature 'steam type' wheel arrangements: a Class 08 is an 0–6–0, for example.

DIESEL Most diesels, however, use notation which counts axles instead of wheels. An 'A' refers to a single powered axle, a 'B' to two powered axles and a 'C' to three, and so on. A '1' refers to a single unpowered axle, present – like the leading and trailing wheels of a steam loco – to distribute the weight. Again, a dash separates the various wheel assemblies (a plus sign signifies that the bogies are permanently coupled or articulated). The 'o' signifies the presence of a traction motor. A Bo-Bo like a Class 25 thus has a pair of four-wheeled bogies, each axle being individually powered. A Class 42/43 Warship, on the other hand, also has a pair of four-wheeled axles, but is a B-B because its axles are powered by the same motor (linked in this case by a Cardan shaft).

A Class 40 is a 1–Co-Co–1, so each bogie has three individually powered axles along with an unpowered set of 'carrying wheels' to help distribute the weight of the locomotive. A Class 31 is an A1A-A1A, each bogie having one powered axle, one 'carrying' axle, and a further powered axle, again so arranged to help distribute the weight of the locomotive and thus reduce the wheel load on the track.

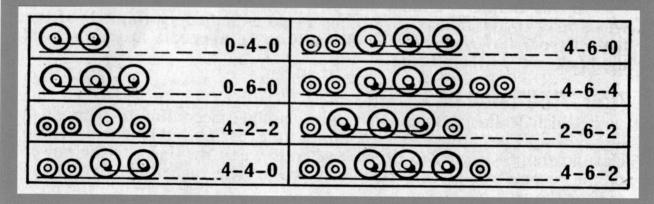

who favoured a 4–6–0 arrangement. At the close of 1926, the LMS sought the loan of No. 5000 'Launceston Castle' from the G.W.R., in order to test it against existing home-grown designs. The 'Castle' performed astonishingly – even on the punishing Cumbrian banks – and presented what seemed to be an obvious solution. The L.M.S. duly approached the Great Western with a view to either buying 'ready-to-run' Castles, or borrowing the plans so that it could build its own version. However, the G.W.R. lacked the requisite workshop capacity and was unwilling to release its paperwork. The honour then fell to the Southern, which supplied copies of that for its Lord Nelson class. After modification at Derby, the plans were sent to the North British Locomotive Company of Glasgow, along with an order for 50 locomotives. The first 4–6–0, No.6100 'Royal Scot', entered service 1927. It was put to work on the express service from Euston to Glasgow which bore its name.

LEFT A team of workers cheer the steam locomotive 'Coronation', 25 May 1937.

BELOW A fireman stokes the furnace in the cab of an L.M.S. Black Five 4-6-0 engine, 1936.

Although successful, they would soon be eclipsed (rather ironically) by the Princess Royal class – a fleet of Pacific locomotives built under the aegis of Fowler's successor, William Stanier (1876–1965) – a Swindon man who was brought in after Ernest Lemon's brief interregnum appointment to reform L.M.S. locomotive policy and calm the troubled waters of pre-Grouping rivalry, which persisted even in 1933.

For many, the arrival of Stanier marks the beginning of the golden age of the L.M.S, although this had really begun in 1932, when the business was reorganised to allow its commercial managers to take the lead over the operating department. This put the emphasis on the customer in a fashion not dissimilar to British Rail when it 'sectorised' in the 1980s. As a result, maintenance schedules were reorganised to improve locomotive and rolling stock availability.

Special fares (like the 'cheap day return') were introduced to encourage travel. Excursion traffic also increased, the company providing special trains to cater for the FA Cup Final, the Grand National and even the Blackpool Illuminations! A number of initiatives were launched to make train travel more attractive in general, including more comfortable corridor coaching stock and accelerated timings. Companies holding large freight accounts with the L.M.S. received reduced-price season tickets for nominated employees, while commercial travellers, fishermen and conveyors of racing pigeons were all tempted with various offers. Passenger miles consequently rose from 6,500 million in 1932 to 8,500 million by 1937. This year was also to see the bursting forth of art deco splendour, in the form of the 'Coronation Scot', a crack express inaugurated to celebrate the accession of King George VI. It took 6½ hours to swish passengers from Euston to Glasgow in luxury, and was hauled by the most powerful locomotive in the country: Stanier's streamlined Princess Coronation class. Finished – like

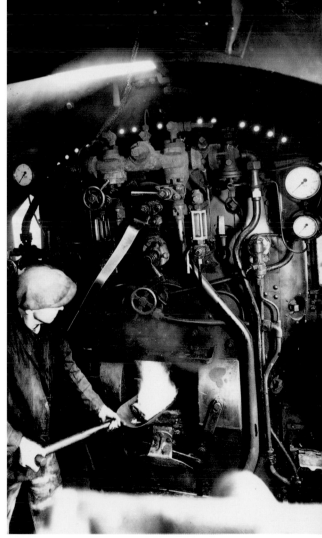

A page from the A.C.E.

THE
ATLANTIC COAST EXPRESS
By S. P. B. MAIS
Decorated by ANNA ZINKEISEN

My object in this book is quite simple. It is to make you look out of the carriage window. You may object to this that you can't possibly read a book and look out of the window at the same time. Well, here for once, you can. This book will help you to look out of the window.

You may say that you see no point in looking out of the carriage window because you know every point of interest already.

If you're so sure about that I would ask you to spot the photographs of scenes taken from the carriage window that are included in this book and if you can accurately place them all you needn't worry to read any more.

You may say that you won't look out of the carriage window because there is nothing particular to see. May I say, Sir, that I have travelled through many countries at many seasons of the year, but I have never been more moved by the beauty of what I have seen from the carriage window than I was on that golden early morning on the last day of December when I looked down from the moor bathed in sunlight, with fields all about me white with rime, on two sinuous snake-like ribbons of white billowy mist that traced out the course of the rivers Tavy and Tamar, five hundred feet below the railway line. It was as majestic as Switzerland.

Nothing to see?

WHAT TO SEE FROM THE WINDOWS OF THE
ATLANTIC COAST EXPRESS
ON SALE + PRICE 2'6
AT BOOKSTALLS OF THE
SOUTHERN RAILWAY

ABOVE Poster produced for the Southern Railway (S.R.) to promote their Atlantic Coast Express service. It shows the opening page of S P B Mais' book *What to see from the windows of the Atlantic Coast Express*, which encouraged readers to observe the landmarks and natural beauty of the countryside crossed by the Atlantic Coast Express.

the coaches – in an attractive shade of 'Caledonian Railway blue', their streamline casing was eye-catching but fitted largely for publicity purposes. Stanier's belief that it added unnecessary weight and made maintenance more difficult meant that subsequent Coronations were built with smoke deflectors instead, while a number of early examples later had their casings removed. Whether wasteful or wonderful, thanks to the skill of the Tyseley Locomotive Works, you can judge for yourself again, as No. 6229 'Duchess of Hamilton' was 're-streamlined' in 2009 and is currently on display at the National Railway Museum, York.

Towards the end of their careers in the 1950s and 60s, members of the Princess Coronation class found themselves relegated to less glamorous duties, such as parcels and freight workings. This would have seemed anathema in the 1930s, these sorts of duties being then in the capable hands of Black Fives, 8F 2–8–0s and Fowler 4Fs. But freight was very important to the L.M.S., accounting for some 60 per cent of its takings. Of particular note were the long, snaking trains of mineral wagons, that took coal from Nottinghamshire to London. The company brought 2,712,000 tons of coal into the capital in 1938 alone.

Where the summer comes soonest
Coal was obviously the lifeblood of the steam-dominated railway industry at this time, but one of the Big Four relied much less on income from its haulage than the rest: the Southern Railway, which was formed from the London and South Western (L.S.W.R.), the London Brighton and South Coast (L.B.S.C.R.) and the South Eastern and Chatham Railways (S.E.C.R.). The company did haul freight – such as milk and cattle from the agricultural West Country and imports from its south coast ports – but passenger traffic was always its main source of revenue; indeed, it carried more than a quarter of Britain's passengers, mainly on its concentrated network of commuter lines around London. This made it a perfect candidate for electrification, which combines low running costs (compared to steam traction) and improved acceleration, allowing the operation of intensive services.

The L.S.W.R. and L.B.S.C.R. had already introduced electric traction to the London area before the Grouping, but the two schemes were incompatible, the L.S.W.R. using third-rail 660V dc, the L.B.S.C.R. favouring a 6,600V ac overhead system (similar to that used by the Midland for its Lancaster–Morecambe route). The Southern decided to adopt the L.S.W.R. system as standard, as it was cheaper to install and the lack of catenary equipment meant that bridges and tunnels did not require alteration.

The London suburban network was fully switched on during 1929, with the conversion of the Brighton line beginning the following year. The new service to the Sussex resort was opened to the public on 1 January 1933 (steam services were withdrawn at the same time) and resulted in a 33 per cent increase in traffic in the first year. Colour-light signalling was also installed, with a new powered signal-box above the carriage repair shops at Brighton replacing six small mechanical installations.

Most of the Southern's 2,390 steam locomotives, like the N15 and H15 classes, were inherited from its constituent companies. From 1924, however, the CME, Richard Maunsell (1868–1944), began a standardisation policy to ease maintenance procedures. In 1926, he introduced his Lord Nelson 4–6–0s, whose existence helped bring the Royal Scots to the L.M.S., (see page 103), while his Schools class is generally regarded as the finest 4–4–0 ever produced in this country. His last design was for an 0–6–0 freight locomotive: the Q class. The first examples were completed in 1937, the year in which Maunsell retired.

Until the arrival of the Pacifics in the 1940s, much of the Southern's continental and holiday traffic was hauled by Maunsell-designed or Maunsell-improved locomotives. One of company's most well-known holiday trains was the 11:00 ex-Waterloo, better known as the Atlantic Coast Express (or simply the ACE). The service began in 1926 and – among millions of other passengers – used to take the young John Betjeman from Waterloo to Cornwall for long summer holidays by the sea (later immortalised in the poet's 1960 verse-autobiography, *Summoned by Bells*). At its peak, through coaches would be detached from the ACE for Bude, Ilfracombe, Seaton, Sidmouth, Exmouth and Padstow. Many of the detached through

ABOVE With its Pullman carriage, fashionable passengers and smart attendant, this Southern Railway poster for 'La Fleche d'Or/Golden Arrow' is a picture of elegance.

LEFT 'SS Canterbury', a Southern Railway (S.R.) ferry approaching the White Cliffs of Dover. She entered service for the South Eastern and Chatham Railway Company in 1901, and continued to carry passengers across the Channel until she was sold in 1926.

portions would be taken to their final destinations by Drummond M7 0–4–4Ts, while the rest of the train continued behind the originating engine to Plymouth.

The Southern Railway also ran a number of luxury Pullman dining services, including several boat trains, such as 'The Cunarder', which ran from London to Southampton, the 'Night Ferry' (for Paris and Brussels), and domestic services like the 'Southern Belle', which was steam-hauled until 1933, (when EMUs took over). On 29 June 1934, the train was renamed the 'Brighton Belle' and continued to feature in the timetable until withdrawal in 1972.

In 1926, a new Pullman service, the 'Flèche d'Or', was introduced between Calais and Paris. Connecting ferry services and trains from Dover to London were provided by the S.R., but the benefits of introducing a more lavish train were soon realised. On 15 May 1929, the new Golden Arrow/ Flèche d'Or was duly inaugurated. The trains left both capital cities at 11:00, that on the English side usually consisting of ten Pullman cars hauled by a Lord Nelson. The run to Dover took 98 minutes and the crossing to Calais was made aboard the 'Canterbury', a new, luxury purpose-built ferry.

Maunsell's successor as CME was O. V. S. Bulleid (1882–1970) , who brought experience gained under Henry Ivatt, and Nigel Gresley, at the Great Northern Railway. Bulleid was a great innovator, who even set about reinventing the wheel for the Southern, his 'boxpok' design replacing traditional spoked wheels on his locomotives, as he felt they gave better all-round support to the tyres. He also designed a chain-driven valve gear mechanism compact enough to fit within the restrictions of his Pacific designs: the Merchant Navy class of 1941 and its lighter variant, which appeared four years later.

The Merchant Navy class was among the first to use welding in the construction process; this enabled easier fabrication of components during the austerity of the war and post-war economies. It also featured a thermic siphon in the firebox (a large tube that allowed water to be heated more quickly and improved boiler circulation). Most visually strikingly, the locomotive boiler was enveloped by Bulleid's air-smoothed sheet steel casing, which was not streamlining, as demonstrated by the extremely flat front end, but a means of lifting exhaust gases away from the cab. The flat sides also enabled the locomotives to be cleaned with a carriage washer, representing an attempt to reduce labour costs. They looked extraordinary, but

RIGHT The Bournemouth Belle, hauled by a Merchant Navy class 4–6–2 locomotive number 21 C 15 'Rotterdam Lloyd' at Winchfield, Hampshire in 1947. The Bournemouth Belle ran from Waterloo to Bournemouth.

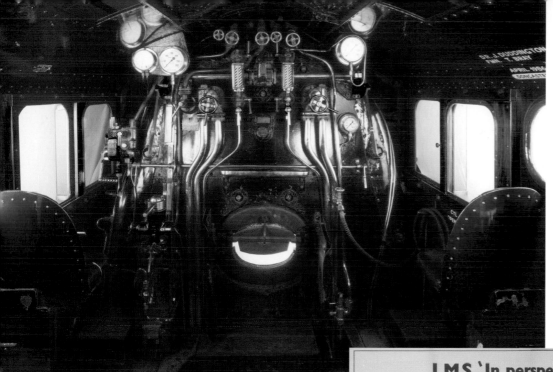

LMS 'In perspective' No 3
The Footplate

How the driver..
STARTS
the engine

1 Adjust Reversing Lever to forward gear

2 Set brake Handle in 'off' position

3 Adjust small & large ejectors to create a vacuum for brake power

4 Open Regulator slightly

How the driver..
STOPS
the engine

1 Close the Regulator

2 Adjust Reversing Lever to 'drift' position

3 Apply Brake

LMS   4-6-2 Coronation Class Locomotive

performed extraordinarily well – most notably on expresses from Waterloo to Southampton, Exeter and Bournemouth, and later on the Southern's many boat trains.

The effects of the Second World War on Britain's railways created a specific operational problem which was hitherto unknown on the S.R. Before the war, 75 per cent of traffic was passenger orientated, compared with 25 per cent freight; during the conflict, roughly the same number of passengers was carried, but freight grew to 60 per cent of total traffic. The company simply did not own enough freight locomotives for such an increase. Bulleid solved this by creating what is considered to be one of the ugliest: the Q1 class. With a tractive effort of 30,080 lbf, these ponderous (yet oddly appealing) beasts were the most powerful 0–6–0 design ever to work in this country. Bulleid had eliminated anything that might be considered unnecessary, including the traditional wheel splashers, but managed to produce 40 with the material required for almost twice that number of more conventional engines.

Steam, speed and slendour

A shortage of goods locomotives had never been an issue for the L.N.E.R., which was responsible for hauling more than one-third of nation's coal, deriving two-thirds of its total income from freight. Its first C.M.E., Nigel (later Sir Nigel) Gresley (1876–1941), designed and built a plethora of 0–6–0, 2–6–0 and 2–8–0 classes throughout his tenure. Gresley had been employed by the Great Northern Railway, one of the L.N.E.R.'s chief constituents, and it was he who was largely responsible for the company's large-engine policy – virtually the opposite of that which had blighted the L.M.S. in its early years. This also helped the L.N.E.R. belie the stigma of its poor London suburban services and reliance on heavy freight, in order to promote

ABOVE A4 class 4–6–2
'Mallard' , No 4468 at
Waterloo, 22nd June 1948

itself as a glamorous operator of fast expresses, where stylish ladies could get their hair coiffured and sharp-suited cads could smoke idly in the restaurant car as they powered up the East Coast Main Line in a streamlined vision of the future. This image was helped considerably down the line by an innovative advertising campaign, which was highly sophisticated and art deco enough to rival even the L.M.S.'s beautiful Princess Coronation class.

This vision of the future came to fruition in 1935, when the 'Silver Jubilee' service began, taking just four hours to travel from Kings Cross to Newcastle at speeds of up to 100 mph. The train included articulated coaches, a feature Gresley had introduced in 1907, and was hauled by a new class of Pacific – the mighty A4.

The A4s were born for high-speed passenger services. Their elegant streamlining improved aerodynamics, thus increasing potential speeds, while serving to lift smoke away from the driver's view. They also featured internal streamlining, as noted in the steam circuit, while higher boiler pressure and the extension of the firebox to form a combustion chamber all contributed to efficiency and a reduction in coal and water consumption.

The most famous of all A4s is No. 4468 'Mallard'. On 3 July 1938, the locomotive attained the world speed record for steam traction by reaching 126 mph on the slight downward grade of Stoke Bank south of Grantham on the East Coast Main Line. This broke the previous record (124 mph), which a German Class 05 had attained two years before.

'Mallard' was one of a small number of A4s that had been built with a double chimney and double Kylchap blastpipe, which improved the draughting and exhaust flow. The locomotive was just five months old, so it was nicely 'run in', allowing free movement without too much wear. The driver on this most auspicious day was Joseph Duddington (a man renowned within the L.N.E.R. for taking calculated risks); his fireman was Tommy Bray. Their record has never been broken.

Despite this achievement, Gresley was not unaware of the possibilities of other forms of traction. In the early 1930s, he attended a demonstration of a diesel-electric shunter and sampled both the German 'Flying Hamburger' and French Bugatti passenger units. During the same period, the L.N.E.R put three diesel-electric railcars and a diesel rail-bus into service.

The L.N.E.R. also owned a surprising variety of electric locomotives and multiple units, having inherited a number from the North Eastern Railway (N.E.R.), which had electrified between Newport and Shildon, along with the Newcastle suburban lines, early in the twentieth century. (The N.E.R.'s Chief Mechanical Engineer, Sir Vincent Raven (1859–1934), had fostered hopes that the East Coast Main Line might be so equipped; sadly this innovation would not be achieved until British Rail completed its own conversion in the early 1990s.)

The N.E.R.'s plans had been borne of a need to compete with electric trams – something which they did with great success. Gresley later provided a specification to Metropolitan-Cammell for new units to replace the NER stock when the latter became life-expired in the 1930s. He also designed a 1,870 HP Bo+Bo electric locomotive for Britain's first main line electrification scheme: the Woodhead route between Manchester, Sheffield and Wath.

This had first been mooted by another L.N.E.R. constituent – the Great Central – before the Great War. No detailed strategy had been devised, but by the 1920s the high levels of heavy freight traffic made steam operation increasingly difficult. These problems remained for the L.N.E.R., which adopted the 1500 volt dc system favoured by its predecessor. Some masts for the overhead line equipment were erected and Gresley's Bo+Bo (No. 6701) was constructed. However, the economic crisis which started the 1930s and the outbreak of war which ended it prevented further progress. As a result, the locomotive was loaned to Netherlands State Railways in 1946, where it was given the affectionate nickname Tommy. The difficulties of operating the Woodhead route were handed to British Railways on nationalisation in 1948. After several years of work, including the necessity to bore a double-track tunnel at Woodhead to replace the twin single-bore tunnels which had been ravaged by steam erosion, the project was finally completed in 1955. It closed in 1981, after a downturn in local coal traffic – the route's main source of income.

ABOVE An A4 class 4-6-2 locomotive No 2509 'Silver Link' at King's Cross station, 16 June 1938. This streamlined locomotive was designed by Sir Nigel Gresley and was built at Doncaster works. It was used to haul passenger trains between London and Scotland. The carriages these locomotives pulled were painted a silver-blue colour, and many of the locomotives were, therefore, given 'silver names'.

The Flying Scotsman

No. 4472 'Flying Scotsman' is probably the most famous locomotive in the world. Built at Doncaster Works to a Gresley design, it entered traffic just after the Grouping in 1923, construction having begun during the Great Northern era. It was first classified as an A1 and carried merely a number (1472) at this stage. Yet the locomotive was something of a flagship locomotive for the L.N.E.R. and was chosen to represent the company at the British Empire Exhibition in both 1924 and 1925.

More importantly, it was also one of five Gresley Pacifics designated to haul the prestigious non-stop 'Flying Scotsman' express from Kings Cross to Edinburgh. It had the honour of heading the first train on 1 May 1928, but there were greater honours to come: on 30 November 1934, while working a light test train, No.4472 (as it was by now) became the first steam locomotive to be officially recorded at 100 mph; the publicity-conscious L.N.E.R. made much of this fact (which has been disputed by devotees of the Great Western ever since).

In 1928, an improved A1, classified 'A3', appeared on L.N.E.R. metals. All A1 Pacifics – like many of their A4 brethren – were subsequently fitted with a double Kylchap chimney to improve performance and efficiency. This caused soft exhaust and smoke drift that tended to obscure the driver's forward vision; the remedy was found in the German-style smoke deflectors, which were fitted from 1960.

'Flying Scotsman' gave three more years' service before being withdrawn by British Railways. Thankfully, it was sold for preservation to Alan Pegler in 1963. After being restored as closely as possible to its original L.N.E.R.

condition, it then worked a number of railtours, including a non-stop run from London to Edinburgh in 1968. Watering facilities for steam locomotives allowed for water-troughs to be used for topping up the tenders en-route and they also used an adapted second 8-wheel tender as an auxiliary water tank.

In 1969, the locomotive went on a promotional tour of the USA, where it was fitted (somewhat incongruously) with a cowcatcher, high-intensity headlamp, bell, air brakes and buckeye couplings. The trip was initially a success, but when its backers withdrew their financial support, Pegler began to lose money and was finally bankrupted in 1972. Fears that 'Flying Scotsman' might be stuck in America or even cut up were quelled in January 1973, when William McAlpine managed to save it and have it shipped home for repair.

In October 1988, the locomotive arrived in Australia to take part in that country's bicentennial celebrations. During the course of the next year, it travelled more than 28,000 miles, including a 442-mile non-stop run from Parkes to Broken Hill in New South Wales – the longest such run by a steam locomotive ever recorded.

After another period of uncertainty, 'Flying Scotsman' was bought by the National Railway Museum, which intends to overhaul it to main line

ABOVE The arrival of the 'Flying Scotsman', at King's Cross Station following its record-breaking run in 1934. It became the first steam locomotive to officially pass the 100 mph (161 km) mark. In the cab are the driver, W Sparshatt (shaking hands), and his fireman, R. Webster.

Of castles and kings

To many railway authors and commentators, the Great Western is to electrification what Greenland is to First Class Cricket. However, at a meeting of the GW Board of Directors on 1 May 1925, the General Manager, Sir Felix Pole, announced that he had been meditating on the possible electrification of the Paddington–Bristol and Paddington–Birmingham routes. A number of references had been made in the House of Commons regarding the potential of such power and he felt that the company ought to look into the commercial aspects as soon as possible. It did, but the consultant's report showed that the return on the capital outlay was far too small for the scheme to be viable.

The Great Western's CME at this time was C. B. Collett (1871–1952), who had

taken over from the charismatic George Jackson Churchward in 1921. Collett had attended a lecture on electrification given by Sir Vincent Raven in January 1923 and revealed in the ensuing debate that his main concern was the cost of the requisite power stations (although he conceded that such a scheme could be made more viable if these installations were built near to a supply of fuel). Though sometimes referred to as merely a 'competent successor' to Churchward, Collett would nevertheless be responsible for designing some of the finest steam locomotives ever to traverse G.W.R. metals and would oversee the introduction of diesel traction to Western lines.

As to the company itself, the Great Western might be said to have been affected the least by the Grouping, being the only one of the Big Four to retain its original identity, organisational structure and main customer base. However, it gained 560 miles of track, 18,000 employees and a further 700 locomotives, many of which were aging 0–6–2Ts which worked heavy coal trains in and around the South Wales valleys, and many of which required urgent replacement. Collett's answer was the 56xx class, which used the Rhymney Railway's relatively modern 0–6–2T as a blueprint and followed the Churchwardian practice of using as many standardised components as possible.

Collett's most famous locomotives were, of course, the celebrated Castles and Kings. The former was a development of Churchward's earlier Star class; 171 were built over a 27-year span from 1923 to 1950. They were noted for superb performance, most remarkably on the 'Cheltenham Flyer' during the 1930s (on 6 June 1932, No. 5006 'Tregenna Castle' covered the 77.25 miles between Swindon and Paddington at an average speed of 81.68 mph – an astonishing feat for the time). Drivers loved them, and described them as the railway equivalent of a Rolls Royce.

During 1924, the doyen of the class, No. 4079 'Caerphilly Castle', was exhibited

SPEED TO THE WEST
CORNWALL DEVON SOMERSET WALES

at the British Empire Exhibition, Wembley, alongside Gresley's 'Flying Scotsman'. The comparatively diminutive Great Western engine was declared to be more powerful than its larger L.N.E.R. rival. This led to locomotive exchange tests between the G.W.R. and L.N.E.R., during which 'Pendennis Castle' (among others) demonstrated the superior fuel and water efficiency of Collett's design. (As we saw earlier, No. 5000 'Launceston Castle' would provide a similar service for the L.M.S.)

Good though the Castles undoubtedly were, they were not powerful enough for heavy, long-distance, non-stop passenger trains like the Cornish Riviera Express. Collett's answer was the King, another 4–6–0, but one which delivered 39,700 lbf tractive effort. After a request from Sir Felix Pole to increase this to above 40,000 lbf, the cylinders were enlarged to a 16¼-in bore, which, along with the use of 6ft 6in driving wheels (as opposed to the company's usual 6ft 8½in variety), brought the figure up to 40,300 lbf (although the increase was removed on all members of the class at their first major overhaul).

The first King, No. 6000 'King George V', appeared in 1927 and was sent on a tour of North America, for the centenary celebrations of the Baltimore and Ohio Railroad, where it impressed all who saw it and earned a beautiful commemorative bell for its trouble. The Kings continued to haul major express trains until well after nationalisation, finally succumbing to the cutter's torch in 1962.

By the 1930s, the price of UK coal had become a grave problem for each of the Big Four: in 1934, it cost 12 shillings 11d per ton; three years later it had risen to 17 shillings. As the G.W.R. consumed in excess of 2 million tons each year, every additional shilling per ton put another £100,000 on its annual coal bill. Such facts led Pole's successor, Sir James Milne, to raise the issue of raising pantographs once again, but – as before – the return on the capital outlay was insufficient for any scheme to be worthwhile. However, this did not limit the company to steam power alone, for Collett was also an early advocate of diesel traction: the G.W.R. had been acquiring internally combusted petrol vehicles since the late Edwardian era, yet it was not until 1933 that an 0–4–0 diesel-mechanical shunter (No. 1) was purchased from John Fowler and Co of Leeds. This was the same year that saw the introduction of the company's first diesel railcar, which had been ordered with two aims in mind: to increase patronage on routes where traffic was not heavy enough to warrant full-length trains, and to provide a cheaper replacement for the G.W.R.'s 'auto' (push-pull) services. Although the initial A.E.C. batch were found to be too light in the frames, the railcars performed well on branch line work and on express services between Birmingham and Cardiff; indeed, it was perhaps only the outbreak of war in 1939 that impeded their proliferation.

The Second World War made the tenure of Collett's successor, F. W. Hawksworth (1884–1976), an uneasy one. His reputation as a paragon of conservatism has persisted even in light of the knowledge that he had to contend not only with yet another coal crisis (which would see its price escalate by a staggering 157 per cent), but also the rest of the war, post-war depression and, eventually, the dark clouds of nationalisation.

His County class 4–6–0 continued the Churchward tradition, but the need to move even heavier trains at even greater speeds was starting to exceed the capabilities of traditional locomotive technology. The battering that the system had taken during the years of conflict compounded the problem by exacerbating lateness and overcrowding. In this climate, there can have been no doubt that the development of a long-term replacement for steam was essential.

Hawksworth considered a paper on main line diesel traction in January 1946, but it was not the answer as far as he was concerned. It should be remembered that the viability of diesel traction had yet to be proven: among other issues, debate was still raging as to the most efficient form of transmission; moreover, there were no equivalent locomotives in this country then available for comparison. Like the G.W.R., the L.M.S. had looked into the subject during 1945, but the resulting North British Bo-Bo (10800) would not be introduced until 1950. For top-link work, the L.M.S. subsequently placed an order with English Electric for the two 1,600hp diesel-electric engines destined to power 10000 and 10001 – yet only the first would appear before nationalisation. On the Southern, Bulleid had approached English Electric even earlier, but the Southern Railway would be the Southern Region before 10201 entered traffic.

Hawksworth's solution was to investigate the gas turbine. The power/weight ratio of a locomotive powered by such means compared very favourably with that of the steam engine; an output of 2,500hp, along with a maximum speed of 90mph and the option of a lighter maintenance regime, made it a highly attractive proposition. In the event, two gas turbine locomotives (Nos. 18000 and 18100) would take to the rails, but as with all ongoing Big Four schemes, it would be left to British Railways to make the next move.

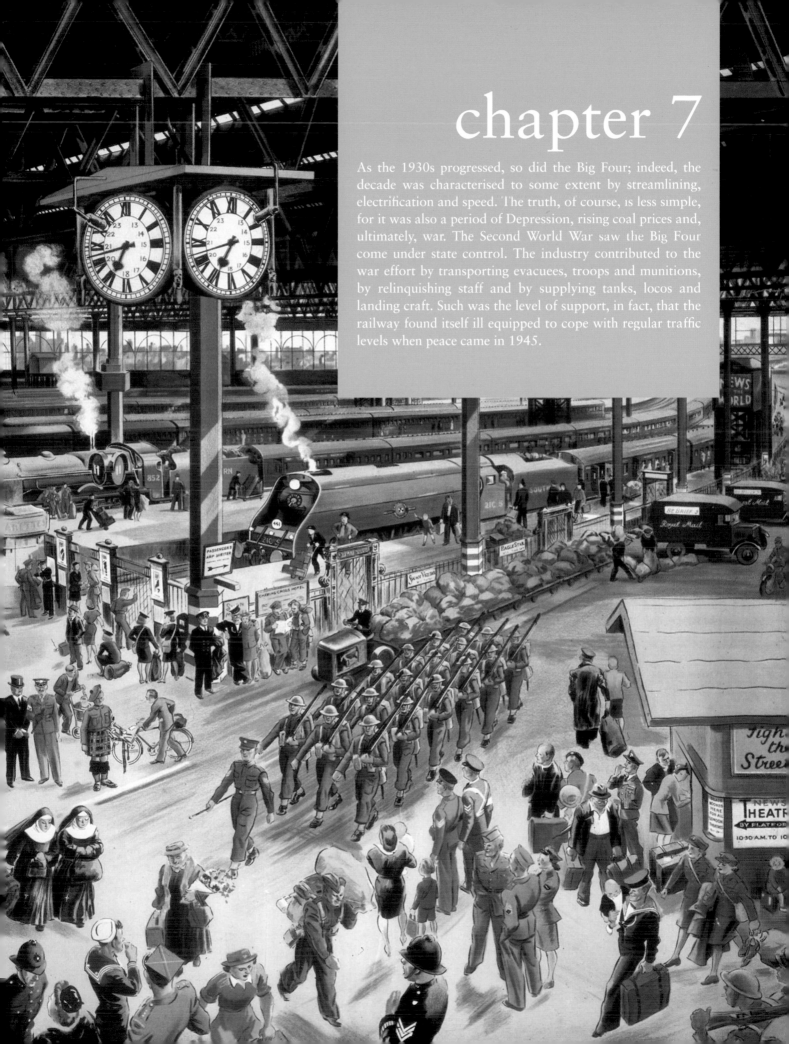

chapter 7

As the 1930s progressed, so did the Big Four; indeed, the decade was characterised to some extent by streamlining, electrification and speed. The truth, of course, is less simple, for it was also a period of Depression, rising coal prices and, ultimately, war. The Second World War saw the Big Four come under state control. The industry contributed to the war effort by transporting evacuees, troops and munitions, by relinquishing staff and by supplying tanks, locos and landing craft. Such was the level of support, in fact, that the railway found itself ill equipped to cope with regular traffic levels when peace came in 1945.

The railways in wartime

The 1930s began uneasily for the Big Four: 'unnatural' alliances made for unnecessary egotism, then, as now, an impediment to progress. Yet as the decade developed, so did the railway, and one might justly describe it as a period of crack expresses, electrification and record-breaking speed runs. Much of this was made possible by the Guarantees and Loans Act of 1934, which provided funds at a low interest rate to help reduce unemployment. It wasn't all Castles, Coronations and Mallards of course, but the many technological innovations that created them are still impressive when one considers that the 1930s were also blighted by the Depression, rising coal prices, the march of fascism and, ultimately, the outbreak of war.

The gathering storm

Although Britain celebrated the Silver Jubilee of King George V in 1935, the year also saw the invasion of Ethiopia by Mussolini's Italy. It was the first sign that fascism was starting to grow teeth; it started to grow legs when Hitler repudiated the Treaty of Versailles, sped up his rearmament programme and introduced conscription. When his troops marched on the demilitarised Rhineland in 1936 and he annexed Austria two years later, war became likely; when he invaded Poland on 1 September 1939, it became inevitable.

Accordingly, the Government took the Big Four into state control – this time with the promise of compensatory income set to an average of that received between 1935 and 1937. It also established a Ministry of Supply, which included a Directorate of Transport Materials, headed by R. A. Riddles (1892–1983), who had been the Mechanical and Electrical Engineer (Scotland) of the L.M.S. Two days later, on 3 September, Prime Minister Neville Chamberlain gave his famous radio broadcast, which announced to the nation that Britain was at war with Germany.

The effect on the system was almost immediate, with rail being the favoured means of evacuating children and pregnant women from towns and cities considered to be at risk from bombing to the comparative safety of the countryside. Almost 1,600 trains carried 600,000 people from London during the first four days of September 1939; 100,000 residents from each of the main industrial areas – Merseyside, Clydebank, Glasgow and Manchester – were also evacuated, while areas like Tyneside and southern ports like Southampton experienced similar operations on a smaller scale.

The adults had to concentrate on the job in hand (which was essentially safeguarding the nation's future). But imagine yourself for a moment standing on a station, labelled like a piece of luggage, torn from the warmth of your parents, unsure of where you are going and – worse still – even less sure of when you would be coming back. You are alone in a sea of children, round-bellied women and a small army of schoolteachers. You probably won't find a magical wardrobe at your destination, like the evacuee children of C. S. Lewis's *Narnia* chronicles, but you may, like some, learn

the odd new skill (such as baking bread or milking cows), and be treated like one of the family by your adopted parents. Alas you may, like others, be beaten for speaking out of turn (or simply for speaking).

The first evacuation train was a Great Western one, leaving Ealing Broadway at 08:30 on 1 September – two days before the declaration. It would be followed by successive trains every ten minutes, which led to severe reductions in regular services. Most freight trains were also cancelled – at least during the first two days – in order to create paths for further evacuation specials. The trains usually carried around 400 – 500 passengers, but there are reports of two running from Rosyth in Scotland with more than 2,000 evacuees between them!

Many children drifted back home during the so-called 'Phoney War' – the seemingly endless period before the German army began to advance towards Denmark and Norway. It's difficult to blame them, but later military action meant that a second wave of evacuation became essential in 1940. This began in May, when 8,000 children were moved in 16 special trains. The following month would see 48,000 taken from towns on the east coast and a further 100,000 from London to Berkshire, Somerset, Wales and the West.

But it wasn't only children whom the railway moved *en masse* during the war. The troops, however, could not 'drift back home'. During the initial manoeuvres, some 10,000 service personnel were conveyed in 22 trains to the King George V dock in Glasgow for passage to the Mediterranean, where they would reinforce garrisons in Cyprus, Alexandria, Gibraltar and Malta. When conscription began in October 1939, even more trains were needed to move men to their billets for rapid training.

ABOVE Evacuees at Maidenhead station, Berkshire, June 1940. When France fell to Germany in June 1940, the Great Western Railway (G.W.R.) ran 96 special trains, conveying nearly 70,000 children from London to the countryside.

PREVIOUS PAGES A Southern Railway poster showing Waterloo Station in wartime. It was produced to mark one hundred years of uninterrupted service during war and peace (1848–1948).

ABOVE Notice board, St Pancras Station, London, 1939, giving information about arrival and departure times, and information to troops that are to be carried by train.

RIGHT Poster produced for British Railways (B.R.) to promote the railways as vital for national defence.

Some were happy to find themselves in a seaside resort like Weston-super-Mare, spending six weeks 'running up and down on the beach' during the day, drinking in local pubs and chatting to local girls at night. Things would soon change when they were billeted elsewhere...

Dunkirk spirit

Yet more traffic was created by the arrival of Canadian troops in December 1939, while the evacuation of the British Expeditionary Force from Dunkirk the following May, which involved the conveyance of 300,000 men over just nine days, required not only 1,000 carriages, but also the acquisition of many railway ships (including the Southern's luxury steam vessel 'Canterbury'). The movement of troops away from Dover was achieved by the use of stabling points for empty coaching stock at Faversham, Queenborough, Ramsgate and Margate, although reports suggest that the congestion was so bad at one point that four trains had to be held as far away from Dover as Willesden.

Redhill saw 80 per cent of the Dunkirk traffic and soon enjoyed new status as a bottleneck, created largely by trains heading from Tonbridge towards Guildford, which had to reverse across the main London–Brighton line. Water cranes ran dry and

coal supplies ran out, as the infrastructure could not cope with the influx of steam locomotives. Many were handled at Earlswood and some even at Three Bridges, which was nine miles away. Nevertheless, most trains were held for a mere four minutes while their engines were exchanged for a freshly prepared one. It was a testament to the organisational and practical skill of the railway.

Some train paths were released by reducing civilian services (trains from London to Glasgow, for example, were cut from 12 each day to six) and by withdrawing the travelling post office (the Night Mail did not cross the border for most of the duration). However, the net effect was actually a *rise* in traffic – and not just passenger: freight trains also increased, in order to supply munitions for ensuing battles, aircraft fuel to RAF stations, and even iron ore from Scotland and the Midlands to the nation's iron and steel works (iron ore imports having ceased). The ore traffic in particular necessitated the speedy construction of new wagons in large numbers.

All these extra trains meant more wear on the track, locomotives and rolling stock. The Big Four had to try to undertake what essential repairs it could with depleted funds – and fewer members of staff. Between them, the companies released nearly 110,000 employees for national service, 90 per cent of whom entered the armed forces. The worsening state of the rolling stock was also exacerbated by the fact that many railway factories lost capacity to the war effort. Horwich and Crewe works supplied 642 tanks; guns and gun mountings were made at Doncaster and Swindon, while the latter – like Eastleigh – also manufactured countless shells, Bailey bridges and ball bearings, along with the landing craft that would eventually be used in the D-Day landings on 6 June 1944.

Staff shortages and overuse meant that some new equipment had to be acquired no matter what. The financial situation was dire and the austerity measures put in place in 1939 limited the railways to constructing mixed traffic 4–6–0 and heavy freight 2–8–0 designs. In December 1941, the Ministry of War Transport decided that Stanier's 8F 2–8–0 was the only locomotive type that could be erected in railway workshops, Churchward's 28xx class being eschewed because of its limited loading

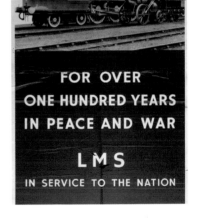

ABOVE Bomb damage at St Pancras Station, London, c 1942.

BELOW Poster highlighting the continual support that the railway provided to the nation, showing a modern Pacific, No. 6235 'City of Birmingham', alongside Stephenson's 'Rocket'.

Stanier 8F 2-8-0s

The 8F 2–8–0 locomotives of the L.M.S. were designed by William Stanier for freight work. The company initially suffered from the Midland Railway's 'small engine policy' (see Chapter 6), which meant that it inherited many locomotives that were unable to cope with heavier trains. Stanier set about tackling this issue when he became Chief Mechanical Engineer in 1932. For the 8F design, he used the same two-cylinder arrangement that he had employed on his earlier Black Five 4–6–0s.

Initially, 126 8Fs were built between 1935 and 1939, but there would be many more after the Ministry of War Transport decided that the class was the only one that could be erected in railway workshops, thanks to their ease of construction, maintenance and all-round reliability. Though they would later be eclipsed by Riddles' cheaper 'austerity' designs, the War Department built 208 between 1940 and 1942. The L.M.S. subsequently erected a further 205 and the other Big Four companies helped fulfil a Railway Executive Committee order, which – coupled with a separate L.N.E.R. request for 68 more – brought the total number of 8Fs to 852. Whilst in the shops at Swindon, Great Western CME F. W. Hawksworth

studied the engines closely and opted to use a slightly modified version of the boiler on his 4-6-0 County class of 1945.

Many 8Fs saw service outside the UK in Palestine, Persia, Iraq, Egypt, Italy and Turkey. Of the 24 locomotives owned by Palestine Railways, 23 were taken over by the Israelis in 1948. The 24th was stranded in the West Bank near Tulkarm and became derelict. Thirty-nine returned from their war duties to Britain and no fewer than 666 were taken into British Railways stock on nationalisation in 1948.

Withdrawals began two years later, the first to meet its maker being No. 48616. One (No. 48009) followed in 1962, but larger inroads were made after 1964. Nevertheless, 150 locomotives survived into 1968 – the last year of standard gauge steam on B.R.. This pales into significance somewhat when one considers that some Turkish 8Fs followed the Modernisation Plan more closely than their UK counterparts by surviving until the 1980s!

Thankfully, several examples have been preserved. While some remain in 'scrapyard' condition, ex-L.M.S. No. 8151 is certified for mainline use in the UK, ensuring that enthusiasts will be able to enjoy their characteristic Stanier rhythm for years to come.

ABOVE LEFT Ex-LMS 8F No. 48305 at Barry scrap yard in December 1975, still largely intact after half a dozen years' neglect, but with clear signs that salvation is imminent.

ABOVE RIGHT The fully restored Stanier 8F 48305 now operating on the Great Central Railway at Loughborough.

gauge. The L.M.S. built 30 8Fs at Crewe and 75 at Horwich, although many more were constructed by the G.W.R., L.N.E.R. and Southern Railway (see opposite). However, the 8Fs were later found to be too labour intensive and required too much steel. As a result, Riddles produced two 'Austerity' designs – a 2–8–0 and a 2–10–0 – which, while intended for use abroad, would see active service at home. They were joined in 1943 by American S.160 2–8–0s, a class used across the country after modification by the Great Western.

All the Big Four companies suffered from the efforts of the Luftwaffe at some stage of the conflict. The Southern, being on Britain's front line, was also involved in the fall out of the Battle of Britain. On 10 July 1940 – the first day of the 'Battle' – a train was bombed near Newhaven, killing the driver and injuring the guard, while on 7 September, an incendiary device struck the approaches to Waterloo at Vauxhall, penetrating the viaduct before exploding and causing so much damage that the station had to be closed. Waterloo would be hit again in May 1941, when over 50 bombs were involved, many of which penetrated a spirits store beneath the platforms, causing a major fire.

The V-1 and V-2 flying bombs posed a terrible threat towards the end of the war. The original 'doodlebug' campaign began in the summer of 1944. On 17 June, one of these unnerving, buzzing missiles struck a freight train on a bridge between Elephant and Castle and Loughborough Junction in London; another destroyed the end of the

BELOW British Tommies complete with their own accompanist are photographed here as they leave England for the Western Front in September 1939.

O.V.S. Bulleid

Oliver Vaughan Snell Bulleid was probably the most innovative of all wartime Chief Mechanical Engineers. He was born in Invercargill, New Zealand to British parents in 1882, but returned to Wales with his mother on the death of his father in 1889. At 18, he joined the Great Northern Railway (G.N.R.) at Doncaster as an apprentice to H. A. Ivatt later becoming, the assistant to the Locomotive Running Superintendent, before accepting a post as Doncaster Works manager.

In 1908, he left the rail industry to work in Paris for the French division of Westinghouse, and returned to G.N.R. in 1912 as Personal Assistant to the Chief Mechanical Engineer (CME), one Nigel Gresley.

During the Great War, Bulleid joined the British Army, rising to the rank of Major in the rail transport corp. He later returned to the Great Northern to manage the Wagon and Carriage works. After the Grouping, Gresley remained CME of the newly formed L.N.E.R. and brought Bulleid back to Doncaster to be his assistant once more. He played a significant part in the production of some of Gresley's designs, notably his P1 and P2 2–8–2s and the U1 Garratt No. 2395 (later No. 9999). In 1937, he fulfilled his destiny by becoming CME of the Southern Railway.

It was now that Bulleid flourished, gaining approval in 1938 for his most famous of designs – the Merchant Navy Pacific class, the first of which appeared in 1941. As noted in Chapter 6 they were among the first locomotives to use welding in the construction process and featured a thermic siphon in the firebox (a large tube which allowed water to be heated more quickly and improved boiler circulation). Most striking visually, the locomotives were enveloped by Bulleid's air-smoothed sheet steel casing, a trait which ensured they stood apart from virtually everything else on the network. A smaller variant, the West Country/Battle of Britain class, followed in 1945; his wartime 'austerity' freight 0–6–0 – the equally striking Q1 class – had appeared in 1942.

Bulleid also took an active role in the Southern's electrification projects, designing several multiple units and three main line electric locomotives (Nos. 20001–20003) in collaboration with Chief Electrical Engineer, Alfred Raworth.

His last steam locomotive design for the S.R. was the unconventional 'Leader,' which also appeared after nationalisation. Its boiler and tender were housed in a diesel-like double-ended body; power was via two three-cylinder, six-wheeled steam bogies, the axles of which were connected by gears. The class was not successful, but the 1,750hp diesel-electric locomotives for which Bulleid provided the mechanical design (10201-3), formed the basis of B.R.'s later English Electric Type 4s (Class 40).

In 1949, Bulleid crossed the water to Ireland to become CME of Córas Iompair Éireann. He retired in 1958, moved to Devon and later to Malta, where he died in 1970 aged 87.

Hungerford Bridge the following day, preventing the normal passage of trains for six months. The later V-2 rockets wrought further havoc, not least in March 1945, when a block of flats at Deptford owned by the S.R. for housing staff and their families, was bombed. A quarter of the dwellings were demolished and 51 people were killed.

Cometh the hour.

As one might expect, heroism was rife during the Second World War, with deceptively ordinary people finding the capacity within themselves for bravery, selflessness and often both. With this in mind, three railwaymen were awarded the George Cross during the conflict. One was Norman Tunna, a shunter at the G.W.R. marshalling yard in Birkenhead. On the night of 26 September 1940, a large number of incendiary bombs fell on and around the goods station and sidings. Tunna kept calm and carried on, but found two burning incendiaries within a sheeted open wagon of 250lb bombs. He tried to douse the flames, but as they licked higher, he jumped aboard and released the incendiary, which he threw aside with all his might. He then joined his colleagues in spraying the bombs with water until they had cooled to a safe temperature.

The other two medals were awarded to the L.N.E.R. men who had been involved in the Soham incident of 2 June 1944. A fire developed on the leading wagon of a 51-wagon ammunition train, which was travelling at low speed past the Cambridgeshire town as it headed for Ipswich. The wagon was carrying 44 500lb bombs. The driver, Benjamin Gimbert, brought the train to a halt and instructed his fireman, James Nightall, to uncouple it – something which Nightall managed with great speed. Gimbert then started to draw the wagon away and had moved it about 140 yards (still alongside the platforms at Soham) when the bombs went off. The explosion killed Nightall instantaneously; Gimbert, while badly injured, managed to survive. Although the station buildings were nearly destroyed and there was damage to 700 properties within 900 yards of the blast, the L.N.E.R. men saved the town a much worse fate. As Lieutenant-Colonel Wilson wrote in his report on the accident: 'the two enginemen acted in accordance with the highest traditions of the Railway Service, and [...] were successful in preventing an incomparably greater disaster'. Soham signalbox was subsequently repaired and remained in service into the 1990s. It still bore the scars of that dramatic night right to the end, when it was finally made obsolete by the inexorable progress of modern signalling renewals.

The Big Four emerged from the war in a lamentable state, having been run into the ground by the heavy traffic necessitated by conflict. Although a few track improvements had been made to ease the flow of troops and military equipment, and although some new locomotives had been built, investment had virtually been at a standstill since 1939. Within weeks of VE Day, a desire for social change and the prevailing economic climate led to a landslide Labour victory in the 1945 General Election. One of the new government's major achievements was to launch a programme to nationalise public services. The Bank of England came first in 1946, followed by Cable and Wireless Ltd and the coal industry in 1947. The next year saw the formation of British Railways (B.R.), when the G.W.R., L.M.S., L.N.E.R. and Southern were taken into state ownership from 1st January 1948.

The Naming Ceremony of the "West Country" Class Locomotive

"DORCHESTER"

will be performed by

Councillor H. G. LONGMAN, Mayor of Dorchester

at DORCHESTER STATION

THURSDAY, 23rd SEPTEMBER, 1948, at 2 p.m.

SOUTHERN RAILWAY

ABOVE Poster produced for Southern Railway (S.R.) to advertise the naming ceremony of the new West Country class locomotive, the 'Dorchester', which was designed by O.V.S. Bulleid. See box opposite.

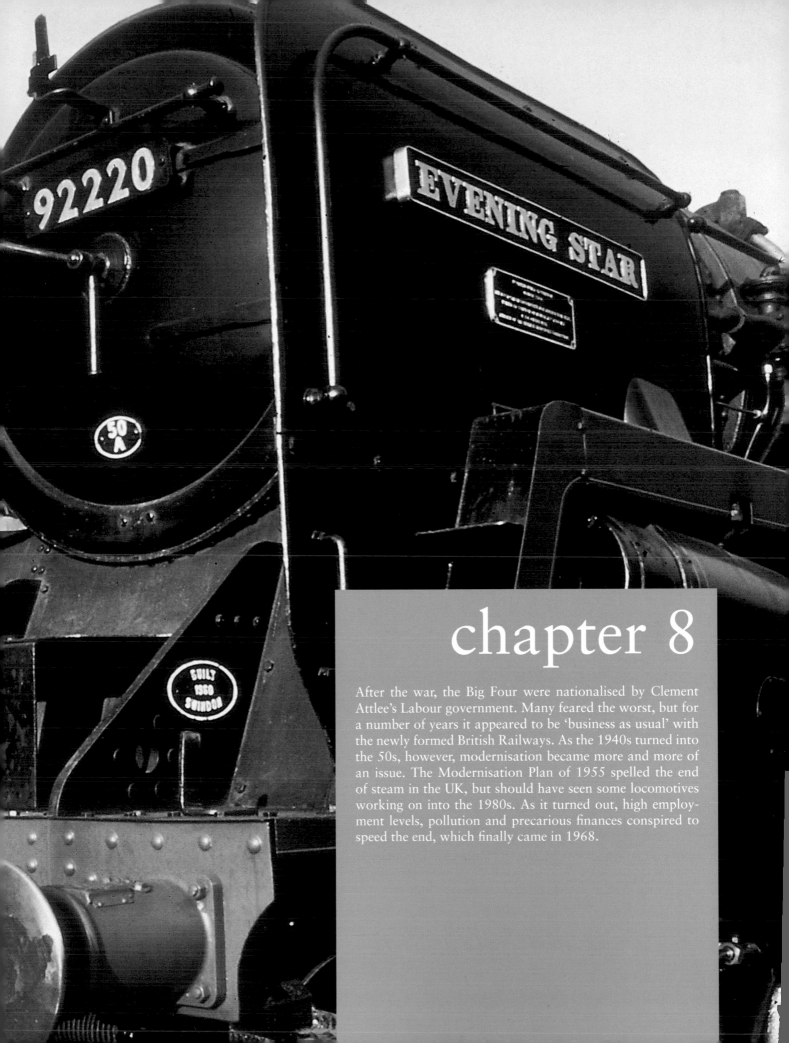

chapter 8

After the war, the Big Four were nationalised by Clement Attlee's Labour government. Many feared the worst, but for a number of years it appeared to be 'business as usual' with the newly formed British Railways. As the 1940s turned into the 50s, however, modernisation became more and more of an issue. The Modernisation Plan of 1955 spelled the end of steam in the UK, but should have seen some locomotives working on into the 1980s. As it turned out, high employment levels, pollution and precarious finances conspired to speed the end, which finally came in 1968.

The nationalised years of steam

PREVIOUS PAGES British Railways (B.R.) 9F 2–10–0 No. 92220 'Evening Star'. This locomotive was the last steam locomotive to be built for British Railways (1960) and was designed by R.A. Riddles.

OPPOSITE B.R. Standard Class 4 2–6–4T No. 80065 with a special train at Bath Road, Chiswick, in November 1956.

Although under State control during the Second World War, nationalisation in 1948 marked the official death of the Big Four, the companies being reborn as the six regions of British Railways (B.R.). Yet the layer cake of British transport was more complicated than this may suggest, for B.R. answered to the Railway Executive, which answered to the British Transport Commission (BTC), which answered to the Ministry of Transport.

The BTC was established with the laudable aim of providing 'an efficient, adequate, economical and properly integrated system of public inland transport and port facilities within Great Britain for passengers and goods'. Geddes would have been proud, but the concept would create more problems for the railway than it solved.

B.R. inherited over 20,000 steam engines, 36,000 carriages, a million wagons, 4,000 multiple unit vehicles and a handful of diesel and electric locomotives, virtually all of which had been severely overworked during the years of conflict. Austerity measures had meant that maintenance had been minimal and it soon became clear that the company would not be able to operate efficiently with such 'a poor bag of assets', as the Labour Chancellor Hugh Dalton had described it.

It wasn't the most encouraging remark, but it did have the unwelcome ring of truth. Some of the tank engines in use on the ex-Southern and L.N.E.R. branches, for example, were in such bad shape that new L.M.S.-designed locomotives (Fairburn 2–6–4Ts on the former, Ivatt 2–6–0s on the latter) had to be drafted in to work the timetable. To ease the problem elsewhere, most of the country's major workshops were assigned to producing new batches of existing types, such as Thompson B1s, Castles and Bulleid light Pacifics, which allowed some of the oldest classes to be withdrawn.

All change?

For the public at large, it seemed to be a case of 'business as usual' at first, the most obvious differences being purely cosmetic. After a number of experiments, blue livery was chosen for top-link engines, brunswick green for passenger engines, lined black for mixed traffic and plain black for freight locomotives. Only the first of the four was destined for an early demise, green being the colour of choice for all passenger locomotives until the Midland started turning out some of its Pacifics in the attractive crimson lake hue of old.

Main-line coaches were finished in 'blood and custard' (also known as carmine and cream), with suburban stock appearing in plain crimson and electric multiple units in malachite green. The small number of main-line diesels received a smart coat of

L.N.W.R.-style black with aluminium detailing. With repainting came renumbering, all steam locomotives receiving the addition of a multiple of 10,000 to their existing numbers, depending on the region (bar the Western, whose original cast four-digit number plates remained untouched).

In order to create a sense of identity, the regions were also given a distinctive colour, to use on publicity material and signage. The Western (brown), London Midland (maroon) and Southern (green) received shades that harked back to their parentage; the Scottish Region, however, was given light blue, the Eastern dark blue and the North Eastern, a delightful shade of tangerine.

Raising the standards

The Railway Executive member for Mechanical and Electrical Engineering was R.A. Riddles (see box on page 132). He and his two assistants effectively fulfilled the old Chief Mechanical Engineer role. Riddles knew that the motive power situation would need a more efficient solution than the continuance of pre-war locomotive policies, but saw little virtue in diesel traction, believing the future to lay with electrification. This was a clearly long-term project, however, and practical solutions were needed immediately; he thus decided to develop a range of uncomplicated standard steam classes.

Some have commented that Riddles' decision to appoint two ex-L.M.S. colleagues (R.C. Bond and E.S. Cox) as his assistants was dubious, and that greater cognisance should have been given to Swindon, Doncaster or Eastleigh methods, for example. The Standards certainly leaned L.M.S.-wards, although their story was shaped to at least some extent by the locomotive exchange trials that Riddles initiated in B.R.'s first year of existence.

The programme involved the transfer of engines

'Evening Star'

No. 92220 'Evening Star' is famed for being the last steam locomotive to be built for British Railways. It was erected at Swindon Works in 1960. To commemorate this fact – and of course its status as 'last of the line' – it was not painted black like its classmates, but finished in lined brunswick green. Swindon also bestowed it with a copper-capped double chimney.

The name 'Evening Star' was selected after a competition in the Western Region staff magazine, three entrants coming up with the winning moniker, which was bestowed at a ceremony at Swindon Works on 18 March 1960. The Chairman of the BTC's Western Area Board, R. F. Hanks, gave a stirring speech in which he acknowledged the fine craftsmanship of the men who had built the locomotive, before adding that 'no other product of man's mind has ever exercised such a compelling hold upon the public's imagination as the steam locomotive. No other machine in its day has been a more faithful friend to mankind nor has contributed more to the growth of industry [...]. Those who have lived in the steam age of railways will carry the most nostalgic memories right to the end.' The nameplate was then unveiled by the Western Region General Manager, K. W. C. Grand.

'Evening Star' was allocated to Cardiff Canton on the Western Region and was used most notably on the Somerset and Dorset route, where it regularly touched 90 mph. On 8 September 1962, it hauled the last Pines Express over S and D metals, before the service was diverted via Reading and put in the hands of Brush Type 4 diesel-electrics. Withdrawal came in 1965, after just five years of service.

The lifting of the steam ban on B.R. in 1971 meant that 'Evening Star's return to the main line was inevitable. Sadly, Eric Treacy died at Appleby station while waiting to photograph the locomotive as it worked an enthusiast special seven years later. As Bishop of Wakefield, Treacy had once been asked the best way to get to heaven. His reply had been 'behind a Black Five'; one feels sure that he saw 'Evening Star' as an admirable substitute.

After its boiler certificate expired, 'Evening Star' was put on display at the National Railway Museum in York.

from each of the Big Four to other regions for 'best practice' assessment. This gave
rise to one or two interesting sights, not least of which were caused by the Southern
Region's lack of water troughs, which meant that ex-L.M.S. locomotives had to be
paired with high-capacity War Department tenders, while ex-Southern types found
themselves saddled with those of L.M.S. parentage (which were fitted with water
scoops). By all accounts, the results were somewhat inconclusive, being affected by
the manner in which the various footplate crews handled the different designs. The
former Great Western engines were also hampered by the use of 'hard' Yorkshire coal
(instead of their usual 'softer' Welsh fuel), which had been imposed in an attempt to
test each class under controlled conditions.

The first Standard to be completed was No. 70000 'Britannia', a two-cylinder Pacific
intended for mixed traffic work. Fifty-five of this class were eventually constructed
between 1951 and 1954. While indeed of clear L.M.S. parentage (albeit with a nod
to Stanier's G.W.R. 'upbringing' – not least of which lay in the chimney, which had
been designed at Swindon Works), they incorporated a derivation of the boiler and
trailing wheel arrangement used by Bulleid on his Merchant Navy class. The firebox
featured a rocking grate, which allowed rebuilding of the fire without stopping the
locomotive; a self-cleaning smokebox helped speed up shedding procedures at the
end of the day, while the raised running plates and Walschaerts valve gear eased
lubrication and maintenance.

The Britannias saw service across the country, and were especially beloved by
Eastern Region crews, who appreciated the improved timings afforded by the high
power and low weight of the locomotives. On the London Midland, they gave
consistent performances on Euston to Holyhead trains and the Western's general
dislike of them was contradicted by Cardiff Canton depot, which put them to excellent
use on South Wales expresses.

The Southern initially received two, which it allocated to the prestigious 'Golden
Arrow' service between Dover and Victoria, but gained further examples after the

Merchant Navy class was temporarily withdrawn following the crank axle failure of No. 35020 'Bibby Line' as it was approaching Crewkerne in 1953. This incident also led to other 'foreign' types – like Gresley V2s – appearing on SR metals. (These mighty 2–6–2s had to have their cab steps and steam injector pipes trimmed to meet the Southern's clearance limits.)

The accident was also partly responsible for an extensive rebuilding programme of the Merchant Navy fleet to a more conventional design. This involved the removal of the air-smoothed casing and replacement of the chain-driven valve gear with three sets of Walschaerts valve gear. The first rebuild to re-enter traffic was No. 35018 'British India Line' in 1956; the last was No. 35028 'Clan Line' in 1960. Sixty light Pacifics were also rebuilt (which saw their temporary replacement by ex-L.M.S. and B.R. Standard Class 5s).

In 1952, B.R. produced its own light Pacific – the ten-strong Clan class, which had been developed to operate on lines with a lower route availability than the Britannias could traverse. They found work on the Glasgow and South Western route and the northern reaches of the West Coast Main Line. In 1954, a further Pacific was produced as a possible express passenger prototype. No. 71000 'Duke of Gloucester' was a three-cylinder engine fitted with a modified version of the Britannia boiler, but with a larger firebox. Sadly, its introduction coincided with the decision to focus on diesel and electric traction (see Chapter 9) and no further examples were constructed. It was condemned to be scrapped, but thankfully a group of enthusiasts rescued its rusting remains and rebuilt them into the locomotive that continues to work heritage trains to this day.

Of the 12 Standard classes, arguably the most successful was the 9F 2–10–0, introduced in 1954 for fast and heavy freight work. The locomotives had 5ft driving wheels and a modified Britannia boiler. For a short period, some were employed on express passenger duties, most notably on the Somerset and and Dorset line (S.D.), where they hauled holiday traffic over the steep Mendip hills rather more easily than the Midland 4–4–0s had been able to manage! Enginemen hailed them as the locomotive that could have saved the line from closure, but as the celebrated S.D. driver Donald Beale once lamented, 'they came too late'. In 1960, No.92220 'Evening Star' became the last steam locomotive to be built for B.R. (see box on page 129).

A golden age?

Although the 1950s suffered the Korean War and the Suez crisis, along with rising retail and property prices, they have come to be epitomised by Prime Minister Harold Macmillan's famous comment that 'most of our people have never had it so good'. On the railway, this was reflected by an upturn in passenger numbers and a return to pre-war timings on express trains (the W.R.'s 'Bristolian' service was restored to its 105 minute non-

R.A. Riddles

Born in 1892, Riddles' career began with the London and North Western Railway (L.N.W.R.), which he joined as an apprentice in 1909. While attending evening classes, he took a course in electrical engineering, believing that the future would involve electric traction.

After serving with the Royal Engineers in the Great War, he returned to Crewe in 1920 to oversee the new erecting shop at the Works, before being dispatched to Horwich to study Lancashire and Yorkshire Railway engine shopping methods. He volunteered as a driver in the General Strike (1926) and worked a number of trains from Crewe to Manchester and Carlisle. The insights he gained on the footplate were put to good use when considering the design of his own locomotives.

Riddles was transferred to Euston in 1933 as Locomotive Assistant to the Chief Mechanical Engineer (CME), William Stanier (see page 103), becoming Principal Assistant two years later. He moved to Glasgow as Mechanical and Electrical Engineer – Scotland in 1937, but was disappointed when C.E. Fairburn was appointed as Stanier's Deputy in his absence. During this time, Riddles was seconded to take No. 6220 'Coronation' (actually No.6229 'Duchess of Hamilton' in disguise) to the USA for display at the World's Fair.

He moved to the Ministry of Supply in 1939, but returned to the L.M.S. in 1943 and, on Fairburn's death the following year, applied for the vacant position. The job was given to H.G. Ivatt, with Riddles promoted instead to vice-president of the company.

When the Railway Executive was created in 1947 ahead of nationalisation, Riddles was appointed Member for Mechanical and Electrical Engineering. Between him and his two principal assistants, they covered the role of Chief Mechanical Engineer and oversaw the design of B.R.'s 12 Standard locomotive classes. The first to enter traffic was Pacific No. 70000 'Britannia' in 1951. Various 2–6–0s, 4–6–0s and tank engines followed, as did what may be deemed the masterpiece of the collection – the 9F 2–10–0s. The last 9F, No. 92220 'Evening Star', was built at Swindon in 1960 (see box on page 127). Riddles retired in 1953, and died 30 years later, aged 92.

stop Paddington–Bristol schedule around this time, for example). Many of these trains included new Mark I coaches, which featured L.M.S.-style all-steel construction, the Pullman gangways and buckeye couplings favoured by the L.N.E.R., and a contour which owed something to Bulleid's Southern Railway carriages.

New staff uniforms and stirring publicity material also helped create a spirit, which was perhaps captured best on 23 May 1959, when A4 Pacific No. 60007 'Sir Nigel Gresley' attained a post-war speed record for steam by reaching 112 mph as it descended Stoke Bank with a loaded passenger train.

Another A4, No. 60017 'Silver Fox', featured in an evocative film made by British Transport Films (BTF) called 'Elizabethan Express' (1954), which celebrates a 'long journey gilded by the sun' between Kings Cross and Edinburgh. (The East Coast Main Line's non-stop train had been the famous 'Flying Scotsman' in L.N.E.R. days, but the honour fell to the 'Capitals Limited' in 1948, before the introduction of 'The Elizabethan' in 1953.)

With its poetic voiceover – clearly inspired by Auden's *Night Mail* (1936), but lighter in tone – the film covers aspects of the whole system: from the wheelwrights and maintenance gang responsible for the smooth ride to the 'Howards, the Berts, the Cynthias, the Mables' enjoying it. Although some of the narration is corny by modern standards, and bearing in mind that the film was made to *advertise* the train, there is nevertheless a palpable sense of pride about the whole thing. Railways were clearly, to quote the title of a later BTF production, *The Good Way to Travel*.

And yet, the mood is ultimately elegiac, and as the train reduces speed for a signal, the narrator utters these bittersweet words:

ABOVE No. 60017 'Silver Fox' in 1955. The engine was one of the original four A4s built in 1935 to haul the 'Silver Jubilee' express between King's Cross and Newcastle.

OPPOSITE The Down 'Royal Scot' at Harthope, on the ascent to Beattock summit, hauled by Stanier Pacific No.46250 'City of Lichfield'.

The loud hiss of steam
As the train seems to slow
To the pace of a cloud,
Breaks the afternoon task
And disperses the dream.

For steam, the dream really *was* about to disperse, modernisation being now firmly on the cards. B.R. had produced its own 'Development Programme' in April 1953, which detailed how £500 million would be spent doing just that over a period of 10–20 years (including £160 million for electrification). The Government's own Railways Act, published the following month, muddied the waters a might, but did recognise the need to reduce bureaucracy. It duly abolished the Railway Executive, after which Riddles decided to retire. The BTC's establishment of a modernisation planning committee the following April shows how quickly his policy of 'steam first, electrification second' was abandoned. Many orders for the Standards were cancelled and, in the event, only 999 locomotives were built.

The end of the Railway Executive allowed power to be devolved back down to the regions via associated Area Boards. On the surface, enthusiasts welcomed the evocative colours that started to appear on Mark I coaches (chocolate and cream on the Western, green on the Southern), which harked back to those Good Old Days of the Big Four. But the 1953 Act also served to denationalise the road haulage industry. This, which involved the sale of 24,000 lorries to private speculators, was to have far-reaching consequences for the railway's freight business. Indeed, road competition – which was also starting to affect passenger receipts, thanks to increasing motor car ownership – coupled with rising costs and industrial action in 1955 had turned a £19 million operating surplus into a £17 million deficit. The closure of uneconomic lines would continue, although the process would gain momentum in the next decade.

Steam's last gasp

There are several reasons why the withdrawal of steam occurred with greater speed than planned and most will be discussed in Chapter 10. However, it was seen more and

more as a means of stemming the flow of cash away from B.R.. This issue was raised by a reappraisal of the Modernisation Plan in 1959 and confirmed by the Beeching Report of 1963, which noted that some £15–20m per annum could be saved by exchanging old technology for new. A reduction of 1,174 steam locomotives (from a total of 8,796 in stock at 31 December 1962) was foreseen, although it was recognised that line closures and cutting of loss-making stopping trains would allow many multiple units to be reallocated to steam diagrams and so release 'further locomotives and coaches' to the scrap merchants. As it was, a drop in general traffic levels, brought about by industrial decline and recession, necessitated more withdrawals than had been imagined. The peak year was 1962, when 2,924 locomotives were condemned. Among them were the King class 4–6–0s, which dated from 1927, but now newer designs like the Clan Pacifics were being consigned to history too.

The following year would see the withdrawal of 'Flying Scotsman', although its A3 brethren (like the A4s) would be destined to see at least some of 1966. The last Stanier Pacific to go was No. 46256 'Sir William Stanier FRS', in October 1964. Many engines were in a deplorable state in this final period, there being fewer cleaners to keep the old retainers shining. Name and number plates also began to be removed around this time, although this was remedied a little by enthusiasts, who not only endeavoured to keep a few locomotives clean, but also reinstated some nameplates with a paintbrush! (No. 70045 'Lord Rowallan' was a particularly fine example of the art.)

By 1 January 1967, there were 1,689 steam locomotives on the network, many of the larger examples belonging to the Southern Region. The S.R. had actually come closest to Riddles' ideal scenario, withdrawing steam engines as it electrified area by area, with little need being seen for diesel traction (at least in comparison with the other regions). At the start of the year, only the Waterloo to Bournemouth main line was yet to be 'switched on'. Since 1963, the route had been virtually in the sole charge of Bulleid Pacifics. That glowing summer saw many Southern men have a final fling, and a number of astounding performances were recorded – including more than a few runs at over 100 mph. In July 1967, electric services began operation; although the final stretch to Weymouth would not be electrified until 1988, an ingenious push-pull diesel operation between the two coastal towns meant that the age of steam had finally ended in the south.

The end

At the start of 1968, the total number of steam locomotives stood at just 362. The last enclave was in the North West. Enthusiasts flocked to the area to watch 8Fs haul long stone trains over the Pennines or a Black Five work a local service. The final week of timetabled steam operation ended on 4 August 1968, after which the last sheds – Rose Grove in Burnley, Lostock Hall in Preston, and Carnforth – shut their doors for good.

It was left to the highly expensive '15 guinea special' to close the chapter in style. At 09:10 on 11 August, Black Five No. 45110 eased the train out of Liverpool Lime Street and headed for Manchester Victoria. Here, the 'Five' was replaced by a resplendent No. 70013 'Oliver Cromwell', which took the consist to Carlisle. The first leg of the return journey was in the charge of two 8Fs – Nos. 44871 and 44781 – which handed the train back to No. 45110 at Manchester for the run to Liverpool. The end had come: apart from the occasional run by 'Flying Scotsman' and the narrow gauge engines of the Vale of Rheidol, steam was dead on British Rail. Yet, perchance she only sleepeth...

OPPOSITE ABOVE The last Somerset 7F 2–8–0's standing at Bath Shed on the final day of service, 6th September 1964.

LEFT The Down Waverley Express Stanier 4–6–0 leaving Leeds City Station.

RIGHT Bulleid West Country Pacific No. 34096 'Trevone' emerging from Buckthorn Weston Tunnel. This locomotive was rebuilt by B.R.from its original streamlined condition in the 1950s.

LEFT The A1 Pacifics were designed by A. H. Peppercorn, the last CME of the L.N.E.R. Ordered by that company, but delivered to B.R. between 1948 and 1949, they worked crack expresses until final withdrawal in 1966. Here, No. 60156 'Great Central' sits on the turntable at King's Cross in 1953.

chapter 9

According to the famous *Thomas the Tank Engine* stories by the Rev. Awdry, diesels (or 'dieseasles') are a thoroughly bad lot, because they killed Britain's beloved steam engines. But diesels had been around some time before they became the major motive power source for B.R., each of the Big Four flirting with them in the 1920s and '30s. By the 1950s, there was a clear need for the newly nationalised industry to save money, and dieselisation was seen as a part of the solution. No one knew then that they would be part of a problem by 1968, themselves on borrowed time as standardisation became a buzzword once more.

The coming of diesels

The diesel engine has been with us for over a century and was first used to power a railway vehicle in 1912. Initial trials were not overly successful, but a breakthrough came two years later when the American company General Electric produced a reliable direct-current electrical control system. The United States was not alone in its development of diesel-electric technology; the first unit train of this type actually entered service in Germany in 1933. This, the famous 'Fliegende Hamburger' ('Flying Hamburger'), became the first diesel to attain the much-prized speed of 100 mph. It was powered by Maybach engines, the benefits of which would later be explored by the Western Region.

The Big Four were slower off the mark than the Germans and Americans, the L.M.S. dipping a tentative toe in the water with the purchase of a diesel railcar in 1927 ahead of its later (very successful) experiments with diesel shunters. At around the time the 'Flying Hamburger' was taking off, Armstrong Whitworth also produced a 1-Co-1 800hp locomotive, which was tested on the Newcastle–Carlisle and Newcastle–Berwick routes of the L.N.E.R. The Great Western introduced fast diesel railcar services to some routes during the 1930's, while it, the L.N.E.R. and the Southern would soon join the L.M.S. in exploring the possibilities of diesel shunters. Yet it would not be until the very end of the Big Four era that the diesel would start to become a viable motive power proposition for passenger and freight work. Gresley did, however, build four diesel-electric railcars for the L.N.E.R.

A new era dawns

British Railways (B.R.) inherited the L.M.S. 1,600 hp Co-Co diesel-electric No. 10000 (see Chapter 5). It was soon be joined by a twin (No.10001) and, a little later, by Bulleid's three 1Co-Co1 1,750 hp machines. R.A. Riddles, the Railway Executive member for Mechanical and Electrical Engineering, doubted the reliability of the internal combustion engine, however, seeing electrification as the ultimate goal (at least for the main lines).

As an interim measure to overcome the serious locomotive issues raised by over-work and under-maintenance during the Second World War, Riddles opted to introduce a series of standard steam classes. Something approaching the Riddles ideal seemed possible in April 1953, when B.R. published a 'Development Programme', which detailed how £160 million (of a £500 million total) would be spent on electrification.

But B.R.'s plans were soon thwarted by the Government's own Transport Act, which appeared the following month. Among other things, its purpose was to denationalise the road-haulage industry. Unfortunately, this had the effect of making even more cheap lorries available to speculative road transport companies. This problem had first arisen after the Great War and was responsible for the slow death of wagonload freight in this country.

The Act also led to the abolition of the Railway Executive, after which Riddles decided to retire and the British Transport Commission (BTC) decided to establish a modernisation planning committee. The committee's thoughts were laid out in the *Modernisation and Re-equipment of British Railways* (1955, henceforward the Modernisation Plan). It spelled the end for steam and authorised the construction of 2,500 diesel locomotives and 4,600 diesel multiple unit vehicles, although the BTC was aware that 'careful planning will be required to ensure that, as the existing stock is gradually replaced by diesel or electric power, it is still used to the best advantage'. It was not to be, and the 'useful life in service' of the 'residue of steam traction' did not go beyond 1968.

The Modernisation Plan estimated that £125 million would be needed to provide the requisite number of main-line locomotives. It saw that much 'useful experience' had been gained with the handful of (British) pioneering designs, and asserted that 'in view of the high degree of reliability attained in other countries where diesel traction has been widely adopted, there is no reason to doubt that equally satisfactory results will be realised here'. And so they were, but the process was not without difficulty.

Pilot scheme pioneers

Initially, £10 million was set aside for 171 locomotives of various wheel arrangements and power levels, comprising 160 diesel-electrics and 11 diesel-hydraulic machines. In the event, an order for three more of the latter brought the total number of Pilot Scheme locomotives up to 174. These were to be supplied from six manufacturers – and B.R. itself – in order to test various configurations over three years before

SERVICE TO INDUSTRY

THE GREAT I C I CHEMICAL WORKS AT BILLINGHAM–ON–TEES DEPEND ON BRITISH RAILWAYS FOR THE DELIVERY EACH YEAR OF NEARLY TWO MILLION TONS OF COAL, 150,000 TONS OF OTHER COMMODITIES, AND FOR THE DISPATCH OF THREE-QUARTERS OF A MILLION TONS OF FERTILISERS, CEMENT, BULK LIQUIDS AND OTHER PRODUCTS.

BRITISH RAILWAY

settling on a smaller range of designs on which the company could standardise. The first orders were placed in November 1955, but were augmented by requests for a further 56 diesel-electrics the following September; permission for the Western Region to purchase 115 extra diesel-hydraulics was also granted in February 1957. There were several underlying reasons for the deviation from the original sensible idea (see Chapter 10).

On 18 June 1957, the first Pilot Scheme locomotive was delivered to B.R. An English Electric machine, D8000 fell into the Type A (later Type 1) power category, able to exert 42,000 lb of tractive effort via its 1000 hp engine. Allocated to Willesden Devons Road, it soon outperformed its fellow Type As, the British Thompson Houston D8200s (Class 15) and North British D8400s (Class 16). While intended for working cross-London freight trains, the D8000s' (Class 20) useful turn of speed (75mph) meant that they also saw more passenger work – something which they retained into the 1980s, especially on summer Saturday specials to Skegness (which they invariably worked in pairs). Later class members found further employment on merry-go-round coal trains and empty stock workings out of Euston. While handsome, their design threatened to be their downfall, sighting being so poor when running bonnet-first that they could not be single-manned safely. This led B.R. to order 117 Type 1s (as they now were) from the Clayton Equipment Company. These, the D8500 series (Class 17), featured a centre cab with low engine covers, which (allegedly) afforded good visibility in both directions. However, their Paxman engines experienced camshaft and cylinder head problems and availability remained poor even after extensive modification. B.R. decided to dispense with them (withdrawals beginning in 1968) and opted to order a further 100 D8000s instead.

The second 'Pilot Scheme' design to appear was a Type B (later Type 2) mixed traffic locomotive built by Brush Traction of Loughborough. D5500 was delivered in September 1957 and, after a trial run, was allocated to Stratford depot in London. It would soon be joined by 19 classmates; they did not enjoy a good reputation at first, many Stratford drivers believing their 1,250 Mirrlees engines 'couldn't pull the skin off a rice pudding'. There were also problems with their control gear and, consequently, many failures – including one lamentable episode involving the Royal Train! B.R. thus chose the Sulzer equivalent (Class 24) as its standard Type 2 design. As the 'Brush 2s' had settled into satisfactory routine service on passenger and freight work, however, the Eastern Region decided it wanted more. B.R. therefore ended up with 263 locomotives, but they sounded a different tone in the 1970s from that with which they were born. In 1965, a re-engining programme began, involving the replacement of the Mirrlees units with 12SVT English Electric examples. The first locomotive to be transformed from Class 30 to Class 31 was D5677; the last was the doyen, D5500, which emerged anew in March 1969.

The most powerful Pilot Scheme class (Type C, later Type 4) could trace its lineage directly to the pre-nationalisation prototypes. The 2,000 hp D200 series (Class 40) was a heavyweight machine and, as a result (and like Bulleid's Southern designs), required extra axles on the bogie to keep it within reasonable limits of route availability. The first locomotive, D200 itself, was delivered from English Electric's Vulcan Foundry to the Eastern Region in March 1958, shortly after which a demonstration run was made from Liverpool Street to Norwich and back with a nine-coach set. The remaining nine of the Pilot Scheme order were also allocated to the ER and, for a short time, became top link engines, working such august trains as the 'Flying Scotsman', the 'Master Cutler' and the 'Tyne Tees Pullman'. The Chairman of the BTC, Sir Brian Robertson (see box on page 146) was unimpressed, however, believing the locomotives were insufficiently powered to maintain high speeds when hauling heavy trains.

This theory was proved correct when the loading was anything above seven passenger coaches, but their bulk was a boon when working long unfitted freights. Solid enough for B.R. to order a further 190, they failed to replace steam on the East Coast Main Line expresses (this job falling to the Deltics). They did, however, become a regular feature on the London Midland, where they tackled the steep Camden Bank north of Euston with ease, and where the need for long periods of sustained speed was less prominent. The locomotives enjoyed a long career on B.R., the final examples – bar 40 122 (the former D200), which was retained for enthusiast specials – being withdrawn from service in 1985. A temporary reprieve came with the remodelling of

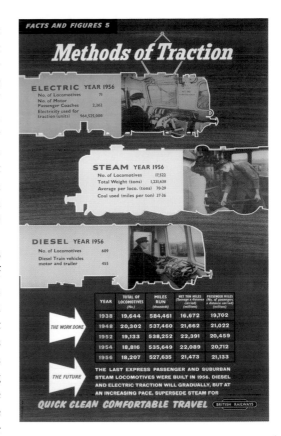

ABOVE Poster produced for (B.R.) comparing the number of electric, steam and diesel locomotives in operation during the year 1956. The poster explains that locomotives powered by diesel and electricity were gradually replacing those powered by steam.

OPPOSITE A poster produced for (B.R.) to advertise the company's services to industry. The poster shows locomotives arriving and departing at the ICI chemical works at Billingham, Stockton-on-Tees. Every year, ICI relied on B.R. to deliver nearly 2 million tons of coal and 150,000 tons of other commodities.

Diesel Electric 'Deltic'

English Electric's Co-Co diesel-electric Deltic preceded B.R.'s own motive power 'pilot scheme', yet led to the construction of one of the most successful, impressive production classes ever to pound British rails. Allotted the number 'DP1' (DP standing for 'diesel prototype'), which it never carried, Deltic was a vision of power in powder blue when it appeared in 1955.

The design was intended to prove that the 18-cylinder Napier-Deltic marine engine ('deltic' referring to its 'delta-like' cylinder configuration) could be used for railway applications. The locomotive featured two, derated from 1,750 hp to 1,650 hp each, giving 3,300 hp in total. This made Deltic the most powerful locomotive in the world at the time.

The styling, with its cream aluminium bodyside beading and curved chevrons, was reminiscent of American locomotives, a trait captured best by the large headlight housing fitted to each nose end (although the lights themselves were never installed). This reflected the fact that English Electric hoped for a flood of export orders. Sadly, these never came, but Deltic worked over B.R. metals for six years.

Trials began on the London Midland Region, the locomotive putting in several impressive 100 mph-plus performances. Deltic was also tested on the Settle and Carlisle route, and was later dispatched to the Eastern Region, whose General Manager Gerard Fiennes realised that the most powerful Pilot Scheme class then under construction would not allow East Coast Main Line principal services to be accelerated by any appreciable extent. Unfortunately, clearance problems between Newcastle and York meant that Deltic had to traverse the West Coast and Waverley routes to get it to Edinburgh. However, it gave notable service on expresses between King's Cross and Doncaster.

A serious phasing-gear oil leak saw the locomotive designated a failure in November 1960. This ultimately led to withdrawal the following March. By this time, however, the 22 modified production versions were entering service with a view to replacing some 55 ex-LNER Pacifics.

Hopes of a move to Canada for more trials (and possible orders) came to nothing, so Deltic was eventually donated to the Science Museum in London. A review in the 1980s led to a new home at the National Railway Museum (NRM), York from October 1993. It currently resides at the NRM's Locomotion site at Shildon (see page 174).

The successful production series (Class 55) started to be phased out in the late 1970s as more High-speed train sets were reassigned to Eastern Region duties. After some fine activity on the 'Hull Executive', the final timetabled service came at the end of 1981, with the last train – an enthusiast special – being hauled from King's Cross to Edinburgh and back by 55 015 'Tulyar' and 55 022 'Royal Scots Grey' respectively on 2 January 1982.

ABOVE The prototype Deltic diesel-electric locomotive. As the result of this prototype's performance, 22 further Deltics were ordered by British Railways to replace 55 steam locomotives on the East Coast main line between London King's Cross and Edinburgh.

Crewe station, which entailed the elimination of various points and crossings to allow 80 mph running over the North Junction. Four Class 40s were selected to work the associated engineering trains, which they did until 1987. The following year saw 40 122 enter the National Railway Museum; six other locomotives were also preserved, one of which (40145) still sees active service on the main line.

Western ways

The Class 40s were not the only Type 4s ordered under the pilot scheme. There were two others, both of which were diesel-hydraulics and both of which were destined for the Western Region (W.R.). The question of why the WR opted for locomotives with hydraulic transmission systems when the BTC (and thus B.R.) had taken the diesel-electric path is partly answered by the fact that there were no plans to electrify

ABOVE Class 40 and 47 diesel-electric locomotives *c.* Crewe Works, 1963.

any Western route. The WR was therefore faced not only with a much longer-term dieselisation programme than was intended for its counterparts, but also a *complete* one. Its hydraulic strategy was an attempt to make the best of this situation.

The comparative lightness of locomotives with hydraulic transmissions and compatible Maybach engines gave them a superior power/weight ratio – a fact that could increase haulage capacity by two coaches. Experience gained with the gas turbine locomotives had also shown electric transmissions to be unreliable, both 18000 and 18100 having suffered from flashovers, traction motor failures and bogie faults – all of which were related to their electrical circuitry.

The case was strengthened by the comment in the Modernisation Plan that loose-coupled freights were to be abolished with the promulgation of continuous brakes. A train fitted with this sort of equipment obviously does not need the deadweight of a locomotive like a Class 40 to help bring it to a halt. As it turned out, this took far longer to implement than anyone had foreseen – indeed, the policy to fit all wagons with automatic brakes was later reversed when the government was seeking ways in which the amount B.R. could borrow to finance the Modernisation Plan might be cut (in the end, non-fully fitted trains were still running well into the 1980s). This single act decreased the potential efficiency of the diesel-hydraulic in one fell swoop.

As well as an order for six Type 2s (D6300–5, later Class 22), an order for four Type 4s (D600–4, later – briefly – Class 41) was placed with the North British Locomotive Company in November 1955. But there was a problem. The BTC's Mechanical Engineering Department had exerted too much influence over the design and had lumbered the WR with the prospect of a weighty 117-ton machine, which defeated somewhat the power/weight ratio advantage. The following January saw the WR receive assent to remedy this by embarking on its own version of the Type 4 (D800–2, Class 42), a scaled-down version of the light-footed German V-200 class.

D800 emerged from Swindon Works in June 1958. After being named 'Sir Brian Robertson' the following month it was put to work on the Cornish Riviera from Paddington to Plymouth. During dynamometer trials, sister loco D801 'Vanguard' showed itself capable of a tractive effort of 48,000 lb at 7mph. A peak transmission efficiency of 82.5 per cent was also recorded. No further D600s were ordered, but there would eventually be 38 Swindon Type 4s (Class 42) and 33 similar locomotives built by North British (Class 43). The hydraulic concept was later developed into the elegant D1000 design (Class 52), while the mixed traffic D7000s (Class 35) would

Sir Brian Robertson

Born in July 1896, Sir Brian Robertson was the eldest son of Sir William Robertson; he was educated at Charterhouse and the Royal Military Academy before serving with the Royal Engineers in France and Italy during the Great War (where he was mentioned in despatches).

From 1945, Robertson was a Deputy Military Governor and, among many other positions, went on to be Commander-in-Chief of the Middle East Land Forces and Governor of the Suez Canal Zone. He retired from the Army for a second time in 1953 to become Chairman of the British Transport Commission. His remit was to provide leadership in what was regarded as an undisciplined organisation and to decentralise the railways. He was certainly a stickler for discipline, as one might expect, but was also at ease with the front-line staff and was well respected by them.

Robertson tried to reorganise the BTC by creating a three-tier system of management, complete with a military-style 'General Staff' – a move that proved to be unpopular with career railway managers. For him, the railway was a public service, which he was charged to deliver to a high standard; he once commented on the 'chasm of difference' between this view and the Conservative Government's notion of the railway as a commercial 'free' transport market competitor. Robertson also supported B.R.'s 1955 Modernisation Plan, which he saw as a way of stemming the flow of cash away from the industry. Sadly, however – and despite being a gifted administrator – he was unable to ensure that the modernisation funds were directed to where they were most needed. Robertson's greatest achievements are perhaps his instigation of the Railway Research Centre at Derby and the British Transport Staff College. In 1958, the Western Region named its first Swindon-built Type 4 diesel-hydraulic locomotive (D800) after him.

After retirement from the BTC in 1961, he was created Baron Robertson of Oakridge. He was succeeded at the BTC by Dr Richard Beeching and died in April 1974, aged 77.

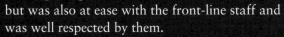

ABOVE A bill sticker puts up a poster on 30 December 1947, announcing the creation of the British Transport Commission.

perform good service on secondary passenger and freight workings – but not for long.

In 1968, the final year of steam, B.R. published a *National Traction Plan*, which outlined its intention to rationalise the locomotive fleet from 28 classes to 15. This dealt a blow to the Western's diesel-hydraulics and many of the smaller, less successful diesel-electrics, like the 'Baby Deltics' (Class 23), 'Metrovicks' (Class 28) and a plethora of Type 1s. By 1972, many of the steam vanquishers would themselves be vanquished.

Electric dreams

The National Traction Plan would have little impact on B.R.'s electric locomotive classes, however, whose own 'pilot scheme' had been rather more sensibly followed.

The BTC had initially acted on Riddles' prime motive power preference quickly, setting up a committee to review existing electrification methods as early as 1948. Its findings led to

the reinstatement of electric services on the Lancaster–Morecambe–Heysham line as an experiment in the single phase, 50-cycle a.c. system. Authorisation was also given for the conversion of the Tilbury and Southend line at 1,500V d.c., and the extension of the same on the Liverpool Street–Shenfield route to Chelmsford and Southend. Although the Southern Region would continue with its third rail d.c. system, and would take delivery of a new fleet of 2,552 hp electric locomotives (the E5000 series, later Class 71) from 1958, the French Railways had shown how a.c. power (at 20kV) offered much greater scope for future development. B.R. duly carried out a survey to assess the costs and the results were outlined in *The System of Electrification for British Railways*, an addendum to the Modernisation Plan published in 1956.

The main part of the report concentrated on the Euston–Manchester–Liverpool route, the electrification of which was calculated to be 4.7 per cent cheaper with a.c. power (£117.8m against £123.6m for d.c.). The a.c. system also benefited from being able to operate via lighter overhead line equipment (OLE). While this required extra (and more expensive) work to provide clearances under bridges and in tunnels, a.c. OLE was easier to erect and so cheaper to install on the whole. In addition, the associated traction had better adhesion, which allowed the use of lighter, more amenable, locomotives that did not waste power in the main resistances for speed control. 'Taking an overall view,' the report concluded, 'the Commission are satisfied that the a.c. system offers substantial economies both in first costs and in annual costs of operation.' Unsurprisingly, a.c. (at 25kV) was adopted as standard for all future non-Southern projects.

The first 25kV locomotive was E1000 (later E2001), which started life as gas turbine No. 18100. It emerged from Metropolitan Vickers in October 1958, re-motored and renumbered, and was put to use on driver training turns on the Wilmslow–Mauldeth Park line. It was soon joined by five 'pilot' classes (AL1-5, later 81-85), which were produced by AEI (AL1), Metropolitan Vickers (AL2), English Electric (AL3) North British (AL4) and B.R. itself (AL5). In all, 100 locomotives were built for assessment. The BTC had learned from the disastrous diesel Pilot Scheme and imposed certain requirements on each of the builders, such as the basic body shape, the axle load (20 tons), weight restriction (80 tons) and wheel arrangement (Bo-Bo).

The first of these 'prescribed' electrics to enter traffic was AL1 E3001 – a vision in electric blue, which was officially handed over to B.R. in November 1959. It was a palpable vision of the future; a new age for the railway was just a block section away.

ABOVE An English Electric Deltic class diesel locomotive hauling an East Coast express in May 1971.

chapter 10

In Britain, 1963 was the year of Profumo, Beatlemania – and Dr Beeching. One might say that 'it was the best of times; it was the worst of times'. Beeching is remembered for the famous 'axe' he wielded over many branch and secondary routes, yet the truth is that more lines were actually closed under his predecessor. The good Doctor also promoted 'liner' trains and managed to reduce B.R.'s deficit by the time he handed over to Stanley Raymond in 1965, after which B.R. consolidated its operations in readiness for further technological development in the 1970s.

The Beeching report and modernisation

The departure of Sir Brian Robertson in June 1961 marked a sea change in the life of B.R. and the beginning of the end for the British Transport Commission (BTC).

Robertson had been outspoken in his opposition to cuts in Government funding. These were suggested by a Select Committee (headed by Sir Ivan Stedeford), which had reported on ways of reducing the amount the BTC would be permitted to borrow to fund the Modernisation Plan. Among its proposed measures were the cancellation of electrification schemes (such as the Birmingham–Lichfield route and the East Coast Main Line) and a reversal of the decision to fit all wagons with continuous brakes (this would have implications for the Western Region – see Chapter 9).

The Stedeford Committee was convened by the Conservative Transport Minister, Ernest Marples. There is a suggestion that a significant proportion of the Conservative Party's 1959 election campaign was funded by those with interests in roads and road haulage and that their reward was the appointment of Marples – who happened to be a successful road-engineering contractor. This aside, the decline in the output of steel and coal the previous year had hit the railways hard and the BTC had no capital to offset its £90 million deficit. However, it had been trying to retrench by closing 'uneconomic' lines and wanted to adhere to the full Modernisation Plan. Marples, and the Government, disagreed; the result was the Stedeford Committee, but a further-reaching result came with the appointment of one of its members as Robertson's successor.

Dr Richard Beeching (1913–1985) was destined to earn great notoriety after the publication of *The Reshaping of British Railways* (henceforward the Beeching Report) in 1963, which set out its author's proposals for stemming the company's losses.

Multiple Choices

It could be argued that, had the government thanked the industry as well financially as it did vocally for its service in the Second World War, there would have been no need for Beeching, and the process of modernisation – vital for industry survival – could have begun much sooner than the mid-1950s. But while the BTC's initial view was that it was 'premature to tackle railway modernisation until progress was made on the acquisition of road transport', attempts were made to economise on branch line operating costs by experimenting with diesel railbuses and multiple units in the early part of that decade.

The benefits of multiple-unit trains had been enjoyed for some years on the Southern (Railway and Region), where a fleet of electric units had been employed on the main lines since the 1930s. Units are cheaper to run in terms of fuel and

ABOVE A Class 5
4–6–0 steam locomotive
alongside a first-generation
Diesel Multiple Unit at
Shrewsbury Station in 1967.

maintenance, and they do not require pointwork for a locomotive to run round rolling stock at terminus stations. They also allow operational flexibility, as several short units can be coupled together for rush-hour trains and then detached again during quieter periods.

The Modernisation Plan recognised these advantages and authorised the construction of 4,600 vehicles. As with the main line locomotive Pilot Scheme, the Government required that contracts for design and manufacture be split between numerous private firms in addition to B.R. itself. The result was – once again – a multitude of different types, some of which were built in small numbers. One of the last designs to survive was the Class 101, built by Metro-Cammell between 1956 and 1959. These operated across the whole country for almost fifty years, the last example being withdrawn from service in December 2003. One of the last designs to survive was the Class 101, built by Metro-Cammell between 1956 and 1959. These operated across the whole country for almost fifty years, the last example being withdrawn from service in December 2003.

Diesel Electric Multiple Units (DEMUs) were also developed during this decade and the next for the non-electrified lines on the Southern Region. Diesel-mechanical and diesel-hydraulic types were judged to have inadequate acceleration, which prevented extensive use as they would have caused delays to other traffic when operated over intensely timetabled routes.

At the end of the 1950s, B.R. introduced its luxury Blue Pullman fleet of main line diesel units (see page 152). These were the forerunners of the highly successful High Speed Trains (HST), of which more anon. These paved the way for the highly successful High Speed Trains (HST), the prototype of which was built in 1972 and attained a world speed record for diesel traction of 143.2 mph the following year. The production series – first introduced on the Western Region in 1976 – introduced regular 125 mph running to Britain. Many remain in service on today's privatised railway.

Blue Pullman

The Blue Pullmans were delivered to B.R. from Metro-Cammell in 1959 and entered service the following year. They gave a clear indication of how passenger traffic would be handled in the future, being the first diesel-electric multiple units to operate with a power car at either end. They also represented an attempt to compete with rising motor-car ownership and domestic flights. As such, they included a number of luxury features, such as full air-conditioning, deeply padded armchairs and an 'at table' service, which included especially selected menus and a wine list. British Transport Films commemorated the launch of these units in Blue Pullman, its beautifully shot cinema short of 1960.

The Blue Pullmans were, by all accounts, a joy to ride on, a smooth pick up on starting, and stable riding at high speeds being ensured by a new type of permanent coupling, which absorbed buffering and drawing loads. The double glazing also added to the effect of 'splendid isolation'. However some Blue Pullmas were criticised for their ride quality.

In order to highlight the new phase of Pullman travel that they represented, the traditional brown and cream livery was replaced by a striking shade of Nanking Blue with white window surrounds. In 1967, the standard yellow safety front end was applied, all of which

was soon replaced by a 'reverse' corporate blue livery, similar to that worn by the prototype High Speed Train.

The London Midland Region (L.M.) received two six-car sets in 1960 to work between Manchester and St Pancras. The Western was allocated three eight-car sets: one for a Paddington–Bristol service, one for a Birmingham turn and one spare, which was put to use on the South Wales Pullman to Swansea from 1961. The completion in 1966 of the West Coast Main Line electrification scheme between Manchester and Euston created an opportunity for a faster electric-locomotive-hauled Pullman service. This saw the L.M. units transferred to the Western in March 1967.

After conversion to work in multiple, the ex-Midland trains initially ran as a 12-car formation on a morning Bristol Temple Meads–Paddington service and afternoon return, between which one six-car set would make a further return trip to Bristol, while the other worked to Oxford and back. This was discontinued in 1969; a plan to roster a set on the 'Golden Hind' – the express dining service between Paddington and Plymouth – also sadly came to nothing.

By 1972, development of first-class accommodation in B.R.'s Mark II carriages had made the supplemental fare for Blue Pullman services seem over-priced and irrelevant to passengers and railway managers; the units were duly withdrawn and the final timetabled train ran on 4 May 1973. A farewell special was also organised by B.R., which worked out and back from Paddington via High Wycombe, Banbury, Leamington Spa, Birmingham New Street, Bristol Temple Meads, Swansea, Cardiff, Bristol Parkway and Slough. As passengers were treated to breakfast, morning coffee, lunch and high tea en route, they certainly went out in style! It is a pity that none of the units were preserved.

Taking a good Beeching

OPPOSITE B.R. poster advertising the six-car Midland Pullman trains.

BELOW Dr Beeching with a copy of his report. *The Reshaping of British Railways.*

But HSTs were for the future, and Beeching's problem was immediate: how could the railway be made profitable? He actually answered this by posing another question: what are the railways for? This he set about answering in his famous report, but before he did so, he simplified many of Robertson's complex management structures and recruited private-sector experts to bring financial – as opposed to military – discipline to the BTC. Further simplification came with the publication of (yet another) Transport Act in 1962, which served to abolish the BTC and establish (from 1 January 1963) a British Railways Board (BRB) with powers to set passenger fares and a little more freedom with freight rates and carriage agreements.

Beeching calculated that £15–20m per annum could be saved by speeding up the process of steam locomotive replacement (see Chapter 6). But other factors were just as instrumental, like the post-war labour shortage. Near full employment had suddenly made dirty jobs like cleaning and firing locomotives much less appealing than hitherto. There was also a growing need to cut down on air pollution and the grime associated with rail travel, while the scarcity of coal remained apparent and the quality of what was available often left much to be desired. Beeching recognised too that his proposed line closures and stopping service withdrawals would permit multiple units to be reallocated to steam diagrams and so release 'further locomotives and coaches' for scrap.

Of course, it is this so-called 'Beeching Axe' for which the report is most well known – despite the fact that the BTC had already created a Branch Lines Committee as early as 1949, and had closed over 3,000 miles of 'unremunerative' lines by 1962 (including the Midland and South Western route from Cheltenham, through Swindon and Marlborough to Andover, which had been of great strategic importance twenty years before).

Beeching understood that the railway 'emerged from the war [...] in a poor physical state' and that 'the surplus on [the] operating account [had] declined progressively' after 1952. The Modernisation Plan failed because 'it did not envisage any basic changes in the scope of railway services or in the general mode of operation of the railway system'. By 1960, however, 'it had become apparent that the effects of modernisation were neither so rapid nor so pronounced as had been forecast, that the downward trend in some railway traffics would persist, and the operating losses were likely to go on increasing unless radical changes were made.'

The radical changes included the closure of a further 6,000 miles of railway, including 2,000 stations and around 250 services. Controversy came with some of the choices – like the Somerset and Dorset line, which closed in 1966, and the Waverley route from Edinburgh to Carlisle (1969). A number of 'last rites' ceremonies were later carried out, with wreathes attached to smokeboxes and pall bearers carrying coffins of memories aboard coaches up and down the land.

Some of the criticism Beeching attracted was not without foundation. For example, his income figures were based on receipts issued at a particular place. This painted a blacker picture for stations more likely to be journey's end than journey's source – like a seaside resort. His approach also failed to recognise how the branches contributed traffic to the core network. Neither did the closures eliminate B.R.'s losses as Beeching had hoped, although their demise might be said to have led to a belated realisation that railways serve a social function, and that they must be subsidised in order to survive and flourish.

One of report's major strengths, however, was its plan to introduce 'liner trains'

'Kestrel'

In 1965, J. F. Harrison (by then effectively B.R.'s CME) realised that the time would come when B.R. would need a single 4,000 hp traction unit, which would require less maintenance than a twin-engined vehicle and could dispense with the need for double heading on freight trains. The Eastern Region was also interested in a 'Super Deltic' to allow speed to be raised beyond 100 mph. These thoughts marked the beginning of the 'Kestrel' project.

The resulting locomotive, numbered HS4000, was built in 1967 by Brush Traction of Loughborough to demonstrate the viability of Harrison's idea and – like Deltic before it – act as an advertisement for possible export orders. The 133-ton Co-Co was fitted with a Sulzer 16LVA24 engine rated at 4,000 hp, which provided a maximum speed of 125 mph. It was finished in a livery of yellow ochre with a broad chocolate brown band about the lower bodyside and was ceremonially handed over to B.R. at Marylebone station in January 1968.

Each of its six axles were powered by an individual traction motor, connection of the axle to the motor being via a reduction gear. The bogie sideframes were a one-piece cast construction, with coil spring suspension, but these were later replaced with modified Class 47 examples in order to comply with B.R.'s decree that all locomotives should have an axle weight of no more than 21 tons. This, however, still left each of Kestrel's axles weighing in at 22.5 tons each – a problem that would eventually lead to the decision to sell the locomotive.

Although officially allocated to Tinsley depot, HS4000 was actually based at Shirebrook, from where it worked a Class 47 diagram. Test runs were conducted with passenger and freight stock, although the latter predominated (especially on coal trains between Mansfield and Whitemoor Yard). After the fitting of its new bogies (and traction motors), Kestrel found itself working a 'Deltic' diagram; a sighting dated 1970 suggests that it was also tested on freightliner trains.

It was withdrawn from service in March 1971 and returned to Brush for refitting ahead of its sale to the Soviet Union. Kestrel was shipped from Cardiff to St Petersburg on 8 July 1971 and gave almost twenty years of service on international passenger services to Romania before withdrawal in 1989.

In many ways, Kestrel was ahead of its time: not until Foster Yeoman introduced the General Motors Class 59s in the late 1980s did it prove possible to haul payloads in excess of 4,600 tons with a single locomotive.

of containerised goods in place of uneconomic wagonload traffic – later embodied in the 'freightliner' concept and brand – and further electrification of the West Coast Main Line from Crewe through to Glasgow, which was finally achieved in 1974.

Modernisation and on...

Of course, modernisation is not always instigated by technology, politics or economics. Sometimes, safety concerns come into play. This explains the increasing mechanisation of track maintenance – which would lead to astonishing reductions in the staff-fatality rate over the next 40 years. As technologies improved, further safety schemes were developed, such as multi-aspect signalling and B.R.'s Automatic Warning System (AWS). The latter, designed to indicate to drivers the status of distant signals, was developed after nationalisation. The Harrow and Wealdstone accident (1952, 112 fatalities) had been caused by a Perth express rear-ending a commuter service after passing a signal at danger in fog. It occurred just as AWS trials were beginning; the incident at Lewisham in 1957 (90 fatalities) also arose from a signal passed at danger (SPAD) in fog, which also led to a rear-end collision. This gave the trials a new urgency and caused the development of AWS to gain momentum, which partly explains why the passenger fatality rate improved considerably from 1957, the average for the period 1958–65 being 7.75 deaths a year.

Some political historians also point to the late 50s/early 60s era as a time when a culture of fear developed in the West regarding the Soviet Union's technological advancements after the launch of Sputnik I (earth's first artificial satellite) in October 1957. This may have led to greater investment in higher education and a determination to "modernise", and may also explain why Philip Hardwick's great Doric arch (1837) at Euston Station was demolished as part of the West Coast Main Line electrification scheme.

Future Poet Laureate John Betjeman tried his best to rally support to save this elegant structure, but – even though the London County Council agreed to reconstruct it on the Euston Road – all plans failed and annihilation began at the end of 1961. However, he was much more successful in saving St Pancras station and a statue was commissioned by London and Continental Railways to celebrate his achievement. The statue is by Martin Jennings and the station was reopened in November 2007 after extensive modernisation and it is now Britain's Eurostar terminal (see pages 148 and 149).

Raising the standards – again

We have already seen how the original Pilot Scheme plans were altered by the placing of further orders in 1956 and 1957 before a single locomotive had been delivered. The main driver for this was the Government, which had wanted B.R.'s deficit cleared more quickly than envisaged. As Beeching wrote, it was expected that 'the substitution of electric and diesel haulage for steam, concentration of marshalling yards, reduction in number and increased mechanisation of goods depots, re-signalling, and the introduction of other modern equipment, would make the railways pay by

reducing costs and attracting more traffic.' This proved to be a costly mistake, although by 1963 some of the designs destined to see the new millennium had started to appear, many of which fell into a new power category.

There had been a realisation that there was a gap in the power range between the Type 2 and Type 4 classes. The result was the Type 3, which covered 1,500 to 1,999 hp. The first Type 3 to appear was D6500, a 1550 hp diesel-electric built by the Birmingham Railway Carriage and Wagon Company for the Southern Region. It entered traffic in December 1959 and was followed by 97 more, the last of which was delivered in 1962. The Class 33s (as they became) were among the first diesels in the country to be equipped with electric train heating. They were soon put to use on a number of passenger workings and were also noted at this time for hauling the Cliffe–Uddeston cement train (double headed) as far as York. Nineteen were later chosen to be fitted with push-pull equipment for working trailer car sets between Weymouth and Bournemouth ahead of full electrification of the line from Waterloo in 1988.

Arguably the most successful Type 3, however, was the English Electric variant – the Class 37. These deep-throated beasts started to appear in 1960 and soon found themselves working all manner of trains across virtually the whole country. In 1965, D6881 and D6882 also underwent high-speed trials on the Western Region. This led to the introduction the next year of eight services diagrammed for two Class 37s, which were permitted to run at 100 mph along certain sections. The coaches rostered for these trains were finished in the new 'blue and grey' livery – introduced, like the name 'British Rail', under Beeching's Corporate Identity Plan of 1964. The use of Class 37s was an indication that, by the mid-1960s, diesel-electric power/weight ratios had caught up with those of the hydraulics. Yet

ABOVE In 1965 the 'new look' colour scheme and arrow logo was introduced for British Rail. There was also a new uniform style, seen here and worn by train guard at Rugby station. Behind is a Class 31 diesel locomotive.

to some enthusiasts, the eventual withdrawal of the W.R.'s Western class Type 4s (Class 52) will always be regarded as 'too soon'.

These 2,700hp locomotives featured beautiful exterior styling by Sir Misha Black of the Design Research Unit (who was also responsible for the B.R. 'double arrow' logo – still used by National Rail today). Many were finished in coaching stock maroon, which made them a stirring sight at the head of Birmingham, South Wales and West of England expresses.

The Westerns (Class 52) started to appear on B.R. from the very end of 1961, only just before the class with which they would initially share W.R. services and which would become the cornerstone of the B.R. fleet for almost fifty years: the Brush Type 4 (Class 47). Though the Pilot Scheme had included two diesel-electric type 4s (Classes 40 and 44), and although both went into mass production, they had their limitations, such as their weight (over 130 tons), for example, which meant they were barred from certain lightly engineered routes. The solution was a new Type 4 specification, which included a maximum weight of 114 tons, a Co-Co wheel arrangement and an engine capable of producing at least 2,500 hp.

After several manufacturers had submitted bids, and some even erected prototypes, the contract eventually went to Brush, which produced 310 locomotives, although B.R.'s Crewe Works built a further 202. They went to work on passenger and freight duties right across the network. All – except a batch of 81 built for freight duties – were fitted with steam heating boilers. Twenty-two (D1500-19, D1960 and D1961) were also fitted with electric train heating (ETH). This type of heating became the norm, so fitment continued on into the 1970s (note that the lack of room inside a Class 52 for ETH was one of the reasons the Westerns were withdrawn as early as they were).

The electric 'pilot scheme' was rather more successful, the experience gained with the AL1-5 classes resulting in a production version – the AL6 (Class 86), 100 of which were built by English Electric and B.R.'s Doncaster Works in 1965 and 1966. The AL6s shared a superstructure design with the AL5s, but were built with one pantograph, which – coupled with the slightly smaller wheels (3ft 9in, as opposed to 4ft) – allowed for an improved internal layout for maintenance purposes. They also featured axle-mounted traction motors (as opposed to the bogie frame-mounted variety), although this led to track damage and poor riding qualities at speeds of 100 mph. The solution came in the form of 'Flexicoil' suspension, the helical springs of which earned the class the nickname Zebedee (after the besprunged character in the Magic Roundabout children's television programme). Fitment began from 1969.

A new era dawns

The 'Beeching Era' officially came to an end in May 1965, when Beeching returned to ICI and was replaced by Stanley Raymond as head of the British Railways Board. Although Beeching's plans would fail to eliminate the railway's working deficit by 1970, he did reduce it from £104 million in 1962 to £67.5 million in 1964, increasing productivity by 26 per cent in the process.

Raymond chose not to put a stop to the line closures (as many had wished), but focussed instead on opening freightliner terminals and endeavouring to dispense with the need for brake vans on freight trains. Further into the future, B.R. would release to traffic its sophisticated English Electric Type 4 (Class 50) to work between Crewe and Glasgow ahead of the first 'Electric Scots' in 1974. These later migrated to the Western Region, displacing more Class 52s from front-line duties. The National Traction Plan of 1968 also started to make inroads into the non-standard, less reliable and uneconomical diesel classes ordered under the Pilot Scheme. The next decade would see the railway as the butt of many ill-informed music hall jokes, yet it also saw the introduction of air conditioned coaching stock to the East Coast Main Line (1971) and surely the apogee of B.R.'s achievement: the Inter-City High Speed Train (HST).

The prototype HST was introduced in 1972 and underwent several trial runs, first on the Eastern Region and later on the Western. In the May of the following year, it attained a speed record for diesel traction of 143.2 mph, thus helping to prove the concept and pave the way for the production series, which entered service in August 1976 to standard schedules. When the timetable changed that October, the HSTs brought regular 125mph travel to Britain for the first time. Although enthusiasts initially hated them – for they were instrumental in the withdrawal of many loco-hauled passenger trains – to anyone younger they were an intoxicating part of the developing railway landscape. B.R. itself saw them as 'worldbeaters', capable of being 'a shop window for Britain'. So highly regarded were they, in fact, that a high-speed trip between Bristol and London was planned in celebration of the Queen's Silver Jubilee in 1977: and so it was that, on 7 May, 253019 reached Paddington from Temple Meads in 68 minutes and 23 seconds – an average speed of 103.3mph, which set (another) world record for diesel traction over a run of this length.

The tilting Advanced Passenger Train (APT) was developed at the same time as the HST, but its life was less charmed than its more traditional counterpart. The original experimental unit (APT-E) saw a return to gas turbine technology in the

form of four 300hp Leyland turbines supplemented by two GEC nose-suspended traction motors. Each vehicle was 70ft long and rode on articulated bogies. It made its inaugural run on 25 July 1972 from Derby to Driffield but was 'blacked' by the train driver's union ASLEF, which objected to the use of a single driver. The unit was subsequently moved to the works at Derby (with the aid of a locomotive inspector). This triggered a one-day strike which kept the APT-E off the main line for over a year. Like the HST, however, it was later trialed on the Western Region and managed to exceed 150 mph on 10 August 1975. By this time, the energy crisis of the early 1970s – which led to huge oil price increases – meant that the gas turbine could never be economically viable as a source of traction.

The prototype units (APT-P) were electrically powered via overhead line equipment. There had been an interim realisation that the biggest requirement for the new trains was on the electrified West Coast Main Line, HSTs (which largely used existing track and signalling) being found to be more than adequate for expansion on the Western and (from 1978) the East Coast Main Line. Unfortunately, political and managerial pressure to show results led to three APT-P trains being launched in 1981 when they were not ready for service. Many technical problems persisted and reliability was low. In the end, the APT-P's never entered passenger service, the whole project being abandoned by pusillanimous government policy. Nevertheless, B.R. incorporated many of its innovative features into the Inter-City 225s, which utilise Class 91 electric locomotives at one end and weighted Driving Van Trailers at the other. These commenced operations between King's Cross and Edinburgh in 1990 – a function they still perform.

Although the design of the successful Eurostars owes much to the French TGVs, the APT's influence may also be seen in the Class 390 'Pendolino' EMUs which currently ply the West Coast Main Line. These of course are a product of the privatised rail industry. The privatisation process began in 1994, when – for the first time in history

– the responsibility for maintaining the track and signals and the responsibility for running the trains were split from each other with the formation of Railtrack. The process was to last for three years as various B.R.-run passenger and freight franchises were sold off. Whether or not this was a wise move will become more apparent as time passes. The last B.R. train was a Railfreight Distribution sector Dollands Moor–Wembley service, hauled by dual-voltage electric 92003 'Beethoven' on 21 November 1997.

The Class 92 was the last locomotive design produced for B.R., being constructed specifically for Channel Tunnel freight services. Although there are discussions under way regarding their conversion to work on 'High Speed 1' – the rail link from the Channel Tunnel to St Pancras station – many indigenous locomotives classes, such as the Class 47s, 56s and 58s, were to be either withdrawn or diminished with the move at the end of the twentieth century towards standardising on (virtually) a single type. That type was the Class 66, a General Motors machine capable of exerting over 3,000hp with a maximum tractive effort of 92,000lb. Since 1999, their numbers have swollen to over 400. Messrs Churchward and Riddles would have been delighted. Probably.

ABOVE Alstom class 390 'Pendolino' nine car 25kV a.c. EMU overhead electric multiple unit.

LEFT A class 92 hauling a container train between Crewe and Alsager.

chapter 11

In this final chapter there is a directory detailing some of the the many heritage railways there are in England, Scotland and Wales. In total there are over 200 heritage railway associations but many of these are museums or Steam centres. This directoy concentrates on heritage railways which fall into three main types, minature, narrow and standard gauge. The directory includes examples of each type but the vast majority fall into the standard gauge and vary in line length from under a mile to over 16 miles. All of the railways rely on volunteers to help run them and you can usually find full details of how you could get involved on the relevant railway website. A large number of them also run driver courses.

Steam preservation railways

PREVIOUS PAGES West Country Class No 34092 'City of Wells' on the Settle and Carlisle line in May 1982 heading towards the Ribblehead Viaduct.

There is something almost magical about a steam railway. Whether the effect is caused by the smell of hot oil, the sound of excess steam lifting the safety valve or the sight of Thomas the Tank Engine coming to life depends largely on the individual's age or choice of reading material. There are, of course, many other aspects of the operation that may also evoke memories for the older visitor or arouse the curiosity of the young who were born too late to remember the 'glory days': the guard's whistle and green flag; the driver's 'greasetop' hat and blue overalls; the signalman's spotless signalbox with its levers for setting the points or controlling the signals; the toot or chime of the engine's whistle as the rods and wheels begin to move. These are all things that were once taken for granted, but which are now largely confined to the locations covered by this guide.

Over the last forty years or so, sites of 'preserved' railways have become increasingly popular as destinations for a day trip, either from home or as part of a holiday. In the early days of the preservation movement most visitors were 'enthusiasts', who had witnessed the rapid decline of the steam locomotive on Britain's railways combined with the closure of a large proportion of the system. More recently, however, although many aficionados are still drawn by the technology, family groups have taken over as the largest visitor category.

'Railway Preservation' means many things to many people and any attempt to define precisely when it began can be the starting point for much discussion, not least among the large, but inevitably aging, band of enthusiasts who can actually remember the early days.

Many will claim that the formation of the Talyllyn Railway Preservation Society in 1950 was the source of the phenomenon. Others will dismiss this assertion by saying that preservation didn't start in earnest until the first successful proposal to re-open a standard-gauge line was made in 1959. However, despite the seeming plausibility of both arguments, you will find in the pages of this directory a number of examples of private lines that were providing a tourist service several years before either example quoted above; where these earlier lines still survive, they are now accepted under the umbrella title of 'preserved railways'.

It is very difficult to generalise on the origins of the sites now used for preserved steam railways, but the vast proportion of preservation centres using standard-gauge (4ft 8½in) are located on closed British Rail lines or at former industrial sites that had been connected to the national system. The majority of locomotives in use at such locations fall into similar categories. They were either purchased direct from British Rail or industrial operators as they were withdrawn from service, or they were rescued from scrap merchants, sometimes

ABOVE An example of a miniature railway 7¼in at Conwy Valley Railway in Wales.

many years after withdrawal. Many of them required large sums of money to be spent before returning to operational use and they continue to consume more money than they do coal!

Disused industrial sites, such as quarries and coal mines, have also been used to establish narrow gauge lines (anything less than 4ft 8½in, but, in practice, not greater than 3ft). There are many narrow gauge branches, each several miles in length, which have an essentially industrial history but which also provided a means of transport for the local population. Miniature lines can be defined broadly as those that are laid to a narrow gauge, usually 15in or less, but where the locomotives are scaled down versions of main-line originals. Not surprisingly, these lines do not have 'miniature' carriages because they would not be able to carry full size people.

The sites used for these lines vary tremendously; some are laid along closed British Rail routes, some are seaside attractions or in theme parks, some are in the grounds of stately homes and some are provided as an additional feature of large garden centres.

Small museums have been established at a number of locations. These can be of great assistance to those interested in such matters, explaining the history of steam railways in general or of the line in particular, putting it into the context of its original purpose.

Virtually all preserved railways, of whatever category, offer a range of attractions beyond simply the trains themselves, encouraging a broad appeal. In addition to normal opening days, many hold special events on or around specific dates, such as St Valentine's Day, Mothers' Day, Easter, Fathers' Day, Halloween, Bonfire Night, Christmas and New Year. There are also attractions aimed at the younger end of the market; these may include taking a ride with such celebrities as Thomas the Tank Engine, Postman Pat or the Mad Hatter. Likewise, for the adults (but with the hope that the children will also come along) there are events concentrating on Rail Mail, Model Railways and Railways at War. Those of a gastronomic disposition will find programmes centred on Real Ale, Cream Teas, Mince Pies and Pullman Dining.

Some form of café or restaurant facility is usually provided; indeed some of the larger concerns have found that there is sufficient demand to justify such provision at several stations along the line. Several have also established good-quality licensed premises serving real ale as well as wines and soft drinks. Gift shops also feature prominently, selling a wide range of giftware.

Websites are an ever expanding source of information on a hugely diverse range of topics related to preserved railways, not only providing details of these special events, but also listing regular timetables, together with information on access by public transport. For each entry a website address is given where one existed at the time of going to press. The UK Heritage Railways website at www.ukhrail.uel.ac.uk is a valuable source of information.

The sites included here are a vital and flourishing part of the tourist industry and the final routes to many of them are well indicated by the familiar brown road signs reserved for such attractions. Because so much reliance is placed on visitors arriving by road, ample car parking will usually be available. However, special events can place a great strain on such facilities, so 'patience' may be the watchword on such occasions. Don't forget that the staff want you to return and will be doing their best to ensure that your visit is enjoyable; most of them will probably be carrying out their duties on a voluntary basis, hoping to enjoy the day as much as you do.

ABOVE An example of a narrow gauge railway 1ft 11.625in at Bala Lake in Wales,

BELOW A standard gauge 4ft 8½in, BR 4MT 2–6–4T No. 80078 on the Swanage Railway (The Purbeck Line) which runs from Swanage to Norden in Dorset.

AMBERLEY WORKING MUSEUM

This 36-acre open-air museum on the site of the former Amberley Chalk Pits holds one of the most extensive collections of narrow gauge rolling stock in the country with 30 locomotives and over 40 varieties of wagon and coach. There are two lines; the first is an industrial demonstration line, while the second carries passengers nearly half a mile in all–too–authentic (unsprung!) quarrymen's coaches. Betchworth Hall houses several locomotives and the Railway Exhibition Hall provides valuable display and restoration space.

With the completion of the restoration of 'Peter', the Museum is able to offer steam locomotive driving experience on the railway. Courses are run once a month and full details can be seen on the website.

HOW TO FIND US: **By car:** 3 miles north of Arundl on B2139 CAR PARKING: Free at Amberley **Nearest Network Rail:** Amberley ADDRESS: Amberley Station, nr. Arundel, West Sussex BN18 9LT TEL: 01798 831370 WEBSITE: www.amberleynarrowgauge.co.uk LINE LENGTH: 500 yds OPENING TIMES: Feb–Oct: 10–5.30 (last entry 4.30) Tues–Sun; daily during school holidays FACILITIES: Restaurant, picnic tables, gift shop DISABLED ACCESS: Wheelchair access

APPLEBY-FRODINGHAM RAILWAY PRESERVATION SOCIETY

This is a true enthusiast's railway, with rail tours run by members of the society for pre-booked visits. It is based in the Corus steelworks at Scunthorpe, which produces about 4 million tonnes of steel a year. There are approximately 100 miles of internal railways on the site.

The Society runs two rail tours, one of 8 miles and one of 15 miles, both of which include a visit to the loco shed, and a brake van tour which visits parts of the railway system not normally accessible. Thre are also brake van tours, which are either timetabled or privately chartered and they tend to cover areas of the site not accesible to hauled coaching stock.

On selected days thorughout the year the railway offers the chance to the public to join the loco crews on the footplate of both steam and diesel locomotives. After eight years of restoration the Hunslet Austerity has been returned to service.

HOW TO FIND US: All visits must be pre-booked on 01652 6578073 ADDRESS: Appleby-Frodingham Railway Preservation Society, P.O. Box 44, Brigg, North Lincolnshire DN20 8XG WEBSITE: www.afrps.co.uk LINE LENGTH: 8 or 15 miles OPENING TIMES: Open only by prior booking. All tours run free of charge, and places are limited FACILITIES: Buffet, gift shop and toilets DISABLED ACCESS: Disabled access to train and toilets.

AVON VALLEY RAILWAY

The Avon Valley Railway is more than just a train ride. Take a six mile round trip on a steam train into the scenic Avon valley and enjoy riverside walks and picnic areas, plus the river boat trips now accessible from the railway's new Avon Riverside station. Back at Bitton station you can admire the work of the volunteers who have painstakingly restored the 1860s building, as well as the locomotives and carriages that operate the train services.

HOW TO FIND US: **By car:** Bitton Station is midway between Bath and Bristol on A431 **Car parking:** Free **Nearest Network Rail:** Train to Keynsham, then 1.5mile walk ADDRESS: Bitton Station, Bath Road, Bristol BS30 6HD TEL: 0117 932 5538 WEBSITE: www.avonvalleyrailway.org LINE LENGTH: 2.5 miles OPENING TIMES: Steam trains operate Easter–end Oct: Sun and public holidays. FACILITIES: Buffet, gift shop and toilets DISABLED ACCESS: Coach converted and toilets at Bitton station.

BATTLEFIELD RAILWAY

Travel through scenic countryside from Shackerstone to visit the site of Bosworth Field, where the bloody Wars of the Roses were settled, and the last king of England to die in battle was slain. The Battlefield Visitor Centre tells the story of that momentous day in 1485. Shackerstone Station dates from 1873, and houses a fascinating collection of local railway history. There is a viewing area overlooking the lines and signal box.

HOW TO FIND US: **By car:** Follow the brown tourist signs from the A444, A447 and B585 CAR PARKING: Free at Shackerstone **Nearest Network Rail:** Amberley ADDRESS: Shackerstone Station, Shackerstone, Leics. CV13 6NW TEL: 01827 880754 WEBSITE: www.battlefield-line-railway.co.uk LINE LENGTH: 5 miles OPENING TIMES: Mar–Nov: FACILITIES: Tea Room, buffets on most trains DISABLED ACCESS: Please phone ahead.

BLUEBELL RAILWAY

The Bluebell Line, is perhaps the country's most famous railway and winds its way through a century of railway tradition. It was the first standard gauge passenger railway to be taken over by enthusiasts and takes it name from the bluebells in the woodlands that adjoin the railway line. The headquarters at Sheffield Park is home to the region's largest locomotive collection (over 30 steam locomotives and many carriages and wagons), as well as a museum of railway memorabilia and a reconstructed signal box. Take a walk around the engine shed and see the magnificent locomotives at close quarters. At Horsted Keynes, there is possibly the finest preserved station in the country along with an award-winning carriage and wagon display.

HOW TO FIND US: **By car:** Sheffield Park is on the A275 **Car parking:** At Sheffield Park and Horsted Keynes **Nearest Network Rail:** East Grinstead ADDRESS: Bluebell Railway, Sheffield Park Station, E.Sussex TN22 3QL TEL: 01825 720800 WEBSITE: www.bluebell-railway.co.uk LENGTH OF LINE: 9 miles OPENING TIMES: W/ends through the year; Daily Apr–Oct and school half terms: FACILITIES: Café, real ale bar, gift shop, all at Sheffield Park DISABLED ACCESS: Wheelchair access,adapted toilets.

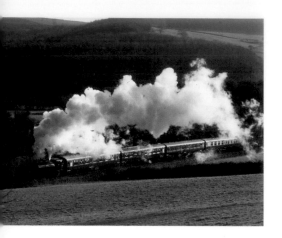

BODMIN AND WENTFORD RAILWAY

Two lines run from the railway's headquarters at Bodmin General, a (restored Great Western Railway station), both affording ample opportunity for picnics, walks and exploration of the Cornish countryside. A three-mile ride leads to Boscarne Junction and the Camel Trail – a popular foot and cycle path. At Colesloggett Halt, on the line to Bodmin Parkway, a footpath leads to the nature trails and cycle tracks of Cardinham Woods. From Bodmin Parkway, you can walk to Lanhydrock, a National Trust property.

HOW TO FIND US: **By car**: Station is on the B3268 **Car parking**: Only at Bodmin General **Nearest Network Rail**: Bodmin Parkway ADDRESS: Bodmin General Station, Bodmin, Cornwall PL31 1AQ TEL: 01208 73666 WEBSITE: www. bodminandwenfordrailway.co.uk LENGTH OF LINE: 6.5 miles OPENING TIMES: Jun–Sep: daily; Mar–May and Oct: selected days FACILITIES: Buffet and souvenir shop DISABLED ACCESS: Car parking outside main entrance, level access to station and ramp on to train with disabled access compartment.

BURE VALLEY RAILWAY

First opened in 1990, the Bure Valley Railway has five steam locomotives operating on this 15in gauge line, Norfolk's longest narrow gauge railway, transporting passengers in upholstered coaches. The journey begins in the old market town of Aylsham, where there are workshops, a small museum and a model railway, and finishes at Wroxham, The Capital of the Broads – combined train and boat excursions are available. Down the entire length of the line there is the Bure Valley walk and cycle path.

There are steam locomotive driver training courses throughout the year.

HOW TO FIND US: **By car**: A140 or A1151 **Car parking**: Free at Wroxham and Aylsham **Nearest Network Rail**: Wroxham ADDRESS: Aylsham Station, Norwich Road, Aylsham, Norfolk NR11 6BW TEL: 01263 733858 WEBSITE: www. bvrw. co.uk LENGTH OF LINE: 9 miles OPENING TIMES: Easter–late Oct FACILITIES: Café, picnic area, shop DISABLED ACCESS: Wheelchair access at both main stations and wheelchair accessible coaches.

CHINNOR AND PRINCES RISBOROUGH RAILWAY

The Chinnor and Princes Riseborough Railway Association was formed in 1989 to restore part of the disused Watlington branch or Icknield Line. Every weekend visitors take a round trip through four miles of charming countryside from Oxfordshire into Buckinghamshire. The Association owns seven locomotives, and there are regular visits by 'guest' engines from around the country.

HOW TO FIND US: **By car**: Chinnor is on the B4009 between Princes Risborough and Junction 6 of the M40 **Car parking**: Free on site **Nearest Network Rail**: Princes Risborough ADDRESS: Chinnor and Princes Risborough Railway Co, Chinnor Station, Station Road, Chinnor, Oxfordshire OX39 4ER INFOLINE: 01844 353535 WEBSITE: www.chinnorrailway.co.uk LENGTH OF LINE: 4 miles OPENING TIMES: Easter–Oct: w/ends; Santa and Mince Pie specials in Dec FACILITIES: Souvenir shop, on-train buffet, picnic area, full service cafeteria at the station DISABLED ACCESS: Call ahead.

CHOLSEY AND WALLINGFORD RAILWAY

This restored line, part of the old Great Western Railway, takes its passengers on a ride through the leafy Oxfordshire countryside. Originally opened in 1866, it is one of the oldest surviving GWR lines in the Thames Valley. The station museum at Wallingford has a collection of local railway memorabilia and a model of the original station with an 'N' gauge model railway. Wallingford, one of the oldest chartered towns in the country is 15 minutes walk away, on the banks of the River Thames. From the station at Cholsey, visit St Mary's Church where the author Agatha Christie is buried.

HOW TO FIND US: **By car:** Wallingford is on A4130 **Car parking:** Ample parking **Nearest Network Rail:** Cholsey ADDRESS: Cholsey and Wallingford Railway, Hithercroft Road, Wallingford, Oxon, OX10 9GQ TEL: 01491 835067 WEBSITE: www.cholsey-wallingford-railway.com LENGTH OF LINE: 2.5 miles OPENING TIMES: trains operate: Easter–Oct; running days are as advertised; phone for special events FACILITIES: Café, shop at Wallingford DISABLED ACCESS: At Wallingford station access from car park and ramp to shop.

CHURNET VALLEY RAILWAY

In the heart of the Staffordshire moorlands, the railway aims to recreate the atmosphere and ambience of a 1950s steam-operated country line. Begin your journey at either Cheddleton Station, with its handsome Grade II Victorian station and many facilities, or the impressive newly re-built Kingsley and Froghall station, complete with award-winning traditional tea rooms. Travel through one of the longest tunnels on a preserved railway and to the jewel in the crown – Consall Station, a replica of a Victorian station.

HOW TO FIND US: **By car:** On the A520 **Car parking:** Opposite the station **Nearest Network Rail:** Stoke-on-Trent ADDRESS: Cheddleton Station, Station Road, Cheddleton, nr Leek, Staffs, ST13 7EE TEL: 01538 360522 WEBSITE: www.churnetvalleyrailway.co.uk LENGTH OF LINE: 5.25 miles OPENING TIMES: Steam trains: late Mar–early Oct, Sun and public holidays; every Wed, Jul and Aug: FACILITIES: Cheddleton: Picnic island, tea rooms, souvenir shop; Kingsley and Froghall Station: tea rooms DISABLED ACCESS: Wheelchair access; train rides by arrangement

COLNE VALLEY RAILWAY

A highly successful reconstruction of a typical Essex country branch line, this attractive railway on the banks of the River Colne now carries as many passengers per year as it did in its heyday. The opulent ambience of the Orient Express is evoked on its Pullman train, featuring beautifully restored coaches. Steam and heritage diesel trains offer rides on Sundays and certain mid-week days in summer holidays. There is free admission to the Farm Park.

HOW TO FIND US: **By car:** NW of Braintree on A1017 **Car parking:** On site **Nearest Network Rail:** Braintree ADDRESS: Yeldham Road, Castle Hedingham, Essex CO9 3DZ TEL: 01787 461174 WEBSITE: www.colnevalleyrailway.co.uk LENGTH OF LINE: 1 mile OPENING TIMES: Mar–Oct: 11–5 FACILITIES: Buffet, picnic area, farm park, Pullman buffet carriage DISABLED ACCESS: Wheelchair access to trains with help from staff.

DARTMOOR RAILWAY

The railway was unexpectedly closed in 2008 and a new company British American Railways now operates both the Dartmoor Railway and the Weardale railway. The Dartmoor railway was restarted in 2009. The railway offers a unique experience with its access to car free Dartmoor National Park. At Meldon you can walk to Meldon Viaduct and see Yes Tor and High Willhays. Work is planned on restoring a disused platform at Yeoford which will give access to Network Rail.

HOW TO FIND US: **By car**: A30 to Okehampton and follow signs for Dartmoor Railway **Car parking**: Free at station **Nearest Network Rail**: Exeter ADDRESS: Dartmoor Railway, Okehampton Station, Station Road, Okehampton, Devon EX20 1EJ TEL: 01837 55637 WEBSITE: www.dartmoorrailway.co.uk LENGTH OF LINE: 15.5 miles OPENING TIMES: All year: W/ends and public holidays; daily during summer FACILITIES: Okehampton: buffet and gift shop open daily; Meldon: coach buffet and visitor centres on days of operation DISABLED ACCESS: All station and trains are wheelchair friendly.

DEAN FOREST RAILWAY

Dean Forest Railway, built in 1809, is the last remnant of the Severn and Wye Railway system. The line currently runs two miles south to the mainline station at Lydney Junction from the headquarters at Norchard Railway Centre and two miles north through the forest to Parkend. At Norchard there is also a museum with an old telephone exchange and a collection of railway memorabilia. The line has five level crossings, three of which are manually operated.

HOW TO FIND US: **By car**: Lydney is on the B4234, signposted off A48 **Car parking**: Free car park at Norchard **Nearest Network Rail**: Lydney ADDRESS: Dean Forest Railway Co. Ltd, Forest Road, Lydney, Glos GL15 4ET TEL: 01594 843423 WEBSITE: www. deanforestrailway.co.uk LENGTH OF LINE: 4.25 miles OPENING TIMES: Sun, Feb–Nov and bank holidays FACILITIES: Shop at Norchard, picnic area, refreshments available on operational days DISABLED ACCESS: Wheelchair access to both museum and trains.

EAST KENT RAILWAY

The original East Kent Railway was built early this century and was one of several lines across the country engineered and run by Colonel H F Stephens in his own distinctive style. He used antiquated locomotives and stock, and the lines were characterised by steep inclines and sharp curves. The museum at Shepherdswell, the railway's headquarters, tells the story of the line and this interesting character. An extension of the line to Wigmore Lane was opened in 2005 and is used on some special events.

HOW TO FIND US: **By car**: A2, follow signs to Shepherdswell. From the A256, take turning for Eythorne and follow signs for EKR **Car parking**: Free on site **Nearest Network Rail**: Shepherdswell ADDRESS: Shepherdswell Station, Shepherdswell, Dover, Kent CT15 7PD TEL: 08457 484950 WEBSITE: www. eastkentrailway.co.uk LENGTH OF LINE: 2 miles OPENING TIMES: Easter–end Sep: w/ends; w/ends in Dec for Santa Specials FACILITIES: Buffet, book and souvenir shop, toilets, visitor centre DISABLED ACCESS: Access to buffet at Shepherdswell.

EAST LANCASHIRE RAILWAY

A wide range of lovingly restored steam and diesel locomotives carry passengers between Heywood, Bury, Ramsbottom and Rawtenstall. At Bury you can visit the new Bury Transport museum which has been re-openend after £2.9 million refit. The railway operates Sunday lunch and evening dinner trains and locomotive driving days. Visit the shops at Dickensian Ramsbottom, or Rawtenstall's Temperance Bar.

HOW TO FIND US: **By car:** A58, just off the M66, Jct 2 **Car parking:** On site **Nearest** Network Rail: Bury **By bus:** From Manchester, Bolton, Rochdale and Burnley ADDRESS: East Lancashire Railway, Bolton Street Station, Bury, Lancashire, BL9 0EY TEL: 0161 764 7790 WEBSITE: www. east-lancs-rly.co.uk LENGTH OF LINE: 12 miles OPENING TIMES: W/ends and public holidays throughout the year; Santa Specials in Dec FACILITIES: Real Ale pub, buffet DISABLED ACCESS: All stations have wheelchair access, and there are disabled toilet facilities at Bury Bolton Street, Ramsbottom and Rawtenstall Stations.

EAST SOMERSET RAILWAY

One of only few remaining all-steam railways in the country, it was founded in 1974 by the artist David Shepherd on the site of the original East Somerset Railway which first started operating in 1858. There is a fine replica Victorian engine shed housing the E.S.R.'s locomotive stock, including GWR 0–6–2T 5637. Visitors are able to view the restoration work going on in the locomotive workshops. There is a nature reserve and art gallery where prints of Mr Shepherd's works are displayed.

HOW TO FIND US: **By car:** Just off A361 **Nearest Network Rail:** Frome ADDRESS: Cranmore Railway Station, Shepton Mallet, Somerset BA4 4QP TEL: 01749 880417 WEBSITE: www.eastsomersetrailway.com LENGTH OF LINE: 3 miles OPENING TIMES: Trains run Jan–Mar and Nov: Sun; Apr, May and Oct: Sat, Sun; Jun and Sep: Wed–Sun; FACILITIES: Licensed restaurant, art gallery, video coach, playground DISABLED ACCESS: Wheelchair access to all public areas and trains.

ECCLESBOURNE VALLEY RAILWAY

The line operates tourist passenger services between Wirksworth and Idridgehay (3.5 miles) and Ravenstor (0.5 mile up a 1 in 27 incline) using Diesel Multiple Units. There are plans to connect to the Midland main line at Duffield (8½ miles) in October 2010, providing a service that will connect with national rail services. The Ecclesbourne Valley is Derbyshire's gentle valley, stretching from the northern outskirts of Derby to Wirksworth, gateway to the Peak District.

HOW TO FIND US: **By car:** Just off B5023 **Car parking:** Only at Wirksworth **Nearest Network Rail:** Matlock ADDRESS: Wirksworth Station, Coldwell Street, Wirksworth, Derbyshire, DE4 4FB TEL: 01629 823076 WEBSITE: www.e-v-r.com LENGTH OF LINE: 4.5 miles OPENING TIMES: W/ends Mar–Oct FACILITIES: Refreshments DISABLED ACCESS: Wheelchair access. Disabled toilets on site.

EMBSAY AND BOLTON ABBEY RAILWAY

A trip aboard this jaunty little steam railway is a great way of exploring the craggy limestone landscape that inspired the Romantic visions of Wordsworth and Turner. Embsay Station,(built in 1888), is home to an extensive collection of tank engines. From here you can travel through the North Yorkshire countryside to the award-winning reconstructed Bolton Abbey Station. The area provides a good base for exploring the dramatic scenery.

HOW TO FIND US: **By car:** Just off the A59 **Car parking:** On site **Nearest Network Rail:** Skipton or Ilkley ADDRESS: Bolton Abbey Station, Skipton, North Yorks BD23 6AF TEL: 01756 710614 WEBSITE: www.embsaybolton abbeyrailway.org.uk LENGTH OF LINE: 4.5 miles OPENING TIMES: Sun through the year, W/ends from Apr to Oct FACILITIES: Bolton Abbey Station: Gift shop, refreshment rooms picnic area; Embsay: Café, gift and bookshop, picnic area DISABLED ACCESS: Wheelchair access

GLOUCESTERSHIRE AND WARWICKSHIRE RAILWAY

The entirely volunteer-run, award-winning railway – often known as the 'Honeybourne line' – once formed part of the Great Western route from Birmingham to Cheltenham. The line had gradually been rebuilt and now offers steam and heritage diesel train rides over 10 miles from Toddington, through Winchcombe and Gotherington, to Cheltenham Race Course Station. The journey, which includes a 700-yard tunnel, offers stunning views of the Cotswolds and the Evesham Vale.

HOW TO FIND US: **By car:** Toddington station is close to the junction of the B4077 (Tewkesbury to Stow) and B4632 (Cheltenham to Broadway); 10 miles east of M5 Jn9: **Car parking:** On site **Nearest** Network Rail: Cheltenham ADDRESS The Railway Station, Toddington, Glos GL54 5DT TEL: 01242 621405 WEBSITE: www. gwsr.com LENGTH OF LINE 10 miles OPENING TIMES W/ends and public holidays, plus Tue, Wed, Thu in school holidays FACILITIES: Book and gift shop, tearoom, buffet cars, garden centre at Toddington DISABLED ACCESS: Wheelchair access in specially converted carriages.

GREAT CENTRAL RAILWAY

The Great Central Railway, once part of a network that ran from Manchester to Marylebone, operates Britain's only double track main line steam railway, aiming to recreate the experience of main line rail travel during the heyday of steam locomotives. The northern terminus is the wonderfully preserved Loughborough Central Station, built in 1897. Beneath the booking hall is a museum of railway artifacts. The engine shed houses a large fleet of restored locomotives. From here, the journey takes in Quorn and Woodhouse Station.

HOW TO FIND US: **By car:** The Station is just off the A6 **Car parking:** Ample roadside parking **Nearest Network Rail:** Loughborough ADDRESS: Great Central Road, Loughborough, Leics LE11 1RW TEL: 01509 230726 WEBSITE: www. gcrailway.co.uk LENGTH OF LINE: 8 miles OPENING TIMES: All year: w/ends; May–Sep: certain weekdays only FACILITIES: Café, gift shop, buffet cars DISABLED ACCESS: Wheelchair access at Quorn and Rothley; especially adapted carriage with accessible toilet facilities.

HEATHERSLAW LIGHT RAILWAY

Enjoy the leisurely pace of yesteryear as you travel along this 15in gauge steam railway from Heatherslaw Mill to Etal Castle (a return trip of about four miles), with views of the River Till and its wildlife. Break your journey and stop off in Etal Village and visit the castle and water mill, watch a working blacksmith and woodturner, and return by a later train. At Heatherslaw there are two model railway layouts ('G' and '00' gauge).

HOW TO FIND US: **By car:** On the B6354 about 12 miles south of Berwick-upon-Tweed, signposted Ford and Etal **Car parking:** On site **Nearest Network Rail:** Berwick-upon-Tweed ADDRESS: Ford Forge, Heatherslaw, Cornhill-on-Tweed, Northumberland TD12 4TJ TEL: 01890 820244 WEBSITE: www.ford-and-etal. co.uk OPENING TIMES: Apr–Oct: daily plus Santa Specials in Dec FACILITIES: Etal: tearooms; Heatherslaw: Café DISABLED ACCESS: Wheelchair access

ISLE OF WIGHT RAILWAY

Passenger trains are operated exclusively using beautifully restored Victorian and Edwardian carriages, usually hauled by locomotives, all of which have spent most of their working lives on the Island. Trains run from Smallbrook Junction (where it connects with Island Line's Ryde to Shanklin electric trains), through Ashey and Haven-street to Wootton Station, a delightful country terminus complete with old wooden booking office.

HOW TO FIND US: **By car:** Clearly signed **Car parking:** Free at Havenstreet Station **Nearest Network Rail:** Island Line to Smallbrook Junction **By bus:** Southern Vectis Route 7 **By ferry:** From Portsmouth (connects with Island Line trains at Ryde) ADDRESS: Havenstreet, Isle of Wight, PO33 4DS TEL: 01983 882204 WEBSITE: www.iwsteamrailway.co.uk LENGTH OF LINE: 5 miles OPENING TIMES: Jun–Sep: daily; Mar–May and Oct: selected days FACILITIES: Licensed café, gift shop DISABLED ACCESS: Call ahead as limited.

KEIGHLEY AND WORTH RAILWAY

One of the few remaining complete branch lines, runs from Keighley to Oxenhope, along a rich seam of West Yorkshire's rail and cultural heritage. Travel via Ingrow, with its award-winning Museum of Rail Travel and work-shops, and Damems, the country's smallest complete station on to Ormiston and Oakworth where The Railway Children was filmed. This is a superb example of an Edwardian Station, complete with authentic advertising signs, gas lighting and coal fires. From here, ride on to Haworth, home to another famous family – the Brontës. There is a station shop and you can walk into the famous village. The line terminates 660 feet above sea level at Oxenhope, where a collection of historic locomotives and coaches can be inspected.

HOW TO FIND US: **By car:** NE of Bradford on A650 **Car parking:** Free **Nearest Network Rail:** Leeds ADDRESS: Haworth, Keighley, West Yorks BD22 8NJ TEL: 01535 645214 WEBSITE www.kwvr.co.uk LENGTH OF LINE: 4.75 miles OPENING TIMES: All year: w/ends and public holidays; Tue–Thu mid Jun–early Jul then daily untill beginning of Sep FACILITIES: Shops, buffets, picnic areas, evening and midday dining trains (advance booking essential: DISABLED ACCESS: Wheelchair access to all station platforms. Full disabled toilets at Haworth station.

KENT AND EAST SUSSEX RAILWAY

The first line to be built under the Light Railways Act of 1896 – and the first full size light railway in the world – the Kent and East Sussex Railway opened in 1900. It has been carefully restored by a team of dedicated volunteers, and now carries passengers in beautifully restored coaches dating from Victorian times to the 1960s through more than 10 scenic miles of Kentish countryside from Tenterden, through Northiam to Bodiam (home of the National Trust's castle). A 'must see' is the Colonel Stephens Railway Museum at Tenterden Town Station.

HOW TO FIND US: **By car**: A28 between Ashford and Hastings **Car parking**: Free parking available at Tenterden and Northiam **Nearest Network Rail**: Ashford ADDRESS: Kent and East Sussex Railway, Tenterden, Kent TN30 6HE TEL: 01580 765155 INFOLINE: 01580 762943 WEBSITE: www.kesr.org.uk LENGTH OF LINE: 10.5 miles OPENING TIMES: W/ends Mar–Oct and bank holidays. Daily early Jul – early Sep FACILITIES: Café DISABLED ACCESS: Disabled parking, adapted toilets, wheelchair access to carriages.

LAKESIDE AND HAVERTHWAITE RAILWAY

This scenic journey starts from the Victorian station at Haverthwaite where steam locomotives haul comfortable coaches on this steeply graded line running through the ever changing lake and river scenery of the beautiful Leven valley. A varied selection of steam and diesel loomotives are on display at Haverthwaite station. From the terminus at Lakeside there is an opportunity to continue your trip aboard one of the Windermere Lake Cruises' steamers.

HOW TO FIND US: **By car**: M6 Jct 36 and follow the signs on the A590 Newby Bridge Road **Car parking**: Fees at both stations **Nearest Network Rail**: Ulverston ADDRESS: Haverthwaite Station, Nr Ulverston, Cumbria LA12 8AL TEL: 01539 531594 WEBSITE: www.lakesiderailway.co.uk LENGTH OF LINE: 3.5 miles OPENING TIMES: Easter school holidays–Oct: daily; specials in Dec FACILITIES: Souvenir shop, picnic area, refreshments DISABLED ACCESS: Access to stations.

LAUNCESTON RAILWAY

The locomotives hauling carriages on this famous narrow gauge railway were built in the 1880s and '90s by the Hunslet Engine Company of Leeds, and worked carrying slate from the mountain quarries of North Wales. Today they carry passengers from the winding hillside streets of Launceston through the glorious Cornish countryside to Newmills. The daily ticket allows plenty of opportunity for a walk along the local pathways or a quiet riverside picnic. The locomotives used were once used on the Dinorwic and Penrhyn railways in North Wales.

HOW TO FIND US: **By car**: Off the A30 **Car parking**: Free at Lauceston **Nearest Network Rail**: Gunnislake ADDRESS: Launceston Steam Railway, St Thomas's Road, Launceston PL15 8DA TEL: 01566 775665 WEBSITE: www.launcestonsr. co.uk LENGTH OF LINE: 2.5 miles OPENING TIMES: Good Friday– Whitsun: Tue and Sun; Whitsun–end Sep: daily except Sat; Oct: half term week FACILITIES: Buffet, gift and book shop DISABLED ACCESS: Wheelchair access to most areas.

LEIGHTON BUZZARD RAILWAY

Situated in Bedfordshire, the railway has one of the largest collection of narrow gauge locomotives in the country and is put through its paces along the tight curves, steep gradients and level crossings of a country-roadside track. Here you can experience the English light railway as it was 80 years ago, with a wide variety of coaches and wagons in use and on display. There are many special events throughout the year, including a Teddy Bears' outing, a Steam Glow night (a night photography event) and the September Steam-Up.

HOW TO FIND US: **By car:** A4146 **Car parking:** Free **Nearest Network Rail:** Leighton Buzzard ADDRESS Pages Park Station, Billington Road, Leighton Buzzard, Beds LU7 4TN TEL: 01525 373888 WEBSITE: www.buzzrail.co.uk LENGTH OF LINE: 3 miles OPENING TIMES: Sun and bank holidays mid Mar–end Oct; Wed in Jun and Jul, Tue–Thu and Sat in Aug FACILITIES: Buffet, shop DISABLED ACCESS: Wheelchair access to trains and toilets.

MID-HANTS RAILWAY

If the Great Central is 'Britain's only mainline steam railway', then the Mid-Hants is surely a contender for leading secondary route. Here Bulleid Pacifics and Urie 4-6-0s may be found breasting the line's challenging gradient, with rakes of attractive green-liveried coaches in tow. The Mid-Hants – or 'Watercress Line' – may be single track, but on a busy day you might pass another train at both of its intermediate stations on the ten-mile run between Arlesford and Alton.

The headquarters of the line – Arlesford – boasts a shop and visitor centre in the beautifully restored goods shed, while refreshments may be taken in the station buffet. At Medstead and Four Marks, the atmosphere is that of a typical, peaceful country station, while Alton has a shop, refreshment facility and access to the national rail network; plans are also afoot to improve the signalling here to allow an even more intensive service to be operated.

HOW TO FIND US: **By car:** Off A31 **Car parking:** At Arlesford and Alton staions **Nearest Network Rail:** Alton ADDRESS: Mid-Hants Railway plc, Railway Station, Arlesford, Hants, SO24 9JG TEL: 01962 733810 WEBSITE: www. watercressline.co.uk LENGTH OF LINE: 10 miles OPENING TIMES: Mar–Jun and Sep–Oct: w/ends and public holidays: Jul and Aug: daily FACILITIES: Café, book and souvenir shops and dining trains DISABLED ACCESS: Access to all trains.

MID NORFOLK RAILWAY

A relative newcomer to the preserved railway scene, the Mid-Norfolk Railway is over 150 years old, and was part of the Great Eastern Railway network. The aim is to create a multi-functional railway serving tourists, freight customers and local passengers. This 11-mile branch line is now open between Dereham and its junction with the main line at Wymondham, linking numerous villages and passing through four river valleys. The clearance work has been completed on the next stage up to North Elmham and there are plans to try and reach Fakenham.

HOW TO FIND US: **By car:** Close to centre of Dereham **Car parking:** Free **Nearest Network Rail:** Wymondham ADDRESS: The Railway Station, Station Road, Dereham, Norfolk, NR19 1DF TEL: 01362 690633 WEBSITE: www.mnr.org.uk LENGTH OF LINE: 11 miles OPENING TIMES: W/ends and Bank Holidays Mar–Oct FACILITIES: Refreshments, souvenir shop and museum DISABLED ACCESS: Wheelchair access to all stations.

NATIONAL RAILWAY MUSEUM

HOW TO FIND US: **By car**: Signed from York's ring road **Car parking**: On site **Nearest Network Rail**: York ADDRESS: Leeman Road, York YO26 4XJ TEL: 08448 153139 WEBSITE: www.nrm.org.uk OPENING TIMES: 10–6 daily FACILITIES: Gift shop,restaurant, café DISABLED ACCESS: Wheelchair access to most parts of the museum, wheelchair loan available.

Anyone over a certain age is bound to remember the original series of Ladybird Books. Published by Wills and Hepworth, the small volumes kept generations of children informed on just about every subject under the sun – from cars to ancient customs, mammals to maps. Transport featured heavily and railways were covered in the self-explanatory title *The Story of Railways*, which gave an excellent history of the subject from the Surrey Iron Railway to the present (which is now of course part of the past). Well, if you imagine that book multiplied by around ten thousand and made three dimensional, you'll have a good idea of what it's like at the National Railway Museum in York.

Beginnings Although the idea of preserving railway vehicles for posterity began in the nineteenth century, the concept of a national collection only really started to take shape after the Big Four were taken into state ownership in 1948. This act brought together several relics – like the G.W.R.'s 'City of Truro' and the Caledonian 4–2–2 No. 123 – under the care of a single curator for the first time. It also allowed further items to be saved and two museums to be opened (at Clapham and Swindon) in addition to the existing one at York.

But the beneficence of the British Transport Commission couldn't last and in 1961 it got a new chairman – Dr Richard Beeching (see Chapter 10) – whose remit was 'to make the railway pay' (or at least stop losing money). Beeching felt, perhaps understandably, that B.R. should not be involving itself with matters of its heritage, when it clearly should be focussing on the future. As the decade progressed, the celebrated author and preservationist L. T. C. Rolt campaigned for the establishment of a National Railway Museum (NRM). After some discussion, agreement was reached under terms outlined in the 1968 Transport Act for British Rail to provide the premises for such a scheme, which would be affiliated to the National Museum of Science and Industry. The site chosen was the old York North locomotive roundhouse alongside the East Coast Main Line – a place which could not be more appropriate. And so it came to pass that the NRM was opened to coincide with the Stockton and Darlington Railway 150th anniversary celebrations in 1975.

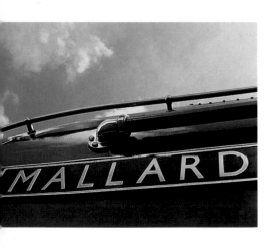

Cathedral of steam? The phrase 'cathedral of steam' is usually applied to major railway termini, but the NRM's Great Hall would easily fit into this category were it not for the fact that it is by no means limited to steam. This cavernous space is home to some of the most famous locomotives in the world, including No.4468 'Mallard', which attained a speed record for steam in 1938 that has never been broken, Stirling's magnificent single-wheeler (No. 1) and Webb's 2–4–0 'Hardwicke', which played such a vital part for the London and North Western Railway in the 'race to the north' of the late 1800s.

One of the longer-term residents is William Stanier's 4–6–2 No. 6229 'Duchess of Hamilton', a Princess Coronation class locomotive of late-30s vintage. After withdrawal from service in February 1964, the locomotive spent several years as a static exhibit at Butlin's Holiday Camp at Minehead in Somerset, but finally came to the NRM in 1976. Following a much-needed overhaul, No. 6229 soon became a regular performer on main line excursions. The expiry of its main line certificate, however, was the end of the locomotive as most of us knew it. Yet an amazing re-birth was soon to take place: in 2009, Duchess of Hamilton emerged in original condition, having been re-streamlined by the Tyseley Locomotive Works. For the first time since 1947, it may be appreciated in all its crimson lake art deco glory.

Another particularly popular Pacific is the Bulleid Merchant Navy No. 35029 *Ellerman Lines*, which has been sectioned to show the internal workings of a steam locomotive. In fact, the full story of the locomotive is told here, from Stephenson's 'Rocket' to the Advanced Passenger Train. The latter is both a testament to B.R. engineering skill and a reproach to the government's lack of belief in it (which is why the train is in a museum and not coming to the end of its working life on the main line).

Other locomotives on display include workhorses like Churchward's G.W.R. 2–8–0 No. 2818, and tank engines such as the Great Northern 0–6–0ST No. 1247 and L.B.S.C.R. Terrier class 'Boxhill'. The diesel era is represented by the first English Electric Type 4 (D200), Brush Type 2 D5500 and diesel-hydraulic D1023 *Western Fusilier* – one of the last of its type to remain in service. Aside from the APT, the history of electric traction is relayed by the North Eastern Railway's Bo-Bo No. 1 of 1902, the later EM1 No. 26020 and 84001, which was built by the North British Locomotive Company as part of B.R.'s second 'pilot scheme' in 1960 (see Chapter 9). For those who wish to compare the exhibits with the very latest motive power, a viewing gallery is provided in The Works, where trains may be seen as they come and go from York station. This part of the museum also includes a number of monitors linked to the York Integrated Electronic Control Centre, which offers a real time window on all the signals in the area.

The rolling stock items on display include early wooden wagonway vehicles from around 1815, along with humble, but more modern mineral wagons, vans and parcel vehicles. Carriages include the stunning 12-wheel first-class dining car built in 1902 for the London and North Western Railway and the North Eastern dynamometer car used on Mallard's record-breaking run.

Some of the more glamorous vehicles are to be found in the Station Hall, which is located in the former goods shed. Examples include the Duke of Sutherlands's private coach of 1899 and a sumptuous Great Western Royal Saloon (No. 9007) which continued in service until 1979. The sea of silks and satins in some of these coaches is a testament to the people who made them. The museum's restaurant is also here, and visitors are invited to 'enjoy a meal…surrounded by trains from a bygone era'. A tempting thought indeed.

The NRM occasionally looks beyond these shores and has imported several major vehicles for display, the rule being that there has to be a connection with Britain. Thus in 1981, the museum accepted a Chinese Class KF7 4–8–4 locomotive, as it was built at the Vulcan Foundry in Newton-le-Willows in 1935, while the Wagon-Lits sleeping car had been used on the famous Paris–London Night Ferry service.

The single exception is the Shinkansen Bullet Train driving trailer, which was donated to the museum by the West Japan Railway Company in 2001 and which now forms part of an award-winning feature. It has the honour of being the only Bullet Train located outside Japan.

Around 100 vehicles may be seen at any one time, the rest being divided between various other museums and heritage railways, along with the NRM's Locomotion site at Shildon, County Durham.

Branching out Locomotion was opened in 2004 to provide extra accommodation for the NRM's expanding array of vehicles. It is situated near the home of Timothy Hackworth, who moved to Shildon in 1825 to become resident engineer to the Stockton and Darlington Railway. Hackworth designed several locomotives for the line, which were built at his Soho Works. This also forms part of the Locomotion complex.

Visitors are greeted by Hackworth's most famous locomotive – 'Sans Pareil', his entry for the 1829 Rainhill Trials. A replica of this 0–4–0 may be found in the main 'Collection' building, which is also home to many other locomotives, such as Gresley's V2 2–6–2 No. 4771 'Green Arrow', the prototype Deltic and E5001, the Southern Region electric (later Class 71) built at Doncaster in 1958 to work boat train services between London and the South Coast. The prototype, gas turbine-powered version of the APT may also be found here.

There are many examples of rolling stock on display, such as a late-Victorian North Eastern Railway snow plough and a 100-ton bogie tank wagon, built by Charles Roberts and Company in 1970.

Locomotion boasts a play area for small children and has green credentials, a wind turbine being used to provide power to the National Grid. There is also a biodiesel bus, which is used to transport visitors around the site without damaging the environment.

Beyond the Locomotive Although it may be the Mallards, Flying Scotsmen and Deltics which most capture our imaginations, railways are about much more than just locomotives and rolling stock. To reflect the sheer magnitude of the subject, the National Collection holds many artefacts, such as tickets, timetables, clocks and furniture. There is also an extensive collection of uniforms, which comprises around 4,800 items (including a splendid green velvet Lancashire and Yorkshire Railway jacket. A new project is being conducted in partnership with the National Association of Decorative and Fine Arts Societies (NADFAS), whose volunteers have been trained and supervised by the NRM's conservators and curators to condition, check and research the collection. This will enable prioritised sections to be digitised for later study.

Among the many railway posters on show are such evocative examples as the jolly fisherman of 'bracing' Skegness and some of the wonderful paintings undertaken by Terence Cuneo for British Railways in the 1950s and 60s. More recent posters, such as the 'Look what you gain when you travel by train' campaign of the 1970s, may also be found here.

The extensive archive of papers, periodicals, engineering drawings and official photographs has recently been supplemented by the work of famous lensmen like Eric Treacy. In addition, the NRM's own photographers have worked to record the contemporary railway scene, including the construction of the Channel Tunnel. Towards the end of the millennium, the NRM began to collect taped recollections of former railway staff for a National Archive of Railway Oral History. These recordings join those made of steam engines by the late Peter Handford.

The museum library houses a significant collection of railway periodicals and official publications. The new Search Engine archive has made these available to a wider range of visitors and also offers a 'drop in' facility for those seeking help with railway related questions – visitors can even watch railway films and DVDs in peace. The Forsythe Collection of British and overseas travel and transport publicity material has recently been acquired. This covers rail, air, road and water transport from the 1940s up to the present century. Work is currently under way to make it more accessible to visitors.

NENE VALLEY RAILWAY

The Nene Valley Railway is one of the country's most famous railways and has been the location for dozens of films and TV programmes, including 'Octopussy', 'Goldeneye' and 'London's Burning'. It is also the home of 'Thomas', perhaps the best loved of all train engines, who has his own special events through the year. Visitors can take a ride starting at Wansford, with its engine shed, unique collection of historic European locomotives, and model railway. The trains pass through scenic Yarwell, on to Ferry Meadows which gives access to the Country Park with acres of meadows, lakes, woods, activity areas and a miniature railway.

HOW TO FIND US: **By car:** Just off the A1 between the A47 and A605 junctions **Car parking:** On-site **Nearest Network Rail:** Peterborough ADDRESS: Wansford Station, Stibbington, Peterborough PE8 6LR TEL: 01780 784444 WEBSITE: www. nvr.org.uk LENGTH OF LINE: 7.5 miles OPENING TIMES: End Feb–Mar: W/ends; Apr–Oct: Wed and w/ends; Jul–Aug: Tue–Sun FACILITIES: Café, museum shop, second hand bookshop DISABLED ACCESS: Wheelchair access to all facilities and trains.

NORTH NORFOLK RAILWAY

The Poppy Line runs on the former Midland and Great Northern Joint Railway track from the Victorian seaside resort of Sheringham to a terminus just outside the Georgian market town of Holt. It is one of Britain's most scenic preserved railways, with spectacular views of coast and heathland. The peak summer service has eight steam return services with a hop-on, hop-off facility. Trains have cycle vans. The midway station at Weybourne is a real Victorian gem, and gives easy access to woodland nature trails and cycle paths across Kelling Heath. In 2010 the line at Sheringham was joined to Network Rail.

HOW TO FIND US: **By car:** Sheringham Station is just by the A149 Cromer–Wells road **Nearest** Network Rail: Sheringham ADDRESS: The Poppy Line, North Norfolk Railway plc, The Station, Sheringham, Norfolk NR26 8RA TEL: 01263 820800 WEBSITE: www.nnr.co.uk : LENGTH OF LINE 5.25 miles OPENING TIMES: Daily Apr–Oct and Santa Specials FACILITIES: Giftshop and buffet at Sheringham DISABLED ACCESS: Wheelchair access, including trains.

NORTH YORKSHIRE MOORS RAILWAY

This line runs through the beautiful North Yorkshire Moors National Park from Pickering, a lovely Yorkshire market town, through Levisham, the gateway to Newton Dale and its stunning glacial valley, Goathland, the scenic rural village featured in TV's Heartbeat; and on to Grosmont, the operational headquarters where various locomotives can be viewed in the engine shed. There are various special events held throughout the year including a Thomas the Tank Engine weekend.

HOW TO FIND US: **By car:** Pickering is on the A170 between Scarborough and Thirsk **Car parking:** Car parks at Pickering, Levisham, Goathland and Grosmont **Nearest Network Rail:** Grosmont ADDRESS: Pickering Station, Pickering, North Yorkshire YO18 7AJ TEL: 01751 472508 WEBSITE: www.nymr.co.uk LENGTH OF LINE: 18 miles OPENING TIMES: Daily late Mar–Oct FACILITIES: Shops and refreshments at Pickering, Goathland and Grosmont DISABLED ACCESS: Wheelchair access at all stations.

PAIGNTON AND DARTMOUTH RAILWAY

This steam railway offers the discerning traveller many options. Take a steam train along the dramatic Torbay coastline from Paignton, travelling through Goodrington and Churston, and along the wooded slopes beside the Dart estuary to Kingswear from where you can take the ferry across to Dartmouth, a river cruise to Totnes and back by open-topped bus to Paignton. Whilst in historic Dartmouth, take a cruise around the harbour.

HOW TO FIND US: **By car:** M5, then follow signs for Paignton **Car parking:** Paignton, Goodrington and Kingswear **Nearest Network Rail:** Paignton ADDRESS: Dart Valley Railway plc, Queen's Park Station, Paignton, Devon TQ4 6AF TEL: 01803 555872 WEBSITE: www.paignton-steamrailway.co.uk LENGTH OF LINE: 7miles OPENING TIMES: Easter–Oct, as well as Santa Specials FACILITIES: Refreshment facilities at Paignton and Kingswear DISABLED ACCESS: Wheelchair access.

PEAK RAILWAY

Nestling in the Derbyshire Dales on the edge of the Peak District National Park, a group of enthusiastic volunteers are restoring the past. From a once barren track bed, five miles of heritage railway has been reinstated between Matlock Riverside and Rowsley South. The railway forms part of the old Midland Railway's line between Manchester Central and London St Pancras, originally opened in 1849 but closed in 1968. From Matlock riverside, the train crosses Cawdor Viaduct over the River Derwent and then meanders through beautiful landscape to Darley Dale and Rowsley South.

HOW TO FIND US: **By car:** M1, take Jct 28 to Matlock **Car parking:** Matlock, Darley Dale and Rowsley South stations **Nearest Network Rail:** Matlock ADDRESS: Matlock Station, Matlock, Derbyshire DE4 3NA TEL: 01629 580381 WEBSITE: www.peakrail.co.uk LENGTH OF LINE: 4 miles OPENING TIMES: Sun throughout the year, Sat Apr–Oct FACILITIES: Cafés, shops, picnic area, Palatine Restaurant Car, children's play area; riverside walks DISABLED ACCESS: Limited wheelchair access.

RAVENGLASS AND ESKDALE RAILWAY

Undoubtedly the most spectacular railway journey in England, travelling from the coast at Ravenglass through the renowned fell-walker Wainwright's 'loveliest valleys' to the foot of the country's highest mountain. There are at least seven trains daily from March to November, linked to walking and cycling packages and with open top and cosy-covered carriages tailored to suit the weather. Once known as 'La'al Ratty', Cumbrian dialect indicating a narrow gauge track, the name has been adopted by a Watervole Stationmaster, a big hit with the children. Many special events are organised during the year.

HOW TO FIND US: **By car:** A595 Western Lake District signposted from Jct 36 and Jct 40 of M6 **Car parking:** On site **Nearest Network Rail:** Ravenglass. ADDRESS: Ravenglass and Eskdale Railway, Ravenglass, Cumbria CA18 1SW TEL: 01229 717171 WEBSITE: www.ravenglass-railway.co.uk LENGTH OF LINE: 7 miles OPENING TIMES: Mid-Mar–Oct: daily; Nov–mid- Mar: trains most w/ends plus holiday periods FACILITIES: Cafés and gift shops at both ends of the line DISABLED ACCESS: Wheelchair access to most trains.

ROMNEY, HYTHE AND DYMCHURCH RAILWAY

The Romney, Hythe and Dymchurch Railway is a true historical oddity; a miniature railway, built in the 1920s for the racing car driver Captain Howey by Count Louis Zborowski an expert in miniature railways. Two locomotives were commissioned and built by Henry Greenly in Colchester by Davey, Paxman and Co. Before they were delivered however, the Count was killed while racing at Monza in the Italian Grand Prix. Howey was left with two locos and the task of finding somewhere to run them. He commissioned Greenly to help him, and it was he that came up with the Romney Marsh. The line opened in 1927 as 'The World's Smallest Public Railway', a triumph of miniature engineering with one-third size locomotives hauling coaches at high speeds across historic Romney March. Today, it can claim the honour of being the world's longest 15in gauge railway.

HOW TO FIND US: **By car**: 3 miles from the M20, Jct 11 **Car parking**: On site **Nearest Network Rail**: Folkestone Central ADDRESS: New Romney Station, Kent TN28 8PL TEL: 01797 363256 WEBSITE: www.rhdr.org.uk LENGTH OF LINE: 13.5 miles OPENING TIMES: W/ends; daily May-Sep; school holidays; Santa specials in Dec FACILITIES: Cafés, picnic areas, gift and souvenir shops. Licensed observation car in service on selected trains DISABLED ACCESS: Wheelchair access on trains, but call in advance; adapted toilets.

SEVERN VALLEY RAILWAY

The Severn Valley Railway not only has more mainline engines that any other preserved railway in the country but, at over 16 miles, is also one of the longest lines. The preservation of the railway started in 1965 where the money was raised to buy the line from Bridgenorth to Alveley which opened in 1970. The line was extended from Alveley to Foley Park and then finally all the way through to Kidderminster in 1984.

The railway starts at Bridgnorth, hub of the Severn Valley network, a bustling market town, and stops off at Hampton Loade, from where you can take a walk, via a privately owned ferry, to the National Trust owned Dudmaston Hall with its extensive, landscaped gardens. One of the highlights is the crossing of the river Severn by means of the Victoria bridge – a massive 200ft single span bridge (as seen in the photograph opposite). Another stop is Highley with its perfectly restored, stone built country station, scene of numerous films and television programmes and a good centre for walks, as is the case with the next stop, Arley. The line continues to Bewdley, which has been described as 'simply one of the most beautiful towns in England'. The final stop is Kidderminster, where there is a Railway Museum.

The Railwaay offers steam experience courses which give the opportunity to drive a large standard gauge railway locomotive under the supervision of qualified staff. There are three levels of steam courses available, each of which is designed to meet the aspirations of those interested in the operation of steam locomotives and there is a diesel course as well..

HOW TO FIND US: **By car**: Bridgnorth is on the A458; Kidderminster is on the A448 **Car parking**: Ample at Kidderminster and Bridgnorth, limited at other stations **Nearest Network Rail**: Kidderminster ADDRESS: The Railway Station, Bewdley, Worcs DY12 1BG TEL: 01299 403816 WEBSITE: www.svr.co.uk LENGTH OF LINE: 16 miles OPENING TIMES: All year: w/ends; mid-May–late Sep: daily FACILITIES: Buffet and bar facilities on trains, station bars, tea rooms, giftshops DISABLED ACCESS: Specially converted coaches available – please book in advance.

SOUTH DEVON RAILWAY

The South Devon line used to run between Totnes and Ashburton and opened in 1872, but never made a profit and eventually closed for freight in 1962. A group of enthusiasts bought the line in 1965 and it re-opened in 1969. Unfortunately the line from Buckfastleigh to Ashburton was lost to the widening of the A38.

The South Devon Railway is one of the best railways in the country for observing and encountering wildlife. It starts at Totnes and runs for seven miles to Buckfastleigh along the east bank of the River Dart – a fast-flowing salmon river, home to herons, swans and kingfishers. At Totnes, visit the Totnes Rare Breeds Centre which is only accessible from the station. Sleepy Staverton station is a reminder of what country stations used to be like whilst at the terminus at Buckfastleigh, you can watch otters swimming and playing from an underwater viewing gallery at the otter sanctuary or walk through clouds of free-flying tropical butterflies at the associated butterfly farm.

The railway offers combined Railway-Buckfast Butterflies and Dartmoor Otter Sanctuary tickets. The station houses the railway museum, workshops and model railway. On some days there is also a miniature railway operating. Nearby is Buckfast Abbey, one of the most visited religious sites in the country and the source of an internationally renowned brand of honey. On most days, a vintage bus links Buckfastleigh station with the Abbey.

HOW TO FIND US: **By car**: Buckfastleigh is on the A38 **Car parking**: On site **Nearest Network Rail**: Totnes ADDRESS: Buckfastleigh Station, Buckfastleigh, Devon TQ11 0DZ TEL: 0845 3451420 WEBSITE: www.southdevon railway.org LENGTH OF LINE: 7 miles OPENING TIMES: Daily Apr–end Oct:; Christmas specials FACILITIES: Café, book and gift shop, shop, children's playground, picnic sites DISABLED ACCESS: Wheelchair access, adapted toilets; a restored carriage has been specially adapted for wheelchairs.

SOUTH TYNEDALE RAILWAY

The journey on England's highest narrow gauge railway begins in Alston, just 20 miles south of Hadrian's Wall, and continues through some beautiful North Pennine scenery to Kirkhaugh. The line was constructed on the trackbed of the former BR Haltwhistle–Alston branch and, it is hoped, will be extended to Slaggyford. Alston itself, a pleasant cobbled town, was once the centre of an important lead-mining district. You can find out more about the area's rich industrial heritage at the nearby Nenthead Mines Heritage Centre.

Since May 2007, a working party consisting of several of the railway's volunteers, have started the groundwork to level part of the old railway trackbed, north of Kirkhaugh station and to lay several lengths of track. It is the intention to continue the track laying up to the Lintley Viaduct.

HOW TO FIND US: **By car**: Alston, just off the A686 Hexham Road **Car parking**: On site **Nearest Network Rail**: Haltwhistle **By bus**: Call Cumbria Journey Planner, Tel: 01228 606000 ADDRESS: The Railway Station, Alston, Cumbria CA9 3JB TEL: 01434 382828 INFOLINE: 01434 381696 WEBSITE: www.strps.org.uk LENGTH OF LINE: 2.25 miles OPENING TIMES: Apr–Oct: w/ends; Jul–Aug: daily; phone for details of other dates FACILITIES: Railway shop, buffet car and café DISABLED ACCESS: A carriage with wheelchair access is available, advance booking recommended.

SWANAGE RAILWAY

Swanage, a sleepy Dorset coastal resort, is the starting point for the Purbeckline, one of the West Country's most picturesque steam railways with glorious scenery and historic locations. The line runs all the way to Norden but there is an opportunity to get off and explore the ruins of the famous Corfe Castle en route. A Royalist stronghold during the Civil War, the castle withstood a Cromwellian siege for six weeks, after which it was largely reduced to rubble by Roundhead gunpowder. At the beautifully restored Victorian station of Corfe Castle there is a Railway Museum with many exhibits from the Southern Railway (open on train operating days only).

The railway offers driving experience days where you can go for a taster experience which lasts about 90 minutes or full day experience driving a diesel.

HOW TO FIND US: **By car:** On the A351 **Car parking:** On site **Nearest Network Rail:** Wareham ADDRESS: Swanage Railway Trust, Station House, Swanage, Dorset BH19 1HB TEL: 01929 425800 WEBSITE: www.swanagerailway.co.uk LENGTH OF LINE: 6 miles OPENING TIMES: All year: w/ends and school holidays; Apr–Oct: daily; Specials in Dec FACILITIES: (Swanage Station) Souvenir shop selling books, videos,railway memorabilia; station buffet serving hot meals and snacks throughout the day DISABLED ACCESS: Wheelchair access onto trains.

TANFIELD RAILWAY

Built in 1725 to carry coal from Newcastle's mines to the ships on the Tyne, this is the oldest surviving railway in the world. Steam trains still operate along a three-mile length of track passing through Causey Woods. Tanfield's oldest surviving building is the 1854 Marley Hill Engine Shed, where visitors can watch the ongoing restoration of engines. In winter, children will enjoy the special North Pole days when the trains puff through the beautiful winter landscape on their way to see Father Christmas.

HOW TO FIND US: **By car:** Off the A6076 **Car parking: On site Nearest Network Rail:** Newcastle ADDRESS: Marley Hill Engine Shed, Sunniside, Gateshead. TEL: 0845 4634938 WEBSITE: www. tanfield-rail way.co.uk LENGTH OF LINE: 3 miles OPENING TIMES: Trains run every Sun throughout the year, public holidays and Wed and Thu during summer school holidays FACILITIES: Most trains have a buffet car, railway shop DISABLED: Manual wheelchair access to some carriages.

WEARDALE RAILWAY

This line was originally built in 1847 to transport limestone to the ironwork at Teeside and by 1895 it had been extended to its final terminus at Wearhead. It was taken over by the Weardale Railway in 1993. The line first started operating trains in 2004 and now runs a regular service throughout the year and the line is owned by an American railway company, Iowa Pacific uisng a newly formed company called British American Railway Services. The service at the moment runs between Wolsingham and Stanhope and there are plans to extend the line a further 18½ miles from Bishop Auckland to Eastgate.

HOW TO FIND US: **By car:** Just off A689 **Car parking:** Free at all stations **Nearest Network Rail:** Bishop Auckland ADDRESS: Weardale Railways, Stanhope Station, Stanhope, Co Durham DL13 2YS TEL: 01388 526203 WEBSITE: www.weardale-railway.org.uk LENGTH OF LINE: 5.5 miles OPERATING TIMES: Easter–Oct: w/ends and public holidays; (see timetable on website) FACILITIES: Café and Souvenir shop DISABLED ACCESS ACCESS: Please call ahead.

WENSLEYDALE RAILWAY

The railway was built in stages during the 19th century to connect the East coast mainline and the Settle/Carlisle line at Garsdale. The railway now runs between Leeming Bar and Redmire which is on the edge of the Yorkshire Dales National Park, a distance of 17 miles which takes about 50 minutes. This is the first part of a project to restore the full 40 miles between Northallerton and Garsdale. From Redmire you can take a vintage bus to Hawes and Garsdale for a day out excursion.

They offer a full day driving package, including welcome and safety briefing, qualified instruction, supervised driver experience on one of their diesel multiple unit (DMU) trains and refreshments, including welcome breakfast and lunch at a local hotel.

HOW TO FIND US: **By car:** Just off the A1 on to the A684 and follow brown signs **Car parking:** Free at Redmire only **Nearest Network Rail:** Northallerton ADDRESS: Leeming Bar Station, Leeming Bar, Northallerton, DL7 9AR TEL: 08454 505474 WEBSITE: www.wensleydalerailway.com LENGTH OF LINE: 17 miles OPENING TIMES: Easter–end Oct: daily FACILITIES: Refreshments, souvenirs DISABLED ACCESS: Full wheelchair access to platforms.

WEST SOMERSET RAILWAY

This charming recreation of a Great Western Railways country branch line is Britain's longest preserved railway. It runs from Bishops Lydeard to Minehead, passing the renowned Quantock Hills and Bristol Channel coast. It is Britain's longest standard gauge railway. There are ten restored stations along the route and you can break your journey at any of them. Many have museums and displays of engine stock. Stogumber, Watchet and Dunster are as picturesque as they are historic, with plenty of picnic spots on the beach.

The West Somerset Railway offers a range of one day and two day railway expereince courses. They also offer a steam experience where you can go behind the scenes and learn about how to prepare a locomotive, the principles of working a steam locomotive, signalling, braking, safety, driving and firing. Guided by an experienced West Somerset Railway Instructor you will haul a train of coaches or freight wagons along part of the entire longest preserved railway in the country.

HOW TO FIND US: **By car:** Bishops Lydeard station is 4 miles from Taunton **Car parking:** On site **Nearest Network Rail:** Taunton **By bus:** 28A ADDRESS: The Railway Station, Minehead, Somerset TA24 5BG TEL: 01643 704996 WEBSITE: www. west-somerset-railway.co.uk OPENING TIMES: Mar–Jan LENGTH OF LINE: 20 miles FACILITIES: Souvenir shops, buffet and buffet car on most trains DISABLED ACCESS: Wheelchair access to all stations except Doniford Halt.

SCOTLAND

CALEDONIAN RAILWAY

This last remaining section of the former Caledonian Railway branch line runs from Brechin Station, the line's only extant terminus and home to a small railway museum, to Bridge of Dun, a good base for walks along the River Esk to the Montrose Basin Bird Sanctuary. Also in the vicinity is the House of Dun, an early 18th-century building owned and run by the National Trust for Scotland. Steam and diesel locomotives are in service on the line. Events such as A Day out with Thomas and Santa Specials are aranged. There is also a model railway at Brechin station.

HOW TO FIND US: **By car**: Brechin is on the A933 and just off the A90 **Car parking**: On site **Nearest Network Rail**: Montrose ADDRESS: The Station, 2 Park Road, Brechin, Angus DD7 7AF TEL: 01674 810318 WEBSITE: www.caledonian-railway.co.uk LENGTH OF LINE: 4 miles OPENING TIMES: End May–Sep: Sun; phone for information on special events FACILITIES: Souvenir shop and picnic site DISABLED ACCESS: Wheelchair access to all trains and assistance (please phone ahead).

MULL RAILWAY

Scotland's first island passenger railway is served by two steam engines, 'Lady of the Isles' and 'Victoria'. There are also four other locomotives. The railway is home to the Balamory Express, well-known from the children's programme. From the Old Pier Station at Craignure the trains climb up to the stately home of Torosay Castle with its archive room and 12-acres of gardens and woodland walks. On the journey there are beautiful views of Ben Nevis, the Glencoe Hills, the Island of Lismore and Duart Castle.

HOW TO FIND US: **By ferry**: Caledonian Macbrayne: 01680 812343 **By car**: At Craignure Ferry Terminal, turn left on the A849, signposted **Nearest Network Rail**: Oban, then take the ferry **Car parking**: Free at Craignure station ADDRESS: Craignure, Isle of Mull, PA65 6AY TEL: 01680 812494/812567 WEBSITE: www.mullrail.co.uk LENGTH OF LINE: 1.25 miles OPENING TIMES: Easter–late Oct FACILITIES: Small shop at Craignure station DISABLED ACCESS: Wheelchair access.

STRATHSPEY RAILWAY

Scotland's 'Steam Railway in The Highlands'. The Strathspey Steam Railway operates from the modern Highland holiday resort of Aviemore to the attractive village of Boat of Garten and Broomhill. This wonderful trip over heather clad moor and by the winding River Spey provides splendid views of the Cairngorm Mountain Range. Broomhill is the location for the station scenes at 'Glenbogle' in 'Monarch of the Glen' (television series) and is 3.5 miles on the A95 from Grantown on Spey, the railway's ultimate goal.

HOW TO FIND US: **By car**: Aviemore is off the A9 on the B9152. **Car parking**: Free at all stations **Nearest Network Rail**: Aviemore ADDRESS: Strathspey Steam Railway Co. Ltd, Dalfaber Road, Aviemore, Invernessshire PH22 1PY TEL: 01479 810725 WEBSITE: www.strath speyrailway.co.uk LENGTH OF LINE: 9.5 miles OPENING TIMES: Apr, May and Oct: Sun and Wed; May and Oct: Sat and Thu; Easter, end May–end Sep: daily FACILITIES: Buffet/Dining Car on most trains, souvenir shop at Aviemore and Boat of Garten stations DISABLED ACCESS: Wheelchair access at all stations.

BALA LAKE RAILWAY

This excellent little line, built to link the industrial borderlands with the Cambrian coastal resorts, runs along the shoreline of Wales' largest natural lake. The ride offers unforgettable views of deep river valleys, tranquil water meadows, sheep-dotted hillsides and, of course, the majestic splendour of Bala Lake itself. The headquarters at Llanuwchllyn features an original Great Western signal box, while the main intermediate station, at pretty Llangower, is a popular picnic and walking spot. The more active among you may like to try the range of watersports available at Bala Lake.

HOW TO FIND US: **By car**: Just off the A494 Bala to Dollgellau road **Car parking**: On site **Nearest Network Rail**: Barmouth and Wrexham ADDRESS: The Station, Llanuwchllyn, Gwynedd LL23 7DD TEL: 01678 540666 WEBSITE: www. bala-lake-railway.co.uk LENGTH OF LINE: 4.5 miles OPENING TIMES: Mid-Apr–early Oct FACILITIES: Refreshments and souvenir shop DISABLED ACCESS: Facilities available on most trains.

BRECON MOUNTAIN RAILWAY

Built on the trackbed of the former Brecon and Merthyr Railway, this narrow gauge passenger-carrying steam railway winds its way through the beautiful Brecon Beacons National Park in South Wales. You can watch old steam locomotives being repaired in the station workshop, take a picnic overlooking the magnificent Taf Fechan Reservoir or pay a visit to Cyfarthfa Castle, a splendid Regency Gothic mansion set in wonderful manicured gardens.

HOW TO FIND US: **By car**: Just off A465 Heads of The Valleys trunk road **Car parking**: On site **Nearest Network Rail**: Merthyr ADDRESS: Pant Station, Dowlais, Merthyr Tydfil CF48 2UP TEL: 01685 722988 WEBSITE: www. breconmountainrailway.co.uk LENGTH OF LINE: 5 miles OPENING TIMES: End Apr–Sep: most days; Oct: some days; phone for details FACILITIES: Café and souvenir shop at Pant, café at Pontsticill DISABLED ACCESS: Wheelchair-adapted carriage, ramps, adapted toilets.

CONWY VALLEY RAILWAY

This friendly, cheerful museum holds a fascinating collection of railway stock and memorabilia. There's a mile-long miniature railway and a 15ins electric tramcar (0.5 mile trip) available daily for passenger rides. The railway runs from Llandudno to Blaenau Ffestiniog and there is a breathtaking range of scenery, from the historic castle at Conwy, through estuary rich in wildlife, to gentle slopes that give way to majestic crags as the train crosses the Lledr by the dramatic Gethin's viaduct. A nearby attraction is Dolwyddelan Castle, the reputed birthplace of Llewelyn the Great.

HOW TO FIND US: **By car**: Betws-y-Coed is on the B5106 **Car parking**: On site **Nearest Network Rail**: Betws-y-Coed ADDRESS: The Old Goods Yard, Betws-y-Coed, Conwy LL24 0AL TEL: 01690 710568 WEBSITE: www.conwyvalleyrailway. co.uk OPENING TIMES: All year: Daily 10–5.30 LENGTH OF LINE: 1 mile round trip FACILITIES: Buffet car refreshments, museum, book shop, model and gift shop, picnic area DISABLED ACCESS: Wheelchair access, adapted toilets.

FFESTINIOG RAILWAY

The railway is the oldest independent railway company in the World having been founded in 1832. It was orginally built to transport slate down from the quarries in the mountains around Blaenau Ffestiniog. A very successful line until the loss of transporting slate and fewer and fewer passengers and eventually closed to traffice in 1946. A large group of volunteers worked on restoring the line and it re-openened in 1954. It is now one of Wales' top tourist attractions. The route takes you from Porthmadog all the way to Blaena Ffestiniog at a height of 710ft.

HOW TO FIND US: **By car**: On the A487 Tremadog Road **Car Parking**: On site **Nearest Network Rail**: Porthmadog ADDRESS: Ffestiniog Railway, Harbour Station, Porthmadog LL49 9NF TEL: 01766 516000 WEBSITE: www.festrail.co.uk LENGTH OF LINE: 13.5 miles OPENING TIMES: Mid Mar–Oct: Daily FACILITIES: Café and bar and souvenir shop DISABLED ACCESS: Accessible for wheelchairs

LLANGOLLEN RAILWAY

The Llangollen railway, the only preserved standard gauge line in North Wales, wends its way alongside the River Dee, famous for its salmon, from Llangollen, past the famous Horseshoe Falls, through the 689-yd Berwyn Tunnel to Carrog with its beautifully restored 1950s' terminus. There are many attractive hill and riverside walks from the country stations   from Berwyn a 15 minute walk talks you to the Horseshoe Falls, where the Llangollen Canal leaves the River Dee.

HOW TO FIND US: **By car**: Junction of the A5 and the A539 **Car parking**: Market Street in the town. **Nearest Network Rail**: Ruabon **By bus**: Call 01978 266166 ADDRESS: Llangollen Railway, Abbey Road, Llangollen, Denbighshire, LL20 8SN TEL: 01978 860979 TALKING TIMETABLE: 01978 860951 WEBSITE: www.llangollen-railway.co.uk LENGTH OF LINE: 7.5 miles OPENING TIMES: All year: most w/ends; May–Oct: daily FACILITIES: Souvenir shop and tea shop DISABLED ACCESS: Specially adapted carriage.

SNOWDON MOUNTAIN RAILWAY

When the weather is fine, this is one of the world's great railway journeys. Commencing from the picturesquely situated village of Llanberis, the railway climbs over 3,000ft in the course of the five-mile journey to the summit of Snowdon, highest mountain in England and Wales. Remember to bring warm and waterproof clothing as temperatures at the summit can be several degrees lower. Operating since 1896, the Snowdon Mountain Railway is the only rack and pinion line in the UK, operating on the Abt system and encountering gradients as steep as 1 in 5.5 as it winds its way through the wild and rugged landscape of Snowdonia.

HOW TO FIND US: **By car**: Llanberis Station is on the A4086, **Car parking**: Pay and display at Llanberis **Nearest Network Rail**: Bangor ADDRESS: Snowdon Mountain Railway, Llanberis, Caernarfon, Gwynedd LL55 4TY TEL: 0844 4938120 WEBSITE: www.snowdonrailway.co.uk LENGTH OF LINE: 5 miles OPENING TIMES: Mid-Mar–early Nov: daily; because of snow/ice and winter maintenance requirements, the upper section does not usually open much before mid/late May, until when trains will terminate lower down the mountain FACILITIES: Cafés at Llanberis and Summit DISABLED ACCESS: Wheelchair users are welcome.

TALYLLYN RAILWAY

Due to close in 1950 after 85 years of service, this narrow gauge line was saved by the Talyllyn Railway Preservation Society, the first such organisation in the world. Not only did these enthusiasts ensure the continued survival of one of Wales' best loved railways but they provided inspiration and impetus for literally hundreds of other rail societies over the succeeding decades. The rich industrial heritage that Britain enjoys today is due in no small part to the efforts of the Talyllyn pioneers.

HOW TO FIND US: **By car:** Tywyn is on the A493 **Car parking:** On site **Nearest Network Rail:** Tywyn ADDRESS: Talyllyn Railway, Wharf Station, Tywyn, Gwynedd LL36 9EY TEL: 01654 710472 WEBSITE: www.talyllyn.co.uk LENGTH OF LINE: 7.25 miles OPENING TIMES: Late Feb–Mar: Sun; Apr–Oct: daily; Specials in Dec FACILITIES: Refreshments and souvenirs at Tywyn Wharf DISABLED ACCESS: Wheelchair access with adapted coaches on some trains; please phone ahead.

WELSH HIGHLAND RAILWAY (CAERNARFON)

This spectacular railway runs from Caernarfon and climbs over 650ft on its way to the summit at Pitts Head. On its way it runs through Snowdonia National Park, snaking its way to the summit before it starts its decent to Beddgelert. Down the steep hillside the line descends past Nantmor village, eventually reaching the current terminus at Pont Croesor - from where the trains currently return to Beddgelert and Caernarfon.

HOW TO FIND US: **By car:** Caernarfon is on A487, a few miles south of A55 North Wales expressway **Car parking:** Public car parks in Caernarfon **Nearest Network Rail** Bangor ADDRESS: Ffestiniog Railway, Harbour Station, Portmadog, Gwynedd LL49 9NF TEL: 01766 516000 WEBSITE: www.festrail.co.uk LENGTH OF LINE: 19 miles OPENING TIMES: Easter to end Oct daily FACILITIES: Souvenir shop at Caernarfon. Both Caernarfon and Waunfawr have excellent places to eat. DISABLED ACCESS: Wheelchair access at both stations.

WELSHPOOL AND LLANFAIR RAILWAY

Historic steam locomotives from two continents travel along this eight-mile line, puffing their way through the pretty countryside, past farms and rivers and over startlingly steep hills, giving fantastic views of Welshpool's picturesque scenery. You can take the opportunity to negotiate the hills and bends for yourself on one of the railway's Driving Experience courses, under the patient guidance of an experienced instructor. Canal boat trips are run at Welshpool, and the famous Powis Castle and Gardens are minutes away from the station.

HOW TO FIND US: **By car:** Shrewsbury Dolgellau road A458 **Car parking:** On site **Nearest Network Rail:** Welshpool **By bus:** Midland Red Buses to Welshpool ADDRESS: The Station, Llanfair Caereinion, Powys SY21 0SF TEL: 01938 810441 WEBSITE: www.wllr.org.uk LENGTH OF LINE: 8 miles OPENING TIMES: Apr–Sep: w/ends andpublic holidays; mid-Jul–early Sep and Oct half term holiday: daily FACILITIES: Tea room, book and video shop, both at Llanfair DISABLED ACCESS: Wheelchair access to both trains and platforms.

Select Bibliography

Adam, J., and Whitehouse P., *British Rail Scrapbook 1953*, (Ian Allan, 1978)

Awdry, C., *Encyclopaedia of British Railway Companies*, (PSL., 1990)

Baker, M., *The Waterloo to Weymouth Line*, (Patrick Stephens Ltd., 1987)

Baxter, D., *Victorian Locomotives*, (Moorland, 1978)

Bloom, H., *250 Years of Steam*, (The Windmill Press, 1981)

Boocock, C., *BR Steam in Colour 1948–1968*, (Ian Allan, 1986)

Boocock, C., *British Railways in Colour 1948–1968: A Period of Transition*, (Ian Allan, 1988)

Bowen Cooke, C.J., *British Locomotives*, (1893)

Butcher, A. C., (Editor) *Railways Restored 2010*, (Ian Allan, 2010)

Chacksfield, J.E., *Sir William Stanier: A New Biography*, (Oakwood Press, 2001)

Chacksfield, J.E., and Collett, C.B., *A Competent Successor*, (Oakwood Press, 2002)

Chapman, W.G., *Loco's of the Royal Road*, (GWR, 1936)

Clough, D.N., *Diesel Pioneers*, (Ian Allan, 2005)

Cook, K. J., *Swindon Steam 1921-1951*, (Ian Allan, 1974)

Durrant, A. E., *Swindon Apprentice*, (Runpast Publishing, 1989)

Engel, M., *Eleven Minutes Late – A Train Journey to the Soul of Britain*, (Macmillan, 2009)

Fletcher, M and Taylor, J., *Railways, the Pioneer Years*, (Studio Editions)

Gibbins, E. A., MCIT, *Square Deal Denied*, (Leisure Products, 1998)

Gibbins, E. A. MCIT, *Britain's Railways: The Reality*, (Leisure Products, 2003)

Gibson, J.C., *Great Western Locomotive Design*, (David and Charles, 1984)

Haresnape, B., *British Rail 1948-78 – A Journey by Design*, (Ian Allan, 1979)

Haresnape, B., *British Rail Fleet Survey: 1 Early Prototype and Pilot Scheme Diesel-Electrics*, (Ian Allan, 1981)

Haresnape, B., *British Rail Fleet Survey: 6 Electric Locomotives*, (Ian Allan, 1983)

Heavyside, T., *Steam Renaissance: The Decline and Rise of Steam Locomotives in Britain*, (Bracken Books, 1984)

Henshaw, D., *The Great Railway Conspiracy*, (Hawes: Leading Edge, 1991)

Holcroft, H., *An Outline of Great Western Locomotive Practice 1837–1947*, 2nd edn, (Ian Allan, 1971)

Hylton, S., *The Grand Experiment*, (Ian Allan, 2007)

Kidner, R.W., *The London Tramcar 1861-1952*, (Oakwood, 1951)

Lee, S.J., *Aspects of British Political History 1914–1995*, (Routledge, 1996)

Le Vay B., *Britain from the Rails*, (Bradt, 2009)

Lewis, M.J.T., *Early Wooden Railways*, (Routledge, 1970)

Moran, Lord., *Churchill at War 1940–45*, (Constable and Robinson Ltd., 1966)

Morse, G., *John Betjeman: Reading the Victorians*, (Sussex Academic Press, 2008)

Nock,O.S., (Editor) *Encyclopaedia of Railways*, Octopus, 1977)

Ransom, P.J.G., *The Victorian Railway and How it Evolved*, (Heinemann, 1990)

RCTS., *Locomotives of the Great Western Railway, Part Eleven: The Rail Motor Vehicles and Internal Combustion Locomotives*, (The Railway Correspondence and Travel Society, 1956)

Reed, B., (Editor), *Locomotives in Profile*, (3 volumes), 1971-73

Robertson, K., *The Great Western Railway Gas Turbines – A Myth Exposed*, (Sutton Publishing, 1989)

Robertson, K., *The Changing Railway Scene: Southern Region*, (Ian Allan, 2009)

Rowledge, J. W. P., *Austerity 2-8-0s and 2-10-0s*, (Ian Allan, 1987)

Rubinstein, W.D., *Twentieth-Century Britain: A Political History*, (Palgrave Macmillan, 2003)

RSSB, *Annual Safety Performance Report 2008*, (RSSB, 2009)

Sharman, M., *The Crampton Locomotive*, (1983)

Simmons, J., and Biddle, G., editors, *The Oxford Companion to British Railway History*, 2nd edn, (Oxford University Press, 2003)

Simmons, J., (Editor), *The Railway Traveller's Handy Book*, (Adams and Dart, 1862, 1971 reprint)

Simmons, J., *The Victorian Railway*, Thames and Hudson, 1991)

Snell, J.B., *Early Railways*, (Weidenfield and Nicholason, 1964)

Summers, L. A., *A New Update of Swindon Steam*, (Great Western Society, 2007)

Turner, S., *In Memory of the Class 40s*, (Rail Photorpints, 1985)

Vaughan, A., *The Greatest Railway Blunder*, (Ian Allan, 2009)

Williams, E.S., *Our Iron Roads*, (2 volumes, 1883)

Wilson, F.E., *The British Tram*, (Percival Marshall, 1961)

Wragg, D., *Wartime on the Railways*, (Sutton Publishing, 2006)

Periodicals

Heritage Railway
Steam Railway
Traction
The Railway Magazine
Modern Railways

Index